Rivers of Shadow, Rivers of Sun

Rivers of Shadow, Rivers of Sun

A Fly Fisher's European Journal

Norm Zeigler

Illustrations by Michael Simon

Countrysport Press
Camden, Maine

Copyright © 2004 by Norm Zeigler
All rights reserved.

Dust jacket and interior design by Michael Steere

Printed by Versa Press, Inc. East Peoria, Illinois

5   4   3   2   1

Countrysport Press
Camden, Maine
Book Orders: 800-685-7962
www.countrysportpress.com
a division of Down East Enterprise,
publishers of *Fly Rod & Reel* magazine

ISBN: 0-89272-641-5

Library of Congress Control Number: 2004105583

Cover painting: *Stone Bridge over the Irati* by Michael Stidham

Table of Contents

Acknowledgments

This book would be very different, or maybe no book at all, without the support and advice provided by friends, colleagues, and loved ones. Foremost is my wife, Libby Grimm, my life partner, lover, and most affirmative critic. My longtime fishing buddies Berris Samples, Dave Bryer, and Vic Edwards have been true and caring friends through the best and the hardest of times. Don Tate, Bill Tapply, and Cindi Crain believed in *Rivers of Shadow, Rivers of Sun* when it was still in gestation and were more generous with their time and counsel than I had any right to expect. Nelson Bryant provided years of inspiration with his concise, lyrical columns and offered encouragement when I needed it. Bill Walker has been a valued colleague and steadfast friend for more than two decades. Michael Simon is a kindred spirit whose precisely intuitive chapter drawings transmuted my modest word constructs. To these and to the many others who shared lovely countryside and quicksilver streams; offered companionship, kindness, and hospitality; and imparted their passion for ideas, books, and beautiful, finny creatures: Thank you.

This book is for
Libby, Travis, and Katrina,
the loves of my life.

Prologue

The road would be long. All roads are
long that lead towards one's heart's desire.

—Joseph Conrad, "The Shadow-Line"

If it is possible to distill a life down to a few central themes, mine would be a love of the outdoors, a passion for the written word, and what Joni Mitchell called "the urge for going." More often than might be expected, they have overlapped.

Though there is an intrinsic pleasure to any time spent near mountains, forests, fields, and waters, I have always been most drawn to active pursuits—camping, skiing, sailing, surfing, hiking, hunting. But none of them has held the lifelong allure of fishing.

You could say I was born to fish. When my mom was pregnant with me she spent weekends and many evenings with my dad on Baker's Pond, a glacial kettle hole just below the elbow of Cape Cod. They used an old rowboat, gliding along the edges of the drop-off and casting spinners and spoons to bass, pickerel, and sunfish.

It was spring on the Cape, and over the weeks they watched the first shy, pink mayflowers peek out from under the dead pine needles and oak leaves. They watched the lee shore change sides as the north and northeast winds shifted around to the warm southwesterlies. They watched the first soft green leaves come out on the white oaks and swamp maples. They watched the small-mouths begin to build their nests in the sandy shallows.

Some feelings are in the blood and I wonder if I sensed the motion of the boat on the water, the gentle waves lapping, the thrill of the hunt, the changing of the seasons, and the coming of the warm sun after the bleak, gray winter.

In July I got my first look at the world. Soon the excursions resumed, but now two of us were shorebound, usually reclining on a wool blanket, gazing out across the water or up at the summer sky through the swaying oaks and pines. In the next turn of the cycle, the gales and rains of fall stripped the leaves from the trees, and my first fishing season was over.

It was not so many seasons after these natal angling appercep-tions that my dad put a line in my own hands. Under his guidance, and often in his company, I grew up roving the Cape's rivers, ponds, and seashore with a spinning rod and a hungry heart.

In Nantucket Sound, Pleasant Bay, Chatham Harbor, and myriad tidal creeks and brackish estuaries we caught flounder, tomcod, shad, snapper blues, and—in the spring—big old cow stripers that we lured with live herring. In the flooded former cedar swamp near our house it was pickerel, perch, sunfish, and, rarely, a green black largemouth. By my early teens I could handle a spinning rod like a magic wand.

From *Sports Afield, Field and Stream,* and *Outdoor Life* I learned about another kind of fishing, done with long, wispy rods and tiny, fur-and-feather lures. I read of trout caught in far-off places, in clear streams that tumbled from snow-capped moun-tains. The places were exotic (Wyoming, Montana, California, New Zealand), the methods mysterious and arcane. It was a world away from bait and plugs and the marshes, flats, and dunes I knew.

During my college years, dominated by work and study, I found little time for learning fly fishing. But finally, in my early twenties, I was determined to break the code for this intriguing divertissement that seemed equal parts blood sport, avocation, and secular religion, and that had the aura of a secret brotherhood.

One winter, working at a ski resort in Maine, I bought Joe Brooks's two classics—*Fly Fishing* and *Trout Fishing*. In the long, dark nights, while the snow piled up in the pine woods, I read about back casts, false casts, and roll casts; about the advantages of bamboo and fiberglass; about tippets and dry flies and streamers and nymphs. My girlfriend and I began planning a trip out West, to the country I had first read about a dozen years before.

One weekend, with spring in the air, we drove across Maine to Freeport and L.L. Bean. Back then Bean's was still a rough-hewn sporting goods store, not an upscale boutique. The gear was of high quality; the staff was friendly, knowledgeable, and down-to-earth. All were longtime hunters and fishermen.

We bought a tent, sleeping bags, backpacks, camping accessories, and—most important to me—a complete fly-fishing outfit. The rod was a three-piece, fiberglass backpack special that came in an aluminum tube. It cost $25 and I think the reel was $6.

In a few weeks, back on the Cape, I put together my new outfit for the first time. I drove to the house of a friend who lived on a lake and, standing on his dock with *Fly Fishing* open to the "Casting" chapter, I taught myself the basics—sentence by sentence, paragraph by paragraph.

At first I made all the usual mistakes: cracked the leader like a whip, slapped the line down on the water, let my backcast sag so low that the forward cast hit me in the back of the head. But then the rhythm began to come, the rod and line became extensions of my arm, the loops in the air started to resemble the illustrations in the book.

In the next weeks I returned to that lake three more times, and finally I was ready: I could cast with a fly rod; now it was time to fish.

With spring in full bloom, my girlfriend and I headed off in search of mountains and streams, of wild places and wide-open spaces. We embarked on that quintessentially American quest for the adventure of the open road. And trout.

In the Great Smokies I stalked little rainbows under rhododendron blossoms. In the Colorado Rockies I filled the breakfast frying pan with beaver-pond brook trout. In the Sawtooths I learned to fight bigger rainbows. In the Bitterroots I marveled at the cutthroats' gaudy beauty.

I learned by trial, but more by error. In the Missouri River at Three Forks, I tied a streamer (a Kennebago smelt) to a 6X tippet and broke off a big trout. At a shallow forest lake in the Flathead Valley, I feverishly cast to myriad rise rings and landed a four-pound carp. On the Middle Fork of the Salmon, I cursed in frustration as the current repeatedly dragged my fly under after a brief free-float—until I remembered Joe Brooks's line-mending canon. Near Banff, I futilely flailed away at a fishless torrent that was silver gray with glacial silt.

And in our rovings I made a discovery, a classically hubristic youthful epiphany: Fishing, I divined, was like sex; it was almost always pleasurable. But fly fishing was like sex with someone you love.

By the time we drove back across Canada, I was beginning to learn what it meant to be a fly fisherman. I had picked up the basic ten o'clock–two o'clock cast in twenty minutes. The rest would take a lifetime.

Since my early teens I had suffered from a serious case of that singular affliction the Germans call *Fernweh*—the yearning for faraway places—and our cross-country adventure/*Bildungsreise* caused a major flare-up of my wanderlust. A further longtime complication was the pull of seemingly opposite realms: Europe and the American West.

For a while the conflict remained unresolved, but a couple of years later I again headed out West for the summer, this time alone. Again I camped and spent most of my time chasing trout. But I also lined up a ski-season job in Sun Valley. I would return East for a few weeks to put my things in order, then drive back out. And in the spring, when the snow melted, I would stay on and make a life in the Rockies. For a Cape Cod swamp Yankee, it would be a sea change.

Back on the Cape I prepared for the move, but romantic complications soon ensued and the relocation got hung up like a fly line on a deepwater snag. November came and went, then December slipped away, and my grand plan was just another faded dream.

Two more years passed before I departed my ancestors' glacial sand spit, so bleak and so heartbreakingly lovely. This time I went east—across the Atlantic. And stayed.

In Europe I took a job as a journalist. I felt doubly blessed to be living an expatriate adventure and getting paid for work that was challenging and fun. Travel and the outdoors remained avocations. About the only thing better, I thought, would be to make my living following all three of my fancies. The chance seemed beyond remote. And yet, shortly it came true.

As a "travel and outdoor writer," my assignments ranged from Moscow to Edinburgh, from Copenhagen to the Greek Isles, and to many places in between. I skied the summer glacier at Zermatt and camped in the shadow of the Pyrenees. I hunted geese in Eastern Germany, chamois in the Bavarian Alps, pheasants in Yugoslavia (when there was still a Yugoslavia). And I fished for trout: in Denmark, Poland, Germany, Austria, and other places.

I also covered major breaking news: the exodus of ethnic Germans from the Soviet Union, *glasnost* and *perestroika* under Mikhail Gorbachev, Vice President Al Gore's first official overseas trip (to Warsaw). It was a time of political turmoil and epic change in Europe, a time when those of us who were there felt blessed to be at the epicenter of history. Few people are lucky enough to be paid to do the things they most love, but I knew that I was one. I kept pinching myself and hoping I would not wake up.

They were wonderful years, years of professional satisfaction, of falling in love and starting a family, of being young in exciting times. One day, I thought, I will tell about it.

In that, I know I am not alone. Most journalists harbor the hope that one day they will write something that next week will be more than birdcage liner. There is always the danger of living up to the cliché—i.e., every reporter has a book in him, and that's where most of them should stay.

This is a fly-fishing book. But I hope it is more. Fishing stories alone can be repetitive and boring: Went here, used this, caught that. Often the things that make a trip memorable have little to do with catching fish.

In its variety, vastness, and profusion of wild places, the United States is—as the Germans say—the land of unlimited possibilities (*das Land der unbegrentzten Moeglichkeiten*) for fly fishers. Montana alone is ten thousand square miles bigger than the reunited Germany, one-and-a-half times the size of the United Kingdom, five times the size of Austria. And there are few angling destinations lovelier than the Sawtooths, the Absarokas, the Wind River Range, and the waters that nourish them.

And yet, there are many good reasons for fly fishers to head for Europe. Most Americans see the Continent as a place to soak up art, history, and culture. We think of the Champs Elysee, the Uffizi Gallery, Tivoli Gardens, the Grand Canal, the Trevi Fountain, the Acropolis. It is a largely urban perception that belies the region's wondrous cold-water fishing possibilities: the big rainbows of the Deutscher Traun, Jutland's spring creeks, the freestone streams of the High Pyrenees. And numberless others.

But for me the fishing was always only part of the allure.

What made Europe special were the exhilaration and adventure of travel, the thrill of discovering new waters, and the exotic flavors of foreign places. And, of course, there were the people, diverse in their politics, creeds, traditions, and nationalities, and yet—to paraphrase Kipling—brothers and sisters under their skin.

I deciphered hatches and cast loops with people who were wealthy and complacent, people who were poor and happy, people whose lives were circumscribed by the perverse vicissitudes of history. Kind people, funny people, and people consumed by bitterness, envy, and hate. I fished in the bootsteps of a literary giant, the shadow of a castle, and the specter of a death camp. "You went out to fish, and you found all this other stuff," a novelist friend of mine said.

Some of these stories have few fish in them. But it does not always take great fishing to make a good fishing story (Hemingway, Robert Traver, and Nick Lyons come to mind).

One of my favorite books—Turgenev's *Sportsman's Sketches*—is a collection of hunting stories. But the scenes and story lines paint word pictures of prerevolutionary rural Russia—vast open spaces, a decadent and dying feudal society, arbitrary cruelty and compassion—beyond the mere pursuit of ducks and snipe and grouse.

Some may say this is a book that cannot decide if it is a memoir, a travelogue, or a collection of fish tales. The effect was intentional, though the reader will have to judge whether it is successfully executed.

For anglers seeking detailed instruction on tactics and technique, this book may be a disappointment. There are countless other fly-fishing writers, from Lefty Kreh to Chico Fernandez and Doug Swisher, who are more knowledgeable than I on those subjects. The best one I know is my friend Berris "Bear" Samples, author of *Thirty Days to Better Fly Casting*.

All of the stories here are true and faithfully rendered, to the best of my notes and memory. Where conversations were in German, I have retained German grammar and syntax in the translations to capture the flavor and spirit of the original language. In those instances when the people I met spoke English but were not native speakers, I have repeated their words as they said them. A few names have been changed, in deference to friends and acquaintances who cherish their privacy.

1

Snows of Yesteryear

Back to Berchtesgaden, September 1988

Where are beauty's smiles and tears?
And where the snows of other years?

—Francois Villon

September in the Berchtesgadener Alps is almost always glorious—cloudless blue days and clear nights, the stars so close you can reach them with a flip cast. But when Gus and I pulled up in front of the Berchtesgadener Hof, a cold rain was falling and the mountains were a distant fantasy somewhere beyond the low overcast. Still, with months of anticipation and hundreds of miles of

Autobahn behind us, the weather did little to dampen our mood. When we stepped out of the car the air had the clean smell of rainfall in high country.

Conceived in the glow of VDTs and fluorescent lights, the trip was the product of office dreams and meticulous planning. Equipment had been carefully considered and collected, from backpacks and fishing rods down to boots, socks, and insect repellent. But from the beginning the most important consideration was timing. After going around and around on it for the better part of a week we had settled on late September. Vacation mobs and summer squalls would be long gone and the first snows should be at least a month away. It would be a fitting end to the trout season, which closed September 30.

To a pair of Rhine Valley work hostages, a handful of sun-spangled days spent hiking, fishing, and exploring the mountains seemed a perfect soul strengthener for the coming flannel gray German winter. For weeks we talked about the glories of *Altweibersommer* (literally "old-wives' summer," equivalent to our Indian summer) in the Alps, and we repeated the Bavarians' chauvinistic Austria joke: "The white blue sky laughs over Bavaria. The whole world laughs over Austria." (*Ueber Bayern lacht der weissblauer Himmel. Ueber Oesterreich lacht die ganze Welt.*)

"It's gonna be great, Norm," Gus said. "That beautiful Alpine sun, milkmaids and cowbells in the meadows, and plenty of that great Bavarian beer!"

For me the interlude would also be a trip back in time. Nearly twenty years before, putting part of my college-loan money to what I knew was a better use than paying for semester hours, I had hopped an Icelandic Airlines Constellation to Luxembourg during winter break and had set out to make the best use of a Eurailpass. Berchtesgaden's jagged peaks and twisting valleys had been a high point of my mini-*Bildungsreise*, but I had not been back since.

At eight A.M. on departure day I obsessively rechecked our gear while Gus leaned against the car smoking one last cigarette. "I think we prolly got enough," he laughed. The back of the station wagon was packed halfway to the roof.

We hit the road like Kerouac and Cassady but soon turned into Laurel and Hardy. Two hours from home, on the Autobahn outside Ulm, the engine began making a loud noise, then started to smoke. Gus was driving in the passing lane, so it took about ten seconds to get over into the right lane, then another four or five to pull out of the traffic and onto the shoulder—just in time for the final *klunk*. We got out and opened the hood to find an oil-spattered engine block and a smoking hole where the oil cap should have been. We looked at each other, at the packed car and just stood there with the speed-limitless traffic roaring by a few feet away.

Because a stupid or careless mechanic had forgotten to replace the cap, all the oil had sprayed out. The "idiot light" had lived up to its name and flashed its warning too late, seconds before the engine seized up.

I walked to an emergency call box while Gus waited by the car, and a half-hour later we rode the tow truck into Ulm ahead of our dead Passat. In the meantime we made a pact to put the comical disaster behind us and make the most of the situation.

We took a couple of hours to explore the city: strolling along the Danube, stopping at a kiosk for a hard roll and *Wurst* washed down with beer, and gazing upward at the Gothic cathedral, most of which was covered in scaffolding for renovation.

We quickly found out how relentlessly the city markets itself as Albert Einstein's birthplace: postcards, brochures, guidebooks. Near the granary museum I posed in front of Juergen Goetz's worshipfully irreverent fountain sculpture of the famous physicist as a snail with the earth for a shell, perched atop a rocket, his eyes popping and tongue out *a la* the famous poster.

When we finally changed cars and transferred gear, we had lost half a day from our carefully planned schedule. Neither of us really cared.

Gus was one of the most upbeat people I knew and by the time we got back on the road the blown engine was already just another travel anecdote. Soon, so was Bavaria's laughing, white blue sky. Looming ahead and then closing in over us as we drove farther south was a frowning, dishwater-dun cloud blanket.

It was drizzling when we turned off the Autobahn and onto the narrow, winding local Route 21. In Bad Reichenhall the balconies and shop windows were wet and streaked, the geraniums in the window boxes dripping. At a crosswalk, an old woman stepped carefully over the gutter, umbrella tilted into the wind.

But in another few minutes the road was climbing, climbing, and then descending the pass at Hallthurm, and despite the rain and gray came the feeling of entering a special place, a place apart, that I had first felt riding in on the train in the snows of 1969.

* * *

As its name implies, Berchtesgadener Land is a realm unto itself, a refuge and a natural redoubt with mountain ranges for walls. Surrounded on three sides by Austria (it lies directly south from Salzburg), this tiny bulge in the southern German border was once a semi-independent principality ruled by a prince bishop. Over the centuries its geography and political traditions spawned a quirky, skeptical streak that broke down badly only once. Even today the residents consider themselves not just Germans or Bavarians—and, of course, not Austrians—but Berchtesgadener.

For more than a hundred years, since the early days of mass tourism, Berchtesgaden has drawn an international mix of visitors. Its lodestone is not history, heritage, or national allegiance but natural beauty, much of it now protected within Berchtesgaden National Park.

It is a region dominated by mountains, some with whimsical

or ominous-sounding names: Untersberg, Jenner, Toter Mann (Dead Man), Grosser Teufelshorn (Big Devil's Horn), Grosser Hundstod (Big Dog's Death). This is a craggy, montane landscape where mini-glaciers and ice caves tucked into far-high corners hide pockets of perennial winter—ice and gneiss eternal.

These are the postcard Alps—jagged ridgelines sloping down to pastures and evergreen forests; verdant valleys; onion-domed churches and steep-roofed chalets. On the streets you really can spot women in dirndls, men in knee breeches and loden jackets. Dominating the skyline and the consciousness are the twin spires of the Watzmann, the area's unofficial emblem.

But Berchtesgadener Land is also a region of waters, of glacial freshets and cobbled streams and Alpine lakes, a dynamic micro-hydrosphere amid the stone-and-ice *Berglandschaft*. Five miles south of town, the Watzmann's sheer east wall plunges into Lake Koenigsee's fiordlike depths; six miles to the west, the Hintersee and Taubensee mirror the Hochkalter's rocky hump and the dark firs of the Enchanted Forest (*Zauberwald*). Farther above are the high-mountain lakes: Obersee, Funtensee, Gruensee—drops of liquid topaz among the crags. Like high, cold waters the world over, many of them hold trout.

* * *

After Gus and I checked into the hotel, I did what any fisherman would do: headed for the water. Koenigsee's outlet stream, the Berchtesgadener Ache, flows through town and out past the salt mine before tumbling down toward Mozart's hometown—Salzburg—and its confluence with the Salzach. Not far from the train station it washes over a bed of large stones and spills under the main road bridge before deepening into a large pool.

On an icy January afternoon nineteen years before, I had stopped on the bridge to kiss the first girl I loved and watch the trout holding in the current near the pilings. Afterward, we hiked up in the early darkness to the stone church with its snowy grave-yard. The clerestory windows gave off a yellow gold glow that stood out against the blackening sky, and in the graveyard the crosses and monuments were mounded high with snow that softened their hard edges.

As we climbed back down the icy steps to town, the church bells began to ring, sharp and clear. We did not want to splurge on a restaurant, so we bought a loaf of crusty white bread and a half kilo of *Emmentaler* cheese, and walked back to the guest house in the deepening chill.

Now, standing in a drizzling rain, I remembered how she laughed that I stopped to watch the fish; how the still, cold air prickled the nostrils, little white puffs of breath drifting out over the river, then our cold noses touching, the warmth of our mingled lips. And later, the first few pinprick stars showing over the mountains, the new snow that came in the night and covered the bottle of wine we left on the balcony.

There were still trout beneath the bridge, thick-bodied browns and rainbows that held themselves effortlessly in the slow water where the river spilled down over the rocks into the big pool. Nineteen years was about one human generation. How many trout generations had passed? I wondered.

* * *

Back at the hotel I pulled off my poncho in the entryway and shook off the water under the awning. I went upstairs and put away my gear and knocked on Gus's door. "Come on in, Norm, the door's open," he said.

He was putting film canisters into plastic shopping bags. When he finished he squeezed out the air, tied the ends, and tucked them into the outside pocket of his shoulder bag. "Boy, I sure hope this rain stops," Gus said, "or I'll need an underwater camera." We both laughed.

"Yeah, they didn't tell us all that famous Bavarian sunshine was the liquid kind."

"Did you call Ted?" Gus asked.

"Not yet. Let's do it now."

Ted Hassinger was an American who had lived in Berchtesgaden for three years. I had been given his name by an acquain-
tance who said Ted could tell us "everything you need to know,
and then some."

When I had phoned him a few weeks before, he was full of
enthusiasm. "Call me when you get in," he said, "I'll give you the
whole scoop over *Jaegerschnitzel* and *Helles*."

This time I reached him as he was about to leave the office.
We arranged to meet at a pub restaurant around the corner from
the hotel, and an hour later he showed up on his bike, face and
hair streaming with rainwater but otherwise none the worse for
the weather. Clad in Gore-Tex and Lycra under a rain poncho,
Ted looked like an ad for the healthy mountain life.

We shook hands and ducked into the light and warmth of the
smoky pub, where a half- dozen people greeted Ted as we made
our way to a table. Soon we were quaffing three tall *Helles* and
planning for tomorrow. Gus and I had heard the forecast—more
of the same. But Ted was unrelentingly upbeat about the wait-a-
minute Alpine climate, and the prospects got brighter with each
beer. By the time we wiped up the last of the mushroom sauce
from our *Jaegerschnitzel,* hopes were on their way to expectations.

"Anyway, Ted said, "there's plenty to see and do whatever the
weather." In the morning we would hike the Jenner.

* * *

At breakfast the overcast was down around the hotel eaves, but
Gus still had plenty of his usual "there-must-be-a-pony-some-
where-in-this-manure-pile" good cheer.

"Well Norm, looks like we're in for another adventure," he
said.

Like many people who'd had tough early years, Gus's opti-
mism was partly gratefulness for the positive turn his life had
taken. Born in Frankfurt a few years before World War II, he had
seen the city bombed to rubble around him as a small boy and,
later, had suffered through the privation of the postwar years. At

seventeen, when an offer to sponsor his U.S. immigration visa came from a family friend in the Midwest (a Jewish man who had fled the Nazis), Gus jumped at the chance.

He had never looked back and was now more American than any native. The only reminder of his birth citizenship was a slight speech anomaly—not an accent exactly but a way he elided some words, missed certain letters (like Rs that followed vowels). On the road he was always considerate and his jokes, anecdotes, and observations about life made the travel time pass quickly.

Unlike Gus and Ted, my outlook tended toward the Eeyorian. As I gazed outside at the rain and fog, the idea of heading farther up into the mountains and weather seemed a down-current snag in a mindscape of riffles and rising trout. But, of course, Gus and I were tough and game. After breakfast we finished stuffing our packs and headed out to hook up with Ted.

He met us at the foot of the Jenner wearing shorts below his poncho and a grin above. The overcast had lifted a little, and we could see partway up the mountain. The rain, however, had not let up.

"It's sparkling white up on top," Ted said.

"Snow?" Gus asked.

"Yeah, that's what they say. Above fifteen hundred meters."

Gus looked at me and laughed. "Hea we go," he said. "We'll prolly get caught in a blizzad and be snowed in foa the winta."

"Yeah, it'll make a great story in the spring," I said. " 'Frozen Bodies of Two Americans Found atop Jenner.' "

The situation was funny and we would make the best of it, but we had planned an Indian summer interlude, not an endurance trek. With the rain dripping off my hood, my mind was on the trout holding below the bridge and the sun somewhere above the clouds.

On the way up the mountain the rain changed to sleet around the fourteen-hundred-meter mark, and a thin frosted layer began to show on trees, rocks and meadows. Higher still, evergreen branches sagged under heavy, wet loads; when we climbed out of the forest, the landscape was bare and nearly white, whipped by a cross-mountain wind.

"I guess this is the famous '*weissblauer Himmel*,' " Gus said, squinting into the driving snow.

An hour later we stamped the snow from our boots and stepped into the warmth of the Carl von Stahlhaus, one of the hundreds of *Berghuetten* that dot the German-speaking Alpine region.

With its implication of small, rude shelters, the English translation—"mountain huts"—is deceptively inadequate. These high-altitude guesthouses may sleep upward of a hundred, and most offer food, beverages, and indoor plumbing.

When our feet and hands had thawed, we ate bowls of steaming goulash and black bread (*Bauernbrot*) with half a dozen other storm refugees. Afterward, our stomachs full and faces flushed with heat from the kitchen, the storm was no longer an ordeal but just local weather, outside and beyond us. We kicked back in the dining room with brown half-liter bottles of beer, exchanging thumbnail bios and putting off heading upstairs to the unheated bunk room.

Ted retraced for us his convoluted trail to Berchtesgaden. Growing up in The Big Easy, he had known a boyhood of jazzy urban lifestyles and floodplain geography. It was a world circumscribed by water and watery land: marshes, lowlands, swamps, bayous, and levees. But after graduating as a communications major from the University of New Orleans he had set out on a transatlantic adventure—and never gone home. He had crisscrossed the Continent from the North Sea to the Riviera, from the Aegean to Brittany. But it was in Bavaria that he fell in love with a landscape as different from the Mississippi delta as the dark side of the moon. And there he stayed.

After starting out as a bowling-alley attendant, Ted had worked his way up to assistant press liaison for the Armed Forces

Recreation Centers. He organized and led groups and press crews bent on skiing, hiking, biking, and exploring the Alps. Ted was in the mountains when the nights turned cool and the cows ambled down from summer pastures in a festive procession, bells a-clang. He was there when the season's first real snowfall covered the Jenner's slopes. He was there when the days lengthened again toward the solstice, when riots of wildflowers filled the high meadows. Seldom was he office bound.

"I can't believe I get paid for it," Ted laughed.

Sometimes he did miss New Orleans—family, Cajun food. "But I'd never live there," he said. "I found that if I'm not near mountains, I'm not happy."

When the candles melted down to wax remnants on the rough-pine table, and our last beers were drained to the dregs, we climbed the stairs into the chill and zipped ourselves into sleeping bags.

Later, lying in the dark, the wind howling around the eaves, I saw again the stream and the bridge with the fish holding beneath it. Sunlight played off the water and the trout rose to canary yellow mayflies that drifted, drifted down, spinning on little circular currents with their sailboat wings before disappearing in a splash. Dreams and expectations, I knew. Nineteen years before, there had been others. Many others.

Down the long row of bunks somebody coughed in his sleep, and the sound echoed off the log walls.

* * *

We met in Luxembourg, she returning from a semester in India, I a first-time transatlantic tourist, callow and wide-eyed. Hand in hand we explored castles, cafés, and cobblestone lanes under the leaden skies, fog, and drizzle of the Low Country winter. As for all young lovers with eyes only for each other, the weather was no misfortune of fate, merely an inconsequential backdrop. But finally we headed south.

For most of a day we rode through a landscape of pigments

brown and gray: drab postwar cities, soggy winter forests, and muddy fields. Finally the train began climbing into the Alps—up, up through the dismal, gray soup and out into sunshine and snow and high blue skies. And that is where we stayed. In the next two weeks we stopped in Lucerne, Interlaken, Zermatt.

And Berchtesgaden.

One day we hiked out of town to the salt mine, donning folk costumes to ride the tram into the Salzberg, the mountain filled with salt deposits millions of years old. With sunlight and snow-scape shrinking away behind, and ahead the dimly lit shaft, we laughed and lurched with the swaying cars.

When the track ran out we climbed down and followed the guide farther into the tunnel to a low opening. As we came to it, the hole gaped black and empty, disappearing down, down into rock. Standing beside a narrow plank chute, the guide joked about who would lead the way into mysterious new regions.

"Who will be the brave one?" he asked. "Who among us is the fearless leader?"

We looked at each other and stepped to the front. To the young, the universe's demons are feeble and few. The unseen future, its outcome beyond knowing, is thrilling and new and full of promise, the threat of danger or disappointment remote and un-real. For youth is risk, or it is no youth at all.

We sat at the top of the chute—I in front, her hands around my waist and the others linked up behind—and off we pushed, sliding down into the blackness. "So first love possesses all the im-mediate temperamental assurance" Kierkegaard wrote. "It fears no danger, it defies the whole world."

I could not know then how it would end for us or that I would double my years before life's circle time parade returned me to the place where first love was forever and all that mattered was an-other night in each others' arms.

Two, three, four seconds of rushing blackness and we shot out into a low, cavernous chamber, wanly lit. A moment later the guide slid down, nonchalant and legs crossed for effect, into the midst of laughter.

We followed another tunnel, touching wetted fingertips to sparkling walls for a taste of ancient seas. Then came an eerie raft ride across a stygian salt lake and more twisting passageways. Finally we walked out of the mine, momentarily blinded, into the brilliant winter sunshine.

Now, in the darkness alone, it was *Schnee von gestern* (snows of yesteryear)—long melted and trickled away downgrade into the broader flow. I rolled over in the hard bunk and went to sleep.

*   *   *

When I woke, the view out the window was monochrome white. I slid farther down in the sleeping bag and pulled the drawstring tighter. I did not stick my head back out until Gus shouted.

"Norm, you awake?"

"Yeah, but I wish I was still asleep." I could see my breath.

"Yeah," he laughed, "it still looks like a blizzad out theya."

"Hey great," Ted said, "today we get to see how tough you guys really are."

In the breakfast room we joined the six other overnight guests talking quietly over coffee. We sat down and soon had steaming mugs in front of us. Next came baskets of hard rolls (*Broetchen*); plates of butter, *Wurst*, and cheese; a bowl of currant jam; and three soft-boiled eggs, jauntily upright atop blue-and-white porcelain egg cups. The eggs were soon topped, their whites and runny yolks were scooped out with tiny spoons, and the rest followed.

"Good start to a snowy day," Ted said.

"Yeah," Gus said, "but I don't see anyone rushing out yet into the fresh air. See how they keep looking out the window?" He nodded toward another table. "I think that *weissblauer Himmel*'s still a little too *weiss* foa them."

When we stepped onto the porch the temperature was

twenty-eight degrees. The snow was still coming down hard and a twenty-five-knot wind whipped it along the ridge in slanting lines that approached the horizontal. My gently rising trout seemed more than a few miles down the valley. They seemed a universe away. We shouldered our packs and stepped off the porch into the whiteout and ten inches of new snow.

On our own, Gus and I might have walked into a dead-end ravine or off a cliff, but Ted was an old hand. We took it slowly, feeling our way with our boots. In places the drifts were knee deep, making for tricky going over scree and on some of the steeper inclines.

As the trail switchbacked down, we got into the lee of the mountain out of the worst of the wind. The howling storm diminished to a mere heavy snowfall. We passed a tiny cabin, not much bigger than an outhouse and built of rough-sawn planks; heard a "*Schi heil*" and a laugh; and looked back to see an old woman in the doorway grinning and waving.

When we got to the tree line it looked like a Christmas card: green and white, the lower fir boughs pressed against each other, tips touching the ground. The temperature had risen three or four degrees, and the snowflakes were heavy and wet. As we descended farther, the snow cover began to diminish and the wind died down to a whisper. Around the forty-three-hundred-foot mark, we walked out of the snow into sleety rain. Suddenly the ground was bare, and we began to encounter cows, now down from the high summer meadows. They stood impassive in the rain, with soggy hides and blank bovine stares.

At a turn in the trail we stopped at a squat log hut, unshouldered our packs, and set them under the eaves. Ted stuck his head in the open door, shouted "*Servus*," and ducked inside. A few seconds later he came out laughing, followed by a short, gnomish man with a ruddy face and Brillo Pad hair.

"Herr Rasp," Ted said, and we shook hands all around. Herr

Rasp wore a rubber apron and boots, and he was sweating and grinning a mischievous grin that deepened his crow's-foot wrinkles as it broadened. I couldn't guess his age.

"Herr Rasp would gladly offer us a little refreshment ('*wuerde uns gerne eine kleine Erfrischung anbieten*')," Ted said. Gus and I nodded, biting back smiles, and followed them back inside.

We walked into a tiny kitchen with a washbasin and refrigerator. To the left was a closet-size bathroom, visible through a narrow doorway. To the right the hut opened up into a kind of great room, nearly dark because it had only one tiny window. But in a few seconds, after our eyes had adjusted, we could make out a cast-iron furnace topped by a copper kettle with coils and pipes and gauges sprouting from it. A clear liquid trickled from a half-inch plastic tube into a stainless-steel milk can on the floor. Heat radiating from the furnace filled the building. Now it was clear why Herr Rasp was sweating and kept his front door open on a sleety mountain day.

Ted brought four small glasses from the kitchen, and Herr Rasp lifted a ladle from the wall, lowering it into the milk can to dip out a jiggerful for each of us. He kept the last glass for himself and hoisted it, grinning. "*Servus*," he said.

"*Servus*," we answered in unison, then we all raised the glasses to our lips.

Herr Rasp tossed his back in a single gulp, and Ted took his in two. Gus and I were more cautious, taking a couple of large sips before downing the rest. The liquid fire burned from mouth to stomach, releasing pungent, bitter fumes that rose into the nose and left a medicinal aftertaste. It took me a second to get my breath, but then we all started laughing. Herr Rasp reached out his hand for the glasses and, one by one, poured out another dose. Then we went around the corner to a table and chairs, and he told us his story and the story of *Enzian Schnapps*.

Enzian, or mountain gentian, is a tough, slow-growing perennial herb that thrives in the thin Alpine soil and air, generally between four thousand and six thousand feet. Dairy farmers, noting their cows' avoidance of the plant and its tendency to take over mountain pastures, consider it a noxious weed. But mountain gentian has long been prized by folk healers for its reputed medicinal properties. Although these days the *Schnapps* is marketed as an after-dinner bitters, not a medicine, it is anecdotally recommended as a cure for everything from nervousness to digestive disorders.

It was probably monks who first mass-produced *Enzian Schnapps*, but in the early 17th century the Grassl family distillery, headquartered in Unterau, obtained the exclusive right to harvest the plant and distill *Schnapps* in the Berchtesgadener Alps.

Rasp, a rough-hewn Berchtesgaden native, had operated the company's mountain-hut distillery on the slopes of the Priesberg, the mountain just below the Jenner, for more than a generation. For up to two-and-a-half months each year—from early August to late October—he called the low-slung cabin home. During that time he shared it off and on with up to six root diggers (*Wuerzel-graeber*), who during the day ranged into the mountains with two-pronged hoes and at night crowded into the tiny bunkroom.

Some of the diggers were old-timers who began wandering the mountain meadows as boys and now did it to supplement their pension checks. Many others were students. Herr Rasp showed us a postcard of local hero Peter Angerer, gold-medal winner in the biathlon at the 1984 Winter Olympics in Sarajevo. "He was one of our diggers," he said. "Peter was a good one."

The *Enzian* harvest, Herr Rasp explained, began with the flowering of the plants and usually ended with the first major snowfall. For him, it was a time of the spruce and fir forests, of the deer and chamois and soaring eagles that inhabited the mountains. On many an autumn night he had heard the battles and bugling of the red stags in rut.

He knew the *Enzianhuette* was really a quaint anachronism, producing only a token volume of Grassl's yearly output. But Herr

Rasp took his work seriously. Each year, he said, as long as he could ("*so lange ich noch kann*"), he would return to chop the bitter roots, mix them with yeast and spring water in the fermenting vat, watch and wait for ten or twelve days, distill the sourmash to *Roh-brand* (raw distillate), and repeat the distillation for *Feinbrand.*

The *Rohbrand's* potency, he told us, ranged from about 35 percent alcohol at the start of the distillation process to 5 percent at the end. But the first of the *Feinbrand* that trickled out of the cooling pipe topped 70 percent, an explosive 140 proof.

Herr Rasp had not told us what we had been served, but I had my suspicions and he confirmed them with a sly smile: At 10:15 in the morning we were drinking *Feinbrand.* As we drained our glasses he declaimed about the virtues of regular consumption— "*Regelmaessig trinken, nicht uebermaessig,*" (Drink regularly, but in moderation)—and from the way my head felt, it was clear this was the kind of medicine best administered in small doses.

We shouldered our packs, shook hands all around, and—partially fortified, partially paralyzed—headed off down the mountain in the sleety rain. A hundred yards down the trail I looked back, and Herr Rasp was still watching us from the doorway.

When we reached the valley there was no hint of the fierce snowstorm above. It was just another misty, gray day with a steady rain falling.

*   *   *

Back in town we had time on our hands. The weather still precluded fishing, so we drove around to see some of the sights.

In addition to natural beauty, Berchtesgaden touts many historical and cultural landmarks: cloisters, museums, castles, mountain chapels. But the region's heritage has a side that many locals would just as soon forget.

The Obersalzberg—the heights above the salt mine—now the site of a hotel, once echoed with the tramp of jackboots. From 1933 to 1945 the usually skeptical, independent-minded Berchtesgadener lost their heads as completely as the roaring, swastika-waving mobs in Nuernberg, Berlin, and Munich. For Berchtesgaden—a favorite haunt of Hitler's from his early days as a street agitator—was the de facto summer capital of the Third Reich.

Newsreels, home movies, and still photos show the *Fuehrer* hiking (resplendent in *Lederhose*), greeting adoring folk-costumed admirers, strolling with Mussolini, Goering, and Eva Braun against the backdrop of the mountains, joking with black-uniformed officers.

In the early years of Nazi rule, the building complex on the Obersalzberg housed the Fuehrer's living quarters, the mountain chancellery, and the barracks for his SS bodyguard. But the dictator's wealthier sycophants, among them some of Germany's leading industrialists, thought he deserved more. In 1939, for his fiftieth birthday, they presented him with the key to the *Kehlstein-haus*, built high above the Obersalzberg, atop the rocky pinnacle of the Kehlstein. It would be an aerie for the supreme leader of the Master Race, the *Uebermensch* who was destined to rule the world.

Painstakingly crafted of stone and reached by an elevator built into the mountain, this mountaintop retreat (dubbed the Eagle's Nest by victorious American troops) is a wonder of German engineering. It was here that Hitler, sentimental soul that he was (he loved dogs and Aryan children), gazed out over the peaks of his native Austria (he was born a stone's throw away, over the mountains in Braunau) while planning bloody conquest and genocide.

The mountains were shrouded in fog when Gus and I drove up the switchback road to the hotel. We went inside to get a cup of coffee in the dining room and to gaze out the picture window. But the view over the valley was a uniform, depthless gray. We might as well have been looking at a TV screen after the cable connection had gone out.

Beneath the hotel lay a bunker complex blasted out of the mountain (but never quite completed) when the mighty Nazi war machine began sputtering and stalling on all fronts. The intricate tunnel network was to be a redoubt for the *Fuehrer* and his most fanatical SS followers. From their mountain stronghold they would orchestrate the *Endkampf*—the final battle against advancing Allied troops—like a *Goetterdaemmerung.*

But in the end there was no glorious twilight of the gods, and the man whose name became the 20th century's central metaphor for evil ("Because he lived, fifty million people died," wrote *The New York Times*) died not like an eagle amid the mountains but like a rat underground in Berlin.

With little to see above ground, Gus and I descended into the bunkers. Nineteen years before, full of the hubris and insouciant curiosity of youth, I had viewed the dimly lit concrete shafts as dramatic artifacts of a smashed empire. But now I felt a chill in the tunnels, one that was more than subterranean. We did not stay long in the cavernous maze haunted by murderous ghosts.

The rain did not stop; the clouds did not lift. In the late afternoon, we visited a pub micro-brewery. Washing down potato salad and *Weisswurst* with the yeasty dark beer, I realized I would not fish the clear, tumbling streams of Berchtesgadener Land on this trip. They had been churned into brownish gray torrents, unwadeable and virtually unfishable with a fly. But sometimes you can wait a long time for sunny days, and it is necessary to make the best of the rainy ones.

Fishing can be a good antidote to thinking, and on this trip there had been too little of the one and too much of the other. Too many memories, too much planning, hoping, waiting. What was the cliché? You can't push the river, only go with the flow? Nineteen years before, I could not make first love last. Nor could I now stop the rain.

* * *

The next day we headed out in intermittent drizzle to the Hintersee, a thirty-seven-acre Alpine lake squeezed among the mountains west of Ramsau, at the beginning of the German Alpine Road (*Deutsche Alpenstrasse*). Unlike the streams, the tourist office had assured us, the lake was still *glassklar* (crystal clear). It was unaffected by the rain.

The English translation of Hintersee is "the lake beyond" or "the lake behind." The original connotation was probably "beyond the mountains," but tucked into a moraine pocket at the foot of the eighty-five-hundred-foot Hochkalter, the lake is also beyond the urban stress of densely populated Europe, beyond the tourist kitsch, and beyond the traffic crush of other resorts.

On a close, gray day it seemed beyond the rest of the world, a place *zum nachdenken*—to contemplate: the end of trout fishing for another year; triumphs, letdowns, and lost chances; the ever-changing seasons of life, my own cycle now beyond Indian summer and slipping away to early autumn.

With the chilly temperature and the dearth of insects, spinning gear seemed the logical choice. I had given up hope of fly fishing and just wanted to catch something, anything, to salvage some of my angling dreams. A swirling mountain wind riffled the steel gray surface of the water when I headed out onto the lake in a rented rowboat. I rowed to the middle first, then began exploring.

The Hintersee's shoreline is mostly rocky, with dark evergreens growing down to the water's edge around much of the lake's perimeter. Unlike the Koenigsee, its littoral zone is fairly wide, extending out fifty or sixty feet in many areas. The bottom is mostly glacial sand, with sparse aquatic vegetation. Along the south shore, marshes and bogs creep up to the edge of the Enchanted Forest.

Periodically a veil of showers swept across the lake, nearly obscuring the mountains and shrouding the shoreline in gray. I hunkered down farther and watched the water stream off the hood of my poncho.

I missed my wife and kids, was glad to be heading home tomorrow.

When you are young you are sure what love is: a racing heart and a sweet sickness that consumes your soul. If you are lucky, you learn that it is mostly a lot of other things: shared caring and a mutual future, days by a sickbed, watching in the delivery room, and knowing that you are part of something new, bigger than yourself—a family.

It is fine to remember old love affairs. You never really lose someone you have loved, longed for, and held in the night; she becomes part of you, as you become part of her. And years later you know you are better for it; even for the pain and stillborn dreams.

With the frequent wind shifts, it was easy to fish the lake by casting and drifting. But it soon became evident that the water clarity, while aesthetically pleasing, was a handicap.

When the rain let up and the wind died, the water's surface smoothed out, and trout were visible all around the lake. Along the edge of the shallows, where the bottom sloped steeply into black depths, they floated weightlessly or cruised with the alertness of the aquatic predator.

If I saw them I would cast the spinner or wobbler or spoon to a spot above and in front of them, let it sink to the right depth, and retrieve it past them. Sometimes I could see them follow the lure, giving it a quick once-over before reversing course and shooting off. A few came right up to the boat. But in two-and-a-half hours of continuous casting I had only had one hit.

With dusk approaching, I reeled in the lure, laboriously unfastened the snap swivel, and put the red-and-white spoon back in the tackle box. The cold rain had numbed my fingers to the point that this simple task was reduced to the equivalent of dealing cards with work gloves on. I laid the rod in the stern, swung the bow toward the north, and started rowing.

The rain made a fine hissing noise on the surface of the water, erasing the ripples from the oars and the thin wake made by the boat as it glided toward shore.

My last fishing trip of the year, anticipated as glowing sun, had been supplanted by the cold rain and gray mountain mist of an

out-of-season autumn. But it did not have to end in the frustration of heaving and hauling hardware. I pulled hard on the oars to
push the boat ashore. Then I put away the spinning rod. If it was
to be a fishless day, at least I would have the pleasure of casting a
fly. Despite the cold weather and the absence of any insect hatch,
occasional rises dimpled the surface of the lake between the rain
showers.

As I headed back out, the overcast lifted for the first time that
afternoon, revealing jagged peaks wreathed in mist and a snow
line extending a third of the way down the mountains.

With my fingers still stiff from the cold and damp, it took
nearly ten minutes of fumbling to tie on the leader and fly. But the
cold was soon forgotten in the rhythm of casting and watching for
a strike. Finally, along the dark edge of the Enchanted Forest, a
tiny Royal Coachman disappeared in one of those moments that
are preserved in the mind like snapshots.

The nine-and-a-half-inch brook trout that I lifted into the
boat was as lovely as many a bigger fish, its iridescent speckles all
the more brilliant in contrast to the gray, gloomy day, with its
threat of winter. Sometimes the little things matter most.

After being lowered gently back into the water, the fish fanned
its gills briefly, unsteady in my hand, before scooting away into the
chilly, fathomless depths. It took another ten minutes of pains-
taking effort to change the waterlogged fly.

One more small brookie took a Yellow Mayfly and was
released before, with darkness closing in on the valley and a bone-
chilling cold seeping in, it was time to write an end to trout fishing
for another year.

High above the lake, the last rays of the sun glinted off the
snow-capped Hochkalter. This was just a hint of the beginning, I
knew. In another month the big snows would come to the High
Alps. For seven months they would pile up on the peaks and hills,
and in the forests, fields, and valleys. Finally, around Easter, the
ascending sun would gain the upper hand. Then these snows, like

the long-ago snows of my youth, would melt and run down to swell the trout streams and farther down to merge into bigger rivers and finally into the sea.

As I rowed back to shore, the final impressions of the fading season were the Alpine stillness and the dark evergreens of the Enchanted Forest, shrouded in gray mist. In the clear depths, the trout still cruised along the dropoff.

2

Monte Perdido

Lost, and Found, June 1989

What human being can help another?
Who can enter into another's soul?

—Ivan Turgenev, "Living Relics"

In the heat of the day, the call of the cuckoo had echoed across the valley, but now the chirping of a nearby cricket punctuated the only other night sounds: the high wind in the trees and the rush of the river below the campground. A full moon rising over the Pyrenees, a cool San Miguel beer, and the smell of fresh trout sizzling in the pan completed the scene. It could not be any better if

I had scripted it, I thought. And in a way, I had.

Since breaking onto the European fishing scene a couple of years before, I had made a few memorable excursions. But most of my outings had been in Germany, where the complicated, quasifeudal system of delegated fishing rights and micromanagement could be daunting. Sometimes it took a major research effort just to find out who controlled a section of stream and how to get a permit. I had longed for the American tradition of open public waters. And fresh vistas. Combining wanderlust with some basic research and a little intuition (trout streams and mountains, I knew, often go together), I became intrigued by the idea of Spain.

The popular image of this nation as a hot, sunny land of bullfights, beaches, and fiestas seems far removed from trout fishing. And most of the millions of tourists who flock there each year head for the seashore or a few large cities—Madrid, Seville, Barcelona, Granada. But there is another Spain, the Spain that is the second most mountainous country in Europe (after Switzerland). It is a wild, surprisingly unspoiled land, whose montane topography is patterned with twisting canyons and valleys carved out by swift rivers.

Still, Spain is a big country with a lot more troutless than troutful habitat. Working with the Spanish National Tourist Office, our own modest travel libraries, and tips from friends, my pal Dave and I tried to divine a good area. We pored over brochures, maps, and booklets; read travel guides; and burned up phone lines.

Much of the tourist-office information was vague or sketchy, many of the brochures obviously dated. Some made reference to "good fishing" in a particular region, but often we had to make oblique inferences about angling possibilities from offhand mentions of rivers or river valleys. There was virtually no specific information about how and where.

Complicating the situation was the fact that the regulations were in a state of flux. Until the previous year, there had been one national fishing license. But fourteen years after Fascist President Francisco Franco's death, the country was still making the transition from draconian centralized authority. As part of the trend, control over fish and wildlife had devolved from Madrid to the provinces, and it was now necessary to obtain one license for Catalan, another for Navarre, etc.

Again and again our inquiries pointed to the Pyrenees, the wild, rugged range that snakes along the French border from the Atlantic to the Mediterranean. Finally, picking an area with few towns and roads, we settled on the Rio Ara, north of Huesca. On the map it was just a thin blue squiggle. But it wound down through one of the ruggedest, least populated regions of the High Pyrenees, holding out the promise of feisty browns in cold mountain currents far from the madding crowd. The clincher was that the river's headwaters skirted a national park whose name had an irrestible air of mystery and adventure—*Monte Perdido*. We would go in search of Lost Mountain.

* * *

We set out from Darmstadt full of anticipation on a cloudy, warm June afternoon, eager to quickly put as many miles as possible between us and the Rhein-Main megalopolis. Both Dave and I had moved to the Frankfurt region for a brief career interlude—and stayed ten years.

It was not Paris or Rome or Florence, but it offered most of the best elements of the Western European urban lifestyle—more rooted, relaxed, and ergonomically sane than American cities. I, and later my wife and kids, loved it all: cosmopolitan restaurants; world-class concerts, operas, and ballets; quiet café mornings and *Kaffeeklatsch* afternoons; quirky kiosks and upscale shops; offbeat, pensive films that seldom made it to the United States. And we never feared walking anywhere at any hour of the day or night.

A few months after we married, my wife and I had committed to the region by buying an old farmhouse, ten miles from the Rhine.

The house itself was a two-and-a-half-story, stone-and-stucco, postwar construction with a red tile roof. But what really sold us were the yard and outbuildings.

Connected to the rear of the house, on the north side of the yard, was a series of low, half-timbered structures that had been storage sheds or stalls. These stretched back about fifty feet to a huge old brick barn. It had been partially rebuilt after the war, and three of the six-by-six cross-timbers were still charred from the night in 1944 when the RAF firebombed the town.

The rest of the area between the house and the barn was a paved courtyard, enclosed on the south side by a six-foot brick wall. Slightly off to the north side of center grew a huge old walnut tree whose branches spanned the width of the courtyard.

And in back of the barn was the greatest gift of all: a one-hundred-fifty-foot expanse of rich, alluvial soil with grass, lilac, and forsythia bushes; a strawberry patch; and a vegetable plot. By European standards, it was an estate.

It was a far cry from the white-picket fences, clapboards, and cedar shakes of our native New England. And some of our relatives thought we were nuts; buying a home in a foreign land was bad enough, but this one was what the Germans call *Renovierungsbeduerftig* (literally, ripe for renovation). We moved in during Central Europe's coldest January in fifty years, and the house did not even have any central heating—only kerosene stoves.

But we were young and foolish, full of adventurous longings. Also, we had grand plans: a nursery for our first child (already on the way), new walls and floors, a new bathroom and kitchen, a huge vegetable garden. Anyway, we thought, most homes are temporary. And in the end, home is where your work takes you, where the people you love most and your friends are, and where your heart is. For now, ours was a little town in the Rhine Valley.

Neither of us had set out to be an expatriate, but here we were;

and we were determined to make the most of our few short years before we moved back to the United States. It was as easy as strolling downtown to buy a ticket. For at our doorstep were some of the great cities of the world—Amsterdam, Paris, Hamburg, Munich, Vienna—all less than a day's train ride away.

Closer to home, every fall Frankfurt hosted the world's biggest book fair. In July, Darmstadt made merry for *Heinerfest,* a prevenient, less ostentatious *Oktoberfest.* The library where we checked out books was a Baroque castle where the last empress of Russia, Alexandra von Hessen, had grown up.

Life is full of tradeoffs, and one reason for these genteel amenities, of course, is that Central Europe is among the most densely populated corners of the world.

In *Gray Streets, Bright Rivers* Nick Lyons captured the contradictory pulls of cities and wild places. But for most of us they are merely conflicting, inchoate longings.

We all know people who cannot run from their rural roots fast enough, who never look back once they feel the comforting solidity of pavement beneath their feet. But Dave and I were not such people.

We did suffer from the "how you gonna keep keep 'em down on the farm" syndrome. But both of us were also country boys at heart, lovers of the outdoors and the quietude of open spaces. Dave had grown up amid the cornfields of Clarion, Iowa, and I had spent my boyhood haunting the marshes, estuaries, sand dunes, and scrub-pine woods of Cape Cod.

Dave and I were both in good moods that surged with the speed as we turned onto Autobahn A-5 toward Heidelberg and Basel. It was that old irresistible footloose-and-fancy-free feeling of cruising down the road—air rushing past open windows—on the way to adventure.

As we rolled south through the central German countryside, towns, forests, and summer-green fields flashed past. Just below

Baden-Baden we skirted the evergreen hills of the Black Forest, then crossed over the Rhine and the border at Mulhouse into a flat, open country of farms and lush hardwood forests, with few towns and the wide, uncrowded *autoroute* stretching away into the distance.

South of Lyon the country became drier, the soil thinner as the day faded away, the sun setting behind the rocky, scrub-brush hills of the Rhone Valley. A little before nine, tired and wind-blown, we got off the highway at Tain l'Hermitage, where we found rooms on the main square for ninety francs.

The hotel was slightly down-at-the-heels, but the owners—husband and wife—were pleasant, and downstairs was a small bar that served sandwiches. We ate at a table on the sidewalk out front; after the meal I had a *demiblonde,* and Dave smoked a pipe before we headed up to our rooms.

Mine had one window with metal shutters, and when I opened them I could look out on the square where young couples and pensioners strolled or sat talking under the plane trees. I wanted to leave the shutters open, but the street lamps were too bright.

* * *

In the morning we lingered over coffee and croissants in the sunlit square but finally roused ourselves from our indolence and hit the road a little before nine.

The Rhone Valley—orchards and fields and sprawling, helter-skelter towns with construction and trucking firms and ware-houses on the outskirts—looked more like parts of the American Midwest than the compact and carefully manicured neighbor-land, Germany.

Past Portes les Valence, Livron sur Drome, Montelimar, we were into Provence and the landscape began to have a Mediter-ranean feel: brown and faded green hills punctuating the rocky plateau; cypress, scotch broom, and scrubby brush alternating with carefully tended vineyards and fields of lavender.

The singing tires churned up the miles down the coast highway—Nimes, Montpellier, Narbonne. Just north of Perpignan we glimpsed the sweet blue Mediterranean and said good-bye to endless superhighways.

As we wound up into the Pyrenees Orientales on local route 116, heat and hurry fell away behind; rocky hillsides and arid brush gave way to lush hardwoods and finally evergreens. At the border crossing in Bourg Madame/Puigcerda we looked in vain for an open money exchange and, finding that they had all closed three hours earlier, cursed ourselves for not bringing *pesetas*. We had little food or drink and no way to pay for lodging if we continued on into Spain.

"Think we should spend the night here?" Dave asked.

"Naah, let's wing it," I said. "We can try Andorra, there might be something open there."

Then we were over the divide and heading down the lovely Segre River Valley. "Senor, Espana!" Dave said, grinning and sweeping his arm across the view: mountains green with forests that stretched away, and far below in the canyon the narrow stream, silver blue and glinting in the late sunshine.

At La Seu d'Urgeil we detoured north on 145, and after only ten miles the shopping centers, tourist traps, and glass-and-steel commercial buildings of Andorra rose amid the mountains and forests.

In the midst of wildness, this pint-size city-state—feudal anachronism, duty-free mecca, and avaricious tax haven rolled into one—looked preposterously incongruous. The streets bustled with commerce and consumers lugging boom boxes, TVs, shoes, clothes, and all else back to tour buses. We stopped just long enough to change $100 each and buy two sacks of groceries in a tacky supermarket. When we recrossed the border into Spain, it seemed like a reprieve.

An hour later, we were setting up our tent along a lovely little stream spilling down out of the Serra de Campirme. The campground, just below the village of Castellbo, was neat and orderly: tent and trailer sites spread out among fruit trees and poplars. It had a general store, restaurant, pool, and first-rate showers. At dusk the air was filled with thousands of swallows, dipping and weaving overhead. We cooked beans and franks over the camp stove with a few stars coming out in the blue black sky.

"This is pretty much what we came for," Dave said, lighting his pipe as we relaxed on canvas stools.

"And the fishing," I reminded him.

"Yeah, you came for the fishing, too."

I wondered if the stream had any trout. Probably a few little ones. I wanted to try it in the worst way but had no license. Dave tried to egg me on.

"Go ahead and give it a shot," he laughed. "I hear the Spanish jails aren't so bad since the *generalissimo* kicked off."

* * *

In the morning the grass was heavy with dew, and our breath came out in tiny clouds.

The valley remained in shadow until almost eight, when the sun edged over the mountains. After breakfast we hiked up to the village.

Half a thousand years before, Castellbo had been a vibrant hub. Now it was a jumble of tumbledown stone-and-clay structures atop a rocky hill. The streets were narrow, steep, stone pathways. Most of the buildings had slate roofs, grown over in places with ivy and centuries of moss, and everywhere were roses climbing the walls.

Only a handful of houses showed signs of human habitation. The streets, alleyways, steps, low walls, and empty windows belonged to cats—gray, white, black, black-and-white, and calico—mewing, casting a curious eye, or skittering away over the stones.

Above were the swallows: swooping and weaving over the roofs and between the houses, in and out and around the open, arched windows and the bells of the lovely but crumbling church. Their nests were everywhere, tucked up under eaves and into nooks in the walls.

Before hiking back down to the campground, we walked the town's perimeter path. It offered a continuous panorama of mountains and valley, but we did not see a single person.

When we paid our bill at the campground general store, I asked the owner, Juan Buchaca, how many people lived in Castellbo.

"Forty-five," he said. "Only forty-five."

"Once it was alive," he said, "but now. . . ." He shrugged his shoulders.

I wished I could know more. Who could tell of the communal devotion that raised Castellbo's spare, lovely Romanesque church; of its triumphs and flourishing; of the plagues, wars, neglect, and subjugation it must have endured (as did all of Europe); and of what finally brought it down? When we drove away it was with some wistfulness, for I knew I would likely never know. And never see Castellbo again.

But the next adventure was just down the road. Today we would head for Huesca. It would be an easy drive if we stayed on major roads—route 1313 down the Segre Valley to Lleida, then route 240 across the plains to Huesca—but for us, destination had no precedence.

At Coll de Nargo we turned west onto a dusty gravel track that climbed into the Serra de Boumort. Up and up it wound, mile upon mile of narrow washboard road that switchbacked through canyons, around talus slopes and sheer vertical walls, skirting heart-stopping drops on the outside curves.

We stopped at one precipice to peer down half a thousand feet to a dried-up streambed.

"Long way down," Dave said.

"And a hell of a long way back up," I countered.

"True. But somehow I think if you ended up down there, you wouldn't be in any shape to worry about it."

It was a high, dry, rocky, landscape, dominated by the muted browns, reds, and yellows of soil and rocks. Stands of black pines, growing in sunny glades on the gentler slopes, were the only green.

About ten miles in, we passed a parked car. A man and woman with cameras were observing a flock of butterflies, clustered on pine branches and flitting about the few trees. For the next twenty miles the only other signs of humans were two tiny semi-ghost towns perched on bare pinnacles upslope from the road. We did not stop to explore.

Just before two we drove onto paved road again at Tremp. It had taken us more than three and a half hours to travel a little more than thirty miles. We were hot, sweaty, thirsty, and famished, so the town's single restaurant was a welcome oasis.

There were tables on the sunny patio out front, but inside it was dark and cool, with fans turning slowly overhead. The main door was open for fresh air, but a bead curtain in the dining-room entryway kept the heat outside.

We drank two bottled waters each before the meal came— roast young chicken, French fries, and butter lettuce with tomatoes—and we downed two Cokes apiece with the food.

"Man, that's the longest thirty miles I've traveled in a while," Dave said.

"It was worth it, though, don't you think?"

"Oh yeah, no question. I guess I didn't really realize there was that much wild country left here."

We finished up our meal with *flan*, Spain's ubiquitous, golden-rich, caramely egg custard, and afterward we relaxed in the coolness of the stone building while Dave puffed on a postprandial pipe.

"You ever hear from Jessie?" Dave asked, blowing smoke out the side of his mouth.

The question caught me by surprise. Up to now we had not talked about anything personal. Jessie had been my best friend. A hard-drinking good-old-boy from Brownsville, Tennessee, he was also a gifted humorist with a wit to rival that of the young Mark Twain.

It generally took a lot to get a laugh out of me. But some of his stories about his relatives back in the hill country—hunting coons and possums, getting drunk on radiator whiskey at Christmas dinner, carrying on in the bars and roadhouses—made me laugh so hard they brought tears to my eyes.

Three years before, Jessie's dad had been murdered while grilling steak in his backyard when he tried to outdraw an escaped murderer from a nearby prison. The convict had come around the corner of the house with a gun, and Jessie's father, who had heard about the escape on the radio, had gone for the Colt .44 Magnum strapped to his hip.

The single shot probably killed him, but no one would ever know if he might have been saved. The killer, on the run with another escapee, had kidnapped Jessie's mother, forcing her to drive them across state while her husband bled to death in their backyard.

When Jessie returned from the funeral, the wild and wooly times in Tennessee did not seem so funny any more. His humor, once freewheeling and ironic, was tinged with bitterness and negativism. He started drinking more, going home later after work.

Six months later, his sister's fiancé died in a motorcycle crash a week before their wedding. Jessie wanted her to come live with him and his wife, Sarah. The change could not help but do her good, he said. I thought it was settled, but a week or so later Sarah stopped by to pick vegetables in my back garden.

It was a standing joke between Jessie and me. As usual, I had planted too much and was happy to share it with friends: strawberries, zucchini, summer squash, green beans, radishes, lettuce, sweet corn, tomatoes. It was a regular farmers' market. And Sarah had harvesting down to a science.

"She's figured it saves us $12.37 a week," Jessie told me one day when we were drinking beer out back. "And she puts every penny of it in our savings account."

But this day Sarah had come for more than produce. Instead of just starting to harvest, she initiated a conversation. It struck me as out of character because she was usually shy and reticent, speaking mainly in pleasantries and platitudes.

"Don't you think that when people go through hard times they should just pull themselves up by their bootstraps?" she asked.

"Yeah, I agree with that generally," I said. "You know, our generation, especially, seems like it's made whining into a fine art. But people can't always make it on their own, either."

She persisted. "Right. But isn't it the responsibility of each person to deal with his own problems and find his own, or her own, inner strength?"

I was too dense to make the connection then, but a week later I found out that Jessie's sister would not be coming over to live with them.

A couple of months passed. Jessie was drinking more, often during the day. Sometimes he would ride his bike over to help me in the garden and ask if I had any cold beer. I usually did.

"Sarah thinks I'm out gettin' my aerobic exercise," he said one day. He laughed when he said it but it was a dark, bitter laugh with no trace of levity or joy.

About two weeks later, he showed up at my door looking shaky. When I asked him to come in he declined.

"I just want you to know I'm leaving Sarah," he said. His voice had a husky tone. I stood dumbstruck, unable to think of a reply. "I wanted to ask you and Libby to please look out for her, help her through the hard times." I finally found my tongue.

"Yeah," I said, "of course." I thought he was going to cry and I felt like it myself, but in the end neither of us did.

When I walked him out to his car, Pauline, a coworker of ours, was sitting in the passenger seat. She looked as if she thought I was going to yell at her but I was only surprised. I had missed it completely.

The first few weeks after the breakup, Sarah was at our house nearly every night for dinner and stayed till bedtime. She would do anything to get him back, she said. She would go to counseling. She would change. But it was too late.

A few months later, Jessie and Pauline moved away. Since then, more than a year, Jessie and I had been in touch infrequently.

"I got a letter from him a few months ago," I told Dave.

"What did you think about what happened?" he asked.

"It was a terrible shock for him. For all of us," I said.

Dave had lost his own wife ten years earlier, a sudden death from a supposedly minor illness. Now he was finally dating seriously again. Serena was a coworker who had recently moved out on her heel of a husband.

"I mean cheating on his wife," he said.

I wondered where this was coming from. And where it was going. People cope with tragedy in different ways, and empathy with another person's troubles is never automatic. But it seemed that it should be in Jessie's case.

"Dave, Jessie is one of the best guys I know. People do the best they can. And anyway, I try not to judge. Especially a guy who had a string of horrific things happen to him like he did."

He let it drop and the talk moved back to our trip. So far it was everything we had hoped.

"Guess we'd better hit it," I finally said.

From Temp the roads were a headlong descent, tortile and inevitable, through changing climate zones. At first there was more greenery—meadows and terraced gardens and even fruit trees on some of the hillsides—but within ten miles the countryside began to dry out. Then came olive groves, stretching away on both sides.

After Lleida there was only arid, rolling plain all the way to Huesca.

The city came up on us like a surprise. It had no suburbs and seemed to spring out of the plain fully formed. Suddenly we were bumper-to-bumper in a line of cars. After the mountains, the bustling, hot, dry, dusty city, with its traffic noise and crush of people, was jarring to the senses. We navigated through the center, searching for the campground we had picked from our *Eurocamp* guidebook, and managed to find it on the first try.

The place was close to downtown, on the grounds of the municipal swimming pool, shoehorned into a mixed neighborhood of shops, warehouses, and apartment buildings. Though clean and spacious—with hedges and plane trees—it felt like Times Square compared to Castellbo. A railroad track passed within a few yards on one side.

We were too tired to swim but headed for the shower room to wash off the road dirt. Afterward, we ate in a little restaurant half a block away and then crawled into the tent. Despite the campground's brilliant sodium-vapor lamps and the city's background noise, we fell asleep quickly.

In the black predawn we were shaken awake by a rumbling roar, squealing wheels, and the clank of steel-on-steel as a westbound freight clattered past, its lonesome whistle wail trailing away into the night.

"I thought the Day of Judgment had come," Dave said. A few minutes later he was snoring again, but I did not get back to sleep for a long while. Where was the train headed, I wondered. Pamplona? Burgos? Bilbao? All the way to Santiago de Compostela?

* * *

In the morning, after breakfast, we packed up and headed to the tourist office. My object was a fishing license, but when we got there the workers could provide only advice, pamphlets, and brochures. Because of changes in the law, they could no longer issue licenses, the young woman at the counter explained. For that we would have to go to the government building at Plaza de Cervantes. Too bad, I thought. The year before buying a license would have been so easy. But at least Plaza de Cervantes was only three blocks away. Dave and I figured the errand would take only a few minutes, and he decided to wait in the car.

The government center was a big complex and it took me ten minutes to find the right office. A friendly receptionist asked me to please wait, then disappeared for several minutes. When she returned she had a perplexed look on her face. Since the change in the law the permiting process was a little complicated, she explained—unclear. Unfortunately, the official who issued the licenses, señor so-and-so, was in a meeting and would then be going to lunch. But if I could come back in about two hours, he might be able to help us.

I began to think the Plaza de Cervantes was aptly named, that I was Don Quixote tilting at bureaucratic windmills. I looked at my watch—eleven o'clock—and the thought of being stuck in hot, hectic Huesca until midafternoon renewed my resolve. I did not get down on my knees but made it clear to the receptionist that I was a poor *extranjero* who really wanted to see more of her beautiful country. And to fish.

She disappeared for another few minutes and this time brought back señor so-and-so, a trim, darkly handsome man in his mid-thirties. He shook my hand and led me to his office. While he checked my papers and filled out the license, he smiled in a friendly way; or it might have been amusement at my obvious relief. The last hurdle was a minor one. I would have to get a bank money order for the cost of the license: 1,950 pesetas, about $15. When I looked anxious he assured me there was a bank around the corner.

Dave is one of the more patient men I have known, so when I finally returned to the car he showed neither irritation nor much surprise.

"I thought maybe you got kidnapped or mugged," he said.

"You won't believe how lucky I am to have this," I answered, waving the license in front of him.

"Maybe we should have just left without it. Who's gonna be checking way up in the mountains, anyway?"

It was with a sense of relief that we left the concrete and asphalt of Huesca. Soon, too, the plains, with their shimmering heat and trickles for streams, fell away behind as we climbed into the foothills, then the mountains of the Sera de Guarda.

For some miles the road twisted through a narrow gorge, with vertical cliffs thrusting hundreds of feet into the air. Dave had been fiddling with the radio most of the trip with little success, but suddenly we were getting the BBC World Service, clear as a bell. It was baffling. But it stayed that way for only a couple of miles, then was gone as mysteriously as it had come. Dave, a ham radio aficionado, thought the phenomenon might have been caused by iron deposits in the mountains.

"Or maybe it's the Twilight Zone," I said.

"Naah, then we would have heard Churchill speaking or something," he replied.

We stopped for lunch at Jaca. Dave had worked in Miami for most of a decade before moving to Europe and, trusting his South Florida Spanish, ordered a *tortilla*. But he raised his eyebrows in surprise when the waiter brought not a flat, corn-flour cake but a tomato–cheese omelette.

"Guess we *habla'd* a different kind of *español* in Miami," he chuckled. "Good thing I like omelettes."

From Biescas, we ascended a hair-raising, tortuous route up into the Sera de Tendenera, then drove through a pass and down the other side into the green valley of the Ara. Bypassing the whitewashed hilltop village of Torla, we turned down a gravel road, drove out onto a steel bridge, and stopped over the rushing river.

Upstream, a ridgeline of jagged peaks etched the skyline.

Implacably aloof in its monolithic grandeur, one towered above the rest: *Monte Perdido* was lost no more.

An hour later—our tent tidy and taut amid a new-mown meadow, cumulus clouds piling up against the High Pyrenees—the urban sprawl and cultural affectations of the Rhine–Main megalopolis were as distant as the dark side of the moon.

While Dave organized the gear, I went for a stroll and scouted the river. There were no hatches or risers, but it definitely looked trouty and I picked a starting point for the morning. When I got back, I stopped to watch a mason laying patio stones in front of the camp shower building.

Talk is too propitious a word to describe our interaction, but we did communicate. Though my Spanish was worse than miserable, I was quick on the draw with a pocket dictionary. Hand gestures and dimly remembered high-school Latin filled in a few of the gaps.

He must have been a trout fisherman because he got excited when I pointed toward the river and posed a one-word question: "*Peces?*"

"*Si,*" he said, nodding his head rapidly, "*muchas peces.*"

"*Donde?*"

"*Todo rio,*" he answered, sweeping his arm across the face of *Monte Perdido,* past Torla, and on down the valley.

We wrote out our names for each other. His was Fernando Valenzuela Aznar. He was about my age or a little older. Before I walked back to the tent, we shook hands. He brushed the stone dust from his right hand before offering it.

In the evening, Dave and I drove into Torla. The night was warm and we rode with the windows down. As we wound down the valley in the summer dark, the lights of the town glowed yellow gold against the star-sprinkled sky and the faintly discernable black bulk of the mountains. The scent of new-mown hay was in the air.

It was a pocket-size town, perched atop a steep hill that over-looked the Ara Valley for ten miles in either direction. Gleaming white houses with flowers spilling out of window boxes gave us an idea how Castellbo might once have looked. Or the now-crumbling ghost towns of the Serra de Boumort.

The village was athrob with music and laughter and conversation in the way that Spanish towns come alive after the sun goes down. Small children darted in and out of doorways or chased each other down the cobblestone streets, and in the church square a group of teenagers played out age-old games of flirtation, role-playing, and dominance.

In brightly lit windows, customers bargained with shopkeepers; diners full of animation and amusement harried their waiters, hoisted wineglasses, and plunged with gusto into multicourse meals. As far as I could tell, we were the only foreigners.

We strolled the streets and browsed several handicraft shops, but finally yielded to hunger and picked a restaurant. The entrance was a low door off the main street, but we had to climb a narrow staircase to the dining room. I was disappointed it was on the second floor, meaning we could not observe the street life, but by that time our stomachs had taken over and we sat down at a table anyway. I ordered *paella* and steamed crawfish, and Dave, not a fish lover, opted for lamb. We shared a bottle of wine with the meal, and dessert, of course, was *flan*. Followed by brandy.

A couple of hours later, when we climbed into our sleeping bags back at the campground, I reminded Dave we needed to get an early start in the morning. We had traveled together enough to know each other's quirks. Dave was kind, patient, and accommodating, but was a notoriously slow starter.

"You know," he said, "I'd really like to find out someday if you can think of any other time to get up besides dawn."

* * *

For an angler, the day never holds as much promise as when viewed from midstream at first light. When I stepped into the river the world was still shades of gray. But with the lightening sky, shapes flat and indistinct became bankside willows, yellow and pale green; peaks, ochre and brown and slate; sand and gravel bars, bleached-bone white and flecked with silver mica.

The Ara begins as a trickle among the jagged peaks in and around Ordesa y Monte Perdido National Park. It is here in this wild, inhospitable region of the Spanish–French frontier that the Pyrenees reach their greatest height, with Pico de Posets at 11,065 feet and Pico de Aneto (Spain's second-highest peak) at 11,168 feet.

From a mountain freshet at its source, the Ara soon swells to a swift stream. Near the southwest entrance to the park it converges with the Araza—plunging from the forbidding 10,997-foot summit of Monte Perdido—and, doubling its volume by the confluence, tumbles over smooth-worn rocks toward Torla.

In the morning chill I had pulled a sweatshirt over my standby flannel. But wading in the glacial water I was cold. It was mid-June, not even summer yet, still the early days of a season all too brief. By July the water would warm slightly, the big insect hatches would start. Then the weeks would gain speed, running away into August, down to a swift end. In the High Pyrenees, from September to June the trout are left alone.

I changed flies, blowing on my hands to tie the clinch knot. With the sun edging up over the mountains I hooked and released a ten-inch brown amid a series of small rapids and riffles. A few dozen yards upriver, the only other fisherman on the river at that hour caught four in quick succession on a silver spinner. I watched him slip two into his creel.

I kept casting and moving upstream, working the main flow, but rose nothing. I tried the edges and, as the sun climbed higher, I had a hit, just a small splash behind the fly as it drifted in near the willows. But when I tried the same drift another half-dozen times, there was nothing. I climbed out of the river and sat down to rest among the willows. The day was progressing, the fish were not biting; it was time to move. I headed downstream.

Just above Torla the river is funneled into a narrow canyon where it becomes a deep, swirling, churning torrent, nearly impossible to get to and even harder to fish. But standing on the footbridge below the canyon I knew I had to try.

Non-anglers scoff at tales of detecting fish-rich waters by smell. But I have experienced it many times, from Cape Cod Bay, when a school of blues was nearby, to a mountain lake in Idaho's Sawtooths, where six- to ten-inch brook trout fought each other to hit any fly that was tossed out. On the Ara, the smell of trout hung heavy in the mist-filled gorge above Torla. To fish it, however, was another matter.

The right bank was sheer rock walls—out of the question. But along the left bank for about fifty feet, there was a narrow shelf between the cliffs and the river. I climbed down from the bridge and edged along the rock. I struggled with the problem for most of an hour, but with no room to wade and rock walls thwarting a backcast, it approached an exercise in existential futility. Finally I gave it up as a worthy but unattainable goal.

When the Ara emerges from the canyon south of Torla, its gradient flattens out and it becomes gentler and more accessible.

But it is below Broto, the next village, that the Ara is loveliest and most fishable. A stretch of several miles is reachable from a gravel road that runs along the west bank from Broto south. Here it is a big, smooth-flowing stream with a gravel-and-cobble bed and occasional sandbars. Much of this section is wadeable and the banks are alternately brushy and clear, offering easy access.

The broad, sparsely populated valley, the meandering river, and the mountains are reminiscent of Wyoming. Farther west, in Navarre, the Pyrenees drop several thousand feet and the countryside becomes green and lush, watered by the mists and rains blowing off the Bay of Biscay. But the Aragon Pyrenees are rougher, drier country.

Cliffs and jagged peaks tower above sunlit pine forests, and the region abounds in wildlife. Near Sarvise I watched an eagle spiral down and land a couple of hundred yards upstream. Bears, ibex, chamois, and deer roam the high country. There may even be a few wolves left. The reality belies the cliché of Europe as densely populated and unrelentingly urbanized.

Though the natural landscape resembles the American West, other features—the ancient towns, traditions, timeworn byways—draw sharp distinctions. It is a compelling dual ambience: wildness juxtaposed with the milleniums-old continuity of European civilization. The rivers, the mountains are timeless. And did Roman legionnaires tread this rocky trail? Was it Crusaders who built those fortress walls?

On a late-spring afternoon, the river between Broto and Sarvise is a mercurial ribbon under a platinum sun. After my hard-fishing morning, Dave and I had enjoyed a leisurely lunch. Then we had driven down to Broto, crossed a steel bridge to the west bank, and parked at the edge of the gravel road near the river. Dave had had enough of tagging along, waiting for me to catch something, so he sat in the car fiddling with the radio while I geared up and checked out the river.

Here the Ara was a series of swift riffles and mini-rapids. Viewed from atop the riverside berm, it looked problematic but not unfeasible. But when I stepped in to cross, I found the water deeper than it looked and knew I would be risking a dunking to wade it.

I could see that, about two hundred yards downstream, the river flattened out, so I climbed back up the bank and started walking. The ground became thick with brush and rose in a small hummock as I followed the curve of the river.

After going about a hundred and fifty yards, I pushed through a patch of woods and found myself standing at the edge of a ten-foot sandbank looking down into a slick pool. Directly below, a thirteen- or fourteen-inch brown was casually feeding. I got down on my stomach and watched like a voyeur.

Cut off from the river's main flow by a narrow sandbar, the pool was a tranquil backwater forty feet long and a dozen feet wide. Upstream, a foot-wide channel funneled a swift, slender stream from the greater current into the head of the pool, washing in richly oxygenated water and serving as a fluid conveyer belt of trout food. At the tail of the pool the water *whooshed* out a narrow sluice, back into the main channel.

Barely beneath the surface and three or four feet downstream from the inlet channel, the fish hung suspended in the gentle flow. It held its position effortlessly, barely fanning its tail, tipping up or drifting slightly left or right to sip an insect or examine a piece of flotsam.

The morning's action had been more than slow: It had been nearly dead. I wanted this fish and wracked my brain for a plan. For a couple of hundred feet upstream and down, the bank was too high and steep for me to get down it. I could dap for the trout like a kid on a sunfish pond, but it would be a ludicrous undertaking trying to haul the nice brown up the bank, flopping and bouncing on a flimsy tippet.

Twenty feet to my right, downstream from the fish, a big pine barely clung to the edge of the bank. I marked the spot, then hiked another hundred yards or more downriver. Here the bank was only three feet high, and I eased down its slope into the stream. I was focused on reaching the spot near the pine and made only perfunctory casts as I worked my way upstream. But I could not rush. The bankside channel was near the top of my boots, and toward the middle, the river deepened to fast water over slippery cobbles.

In my impatience—wading hastily and too far between casts—I spooked a trout close by the bank. I did not see the fish until it shot out into the main current. Then I spooked another, almost underfoot. I stopped for half a minute and talked to myself.

"You came a long way. It's been a great trip. Slow down." But the lecture had little effect and in five more minutes I was almost below the pine and watching the water ahead.

I made a couple of casts, moving slowly upstream, then spied a dimple on the water 30 feet ahead. I took another step and my right foot sank into soft sand. I felt a trickle of water down my leg and stepped up onto a rock, still watching the fish and not my footing. Both feet shot out from under me and I fell backward with a splash, ending up sitting in the water up to my chin, slowly floating downstream.

The cold took my breath away for an instant, but I used the rod for balance and quickly regained my feet. My clothes were dripping and clinging like baptismal raiments; my boots were filled to the brim. I started to curse and then laughed and laughed. "Too fish-hungry," I said. "You got too goddamn fish-hungry."

Half a minute later, still intent on stalking the fish, I looked up to see a tough-looking character with a face of old cordovan and a badge pinned to his shirt standing on the bank twenty yards upriver and motioning me over.

As in most places, Spain requires that you carry your license with you but, foolishly, I had left mine in the car. "*Licencias de pesca*," he said when I sloshed ashore. "*Auto*," I answered, pointing up the gravel road. He probably heard it from poachers all the time: "Left my license in the car."

His eyes got dark and I could not understand the words he started yelling. But with the help of his hand gestures I got the picture all right: Keep your license in your shirt pocket.

Then he noticed the fly rod. He checked the tippet and, seeing the dry fly, gave me a quizzical look and nodded. Some of the hardness went out of his eyes. We marched back together, water sloshing out of my boots with every step. Dave was sitting in the car reading and still fiddling with the radio. He watched us coming but did not say anything as we walked up.

When I pulled the license out of the glove compartment, the warden broke into a broad smile and motioned for me to open my fly box. He raised his eyebrows, chuckled, and shook his head at the "*muy grande*" No. 10 Mayflies and yellow Wulffs. But some of the smaller flies—Blue Duns, Gray Duns, and Light Cahills in 14 and 16—were "*muy bueno.*"

He pointed to himself, then the fly box, made a casting motion and held up three fingers: "*Solamente tres.*"

I thought for a moment and could not figure out what he meant. But when he repeated the gesture I got it: The warden fished with only three flies. After a few more minutes of angling talk he headed back down the road to his Land Rover, wishing me luck with a wave and a grin.

When he had gone I sat on a rock, pulled off my boots, and poured out a couple of gallons of water. I took off my pants and shirt and socks, and wrung them out the best I could, laying them out on rocks in the sun and pulling dry ones from my backpack. Then I had a sandwich and a soda while sitting in the car with Dave.

"What was that you said yesterday? 'Who's gonna check way up in the mountains?'" I asked. We both laughed and he told me he had gotten a shot of my dunking.

"I think we should title it 'The Intrepid Angler.'"

"Or 'The Spastic Caster,'" I said.

I returned to the river, still resolutely ignoring the axiom that most trout are caught within a few hours of sunrise or sunset. The sun was warm, the air was dry and brilliantly clear, and I was content to feel the cool surge of the river against my boots and follow the motion of the line against the vast blue sky. As the sun traced its descending arc, curving down toward the jagged skyline, transmuting the river to tarnished silver and finally blue black steel, there were no minutes, no hours, no time even—only change.

At dusk the valleys of the Pyrenees cool quickly as mountain shadows lengthen across them. I had begun to feel the river's chill and was casting by rote, resigned to a fishless finish. Pick up, back, stop, forward, stop, strip . . . pick up, back, stop, forward, stop, strip . . . *SMASH.*

The fish tore across in front of me, thrashing at the surface as it went. In three or four seconds it was surging toward the willows that overhung the right bank. I put on more pressure, stopping the run, but had to ease off and let the trout run when I felt the strain on line and leader. The fish splashed with its tail and then was in under the branches.

I kept the rod high but in a moment the line was caught. I quickly walked up, reeling in the slack. When I bent over and reached under the willow branches to the snag, I could see the flash of the fish among the leaves that trailed in the current. As I gave a tug on the dead branch and broke it loose, the fish shot off downriver, revving the reel spool like a dragster engine before the lights turn green.

Swimming with the current the trout had more power, but in another minute it was finished and I eased it up onto shore. It was a thick, solid fish, with the dark coloration of some wild browns. In the waning light, shimmering bronze against the clean-washed gravel, it was a living piece of the river.

The next morning Dave and I packed up and started the trek back to civilization.

It was not until a couple of months after the trip that I found out Serena and Jessie had carried on a torrid affair for months after his dad was killed. They had almost become a couple, but Jessie had wanted to make one more try to get things right with Sarah.

I thought of the pain and the disrupted lives, and knew there was no answer to the questions who or what was responsible. Or why. Maybe the answer was in one of my favorite Chekhov stories, "Ninochka:"

"In matters of the heart," he wrote, "no one is guilty."

3

Runes, Dunes, and Hamlet's Trout

Jutland's Winds of Spring, May 1990

"It was on the evening of the first day of May,"
the Wind continued. "I came from the west . . .
I had hurried across the heath and over
Jutland's wood-girt eastern coast, and over
the island of Funen, and then I drove across
the great belt, sighing and moaning."

—Hans Christian Andersen, "The Story of the Wind"

A thin white mist rose from the river. A pair of mallards flew low overhead, the hen quacking loudly as they went past, and scaled in downstream. Everywhere trout were rising, some of them leaping clear of the water to snatch insects out of the air.

I picked out an expanding ring twenty feet upriver and laid out a soft cast. The fly landed gently a yard above the fish, floated downstream a couple of feet, and then disappeared in a splash of spray. I yanked up on the rod and the tip bowed down as the fish took off, first zigzagging across the current and then rocketing into the air to tailwalk across the water.

A minute later I eased the fish to the edge of the bank. It was a beautiful little rainbow, ten or eleven inches long. Its silvery pink sides flashed in the disappearing light as I removed the hook from the corner of its jaw. When I slipped it back into the water, it hesitated in the shallows for a couple of seconds, fanning its gills and resting among the reeds, then shot out into the current and disappeared. I dried the fly with a couple of false casts and picked out another riser to cast to. After the gray, fishless German winter and two days of meager questing, I wanted to stretch out this day until it snapped.

It was spring on Denmark's Vejle River, a clear, smooth-flowing stream that meanders down through the hills of eastern Jutland to empty into the Baltic near the city that shares its name. On its way to the sea, the Vejle flows through some of the loveliest countryside in Denmark: hardwood forests, meadows, and—in summer—hillsides purple with heather.

I was fishing a section near Vingsted, about ten miles from the mouth. Here the Vejle was twenty-five feet wide, deep, and placid. The bottom was mostly sandy and firm, but except for a few places along the banks the river was too deep to wade. Fortunately, it was bordered mainly by open pasture, though here and there giant beeches and oaks or brushy willows overhung the shallows. And the Vejle was full of trout.

In a little more than two hours I had caught and released seven rainbows and six browns, hooked and lost at least that many fish, and missed another dozen that struck too short or that escaped because I mistimed setting the hook.

Another rainbow hit, briefly hooked itself, and then tossed the fly in a churning flash. I paused to warm my hands down inside my boots. It had been a soft spring day with temperatures in the high sixties, but with the coming of dusk the thermometer had plummeted. I could see it in the mist that spiraled up as the rapidly cooling air contacted the warmer water. On the horizon the sun was disappearing behind iron gray clouds, backlighting them orange and red.

A little while later the first stars began appearing in the night sky of spring. I walked back to the tent, where Dave was puffing on his pipe while stirring the embers of a dying fire and trying to tune his shortwave radio. It was our first trip together since Monte Perdido.

"Well, where are they?" he asked.

I told him how fast and furious the fishing had been, then remembered I had promised to bring back one or two trout for breakfast.

"I kept thinking the next one would be bigger, and then I forgot all about it," I said.

"Yeah, yeah, you fishermen," Dave laughed. "It's either the big one that got away, or all the little ones that you put back. Either way, the pan's still empty."

I put away my rod and vest, got out of the boots, and joined him at the fire.

"Did you get anything on the radio?"

"Yeah, I had the BBC World Service. And I just started to get Radio Tirana."

"Radio Tirana?"

"Yeah, I'll get it back for you. The announcer is a woman and her English is perfect. Just every once in a while she'll pronounce a ten-dollar word kind of funny, and you can tell she's not American."

He retuned the radio and there it was, a generic American female voice reciting the news in a clear, flat monotone. You had to listen for a few minutes to figure out that there was a certain slant, a selectivity behind the news. But then she said something about the "workers' and peasants' struggle in China" and I had to laugh. Here we were, two Americans in Denmark, sitting around a campfire listing to anachronistic propaganda out of Albania.

"They don't know the Wall fell six months ago," I said.

"They know, but they think they can put it back up," Dave chuckled.

Except for a Dutch family in a little aluminum caravan, we had the campground to ourselves. And their lights were already out. We split a chocolate bar, brushed our teeth with bottled water, and doused the last coals. It was time to crawl into chilly sleeping bags. Though May was waning toward June, the temperature would drop into the low forties under a bell-clear sky.

In ten or fifteen minutes I heard Dave turn over and then begin the rhythmic breathing that meant he was asleep. I was tired, but Radio Tirana had started my mind working.

The previous November my little boy, then four, had been sick with a bad cold when I left on assignment to Yugoslavia with Gus. Because of the bad phones and the frenetic news hack's pace, I talked with my family only once while I was in the Balkans. Travis was still sick, my wife said, but she had taken him to the doctor and he was getting an antibiotic.

Gus and I had no shortwave receiver, and in the hill country west of Sinj the two or three AM and FM stations that came in were Serbo-Croatian. So were the newspapers. It was not until we recrossed the border into Austria five days later that we learned that the Berlin Wall had been breached. Gus's jaw dropped and he shook his head. "Unbelievable," he said, "unbeLIEVable."

The rest of the way back we speculated endlessly about what would happen now. Probably because he had lived through World War II and the descending of the Iron Curtain before emigrating to the United States, Gus was more stunned than I. "I thought that damn thing was gonna' be theah foah anothah thousand yee-ahs," he said.

Excitement was too mild a word to describe what we felt listening to the radio, overhearing some of the conversations at the rest stops and reading the still-incredulous German papers. We were elated at the prospect of the next weeks and months. The possibilities seemed limitless and only good.

But when I got home Travis had not gotten out of bed, could barely open his sunken eyes, and would not eat or drink. The day before, the pediatrician had seen him again and had merely changed his antibiotic.

It was after nine P.M. but I called a physician friend who lived two hours away.

"Describe to me what he looks like, what his symptoms are," he said.

When I had finished he did not pause. "Get him to the hospital," he said. "Now, not in the morning."

When I carried Travis into the emergency room, the duty doctor examined him briefly and immediately hooked him up to an IV. "He has pneumonia," he said, "he must stay here."

Libby and I spent the next ten days alternating at the hospital. The world's focus on the mass jubilation in Berlin and across Germany was only a background blur. The vicissitudes of history meant nothing compared to the life of our little boy. After he came home I had nightmares for months. I was still having them. This was the first time I had been away since then.

Now I stared into the darkness and listened to the night sounds. I had talked to Libby, Travis, and Katrina the day before. I would call again tomorrow. They were safe and warm in their beds. In another half-hour I pushed the dark thoughts back and farther back, and finally I fell asleep.

* * *

The narrow peninsula of Jutland is thrust out from Central

Europe like an index finger pointing the way to the rest of Scandinavia. Caught between cold northern seas—in the west the North Sea, in the east the Baltic—it is a harsh, damp, storm-tossed landscape stark in its beauty and stingy with adornments.

Unlike the Alps and the Pyrenees, Jutland does not look like trout country. The highest rises barely qualify as hills, so there are no freestone streams tumbling out of high country. But much of the peninsula is veined with networks of spring creeks. Joe Brooks's classic, *Fly Fishing*, first clued me in to their fulsome possibilities.

Dave and I had earned our placid hours astream and in camp with a ten-hour drive from central Germany two days before. We were tailgated by BMWs and headlight-flashing Mercedeses on the speed-limitless autobahn. Construction sites and traffic jams held us up outside Kassel, Hannover, and Hamburg. The mollifying factor was the countryside: the evergreen hills of north Hessen, the rolling farms and mixed forests of Lower Saxony.

When we left Darmstadt, the weather was sunny and seventy-five degrees. But within an hour the sky filmed over and turned slate gray, then black. After Hamburg, we drove in a steady rain to the Danish border. When we passed the checkpoint the change was immediate and dramatic. The white-knuckle raceway tension and the urban stress of the German industrial juggernaut fell away. Ahead was a winding country road with few cars and laid-back, courteous drivers. And speed-limit signs.

Even the weather turned auspicious. Within five miles the overcast began to break, and sunlight streamed through holes in the clouds. The rain let up and then shrank away to veils of showers visible far away across a flat, windswept expanse of deep-green pastures and fields of new grain. Holsteins and sheep grazed with bowed heads, and near rambling, red-brick farmhouses rows of poplars leaned permanently away from the prevailing winds.

By the time we set up our tent in a campground south of Skjern, the twilight sky was deep blue, and a brilliant orange sun was sinking into the fens, a trail of vagrant clouds in its wake. The temperature was fifty-five degrees, with a brisk wind whipping in off the North Sea behind the passing cold front.

* * *

My fondness for Denmark dates to 1984, when Libby and I married in Copenhagen's *Raadhus* (City Hall) and spent a week exploring the capital and the rest of Zealand. If you are lucky and in love, a honeymoon lives up to the definition. We were both.

Part of our luck was our good friends Geoff and Kirstin, who made a gift of their city. In their turn-of-the century walk-up two blocks off Raadhuspladsen, we had Copenhagen at our doorstep. We roamed the Stroget and Nyhavn; dined on stuffed grape leaves à la Beirut and fresh Danish flounder; strolled hand in hand beside the harbor, past the Little Mermaid. Later in the week we drove north to view the modern art in the Louisiana museum, toured Fredericksborg Castle, and explored Hamlet's reputed haunts in Helsingor.

We were foreigners, but everywhere we were made to feel at home. For in their world-class capital, as well as in their sleepy, red-brick villages, the Danes are unfailingly friendly and courteous. The country's pace is rural, the national mood upbeat and noncompetitive. And Denmark is one of those few places that seem to give as much thought to living in harmony with the environment as to exploiting it. Even in the cities the air and water are mostly clean.

When our interlude was over, we made the crossing to Puttgarden and stood together on the ferry's windswept stern, watching Zealand's shoreline recede into the ship's wake for ten miles.

* * *

In the night the wind went calm, and when I ducked through the storm flap a little after sunrise the grass was heavy with dew. It was a crisp, clear spring morning with bird sounds—blackbirds, crows, magpies—beginning to fill up the silence. Down toward the river a cock pheasant was crowing with rhythmic regularity, every half-minute. While Dave and I ate breakfast a sighing wind came up high in the trees, then steadied to a fresh northwest breeze. Within an hour the sun disappeared under a high, whitish gray cloud cover.

After we cleaned up the breakfast dishes we drove into Skjern to see about a license for me and to ask about places to fish. The downtown was a cozy, orderly collection of brick homes, shops, and small businesses, and we quickly found the tourist bureau.

When I had called ahead the week before, the mood in the office had been frenetic. Two weeks of sunshine had warmed the winter-chilled waters, sparking massive insect hatches and turning on the trout. The word had quickly spread, bringing an influx of anglers from across Jutland, north Germany, and even Great Britain. "I can feel the fever," tourism assistant Annelise Kongshede had said. "And I do not fish."

But now, she told us, the fishing was a mere shadow of what it had been. With the rain and the passing cold front, the action had slacked off. In fact, it had just about died. I bought a license anyway and, since we were in no rush, paused to listen and learn.

In Denmark, fishing is the national pastime. On riverbanks, canals, beaches, farm ponds, and bridges over little tidewater sloughs—summer, winter, spring, and fall—anglers gather with all manner of gear and bait. During the warmer months many tourists join the natives.

The River Skjern and its tributaries—the Omme, the Gundesbol, the Vorgod, and the Karstoft—draw anglers from across Europe.

"Mostly Germans," Kongshede told us, "but we also have people from Holland, Belgium, England." Americans, she said, were few and far between.

Rainbows, browns, grayling, and sea trout were the big draws for fly fishermen, she said. But a few obstinate souls still pursued the Skjern salmon, reputedly Denmark's only remaining genetically pure native strain, a fish whose numbers had sunk so low as to make tales of hookups and landings seem apocryphal.

When asked where she thought we should go first, Kongshede initially demurred. But when I pressed the issue she relented. "I would say to try the Omme. There were many biting there last week. And it is a beautiful river."

* * *

Unlike eastern Jutland, the Skjern drainage is flat and damp—mostly peat, pasture, and marshland broken up by occasional wooded patches. Willows, reeds, and Queen Anne's lace grow along the river margins, and the black-and-white cattle stand out starkly amid the green pastures.

When we arrived on the Omme at midmorning, a chill wind was blowing upriver and there was not an insect in sight. I started casting from the dike, but the wind kept tying new leader knots I did not need, so I climbed down the bank, stepping carefully to test the river bottom. It was soft but not muddy, and I found I could wade almost to midstream.

On this chilly spring day, fishing with dry flies approached a formalist exercise. Like the rituals of Paris's bereted, Galoise-puffing, bamboo-rod Sartrists, patiently waiting on the Seine *quais,* not for Godot but for gudgeon, it had more to do with method and ambiance than results. Thigh-deep in the cold flow, watercress waving in the current, onrushing clouds above, the sweep of the wind in the willows and sedge, the bending rod and looping line silhouetted against the sky—all merged into a single harmonic, alpha-wave rhythm.

Dave sat in the car smoking his pipe and watching for twenty minutes, then he drove back into town to look for camera gear and a watch battery.

For an hour I cast, stripped, picked up, and cast again, more by rote than conscious intent.

I had stopped thinking about catching anything. But even without fish, the fishing was beautiful.

Then, daydreaming and half watching a coot in the reeds, I missed the rainbow that smacked my Coachman a foot from the opposite bank. But the fish chased the fly down current, and a second later the line came taught with another splash, the rod began to bounce, and a whirling pinkish silver blur churned across the water. Less than a minute later, smiling at the unexpected gift, I released the little trout and went back to my daydreams. No other fish showed before Dave returned around one o'clock.

"What do you say, you ready to give up the hunter-gatherer bit and go put something in your stomach?" he asked.

"I think you've persuaded me."

Back in Skjern, before finding a restaurant we stopped to view one of the town's cherished attractions: a pair of storks, newly returned from North Africa, peering out from their generations-old nest atop the red-brick train station.

Over lunch, Dave remarked on how clean the air was. "Man, after the Rhine Valley I feel like up here you breathe in and your lungs just keep filling forever. It's better than those oxygen stops they have in Tokyo."

When I got back on the river, the overcast gave way to blue sky with a few leftover cirrus. In the evening the sun shone burnished gold through the willows. Just before it sank into the moors, I caught a six-inch grayling on a Light Cahill.

Back at the campground, the breeze dropped to a whisper after sunset and the air felt like frost. But sometime after midnight the wind came up again, this time out of the northeast, and the next morning dawned brisk and brilliant, with a cotton-cloud sky blown down from Russia and Sweden.

On the Omme, the fresh breeze that was quartering downstream and across kept blowing my back cast into the dike, where it would catch on the wild carrot flowers. And the air was filled with willow fluff that kept getting in my nose and eyes.

Again there were no insects, but I still caught two grayling on a Coachman. One was a fat thirteen-incher that I almost kept for lunch. A few minutes later, trying to cast to the far bank, into the teeth of the wind, I waded out to within a few inches of my hip-boot tops, then stepped in a soft spot and sank to my waist. Dave walked over from the car when he saw me sitting on the dike, wringing out my socks.

"Decided to take some of the river with you?"

"Yeah, for sentimental reasons."

We returned to the campground so I could change into dry clothes and hang out my wet things. It was only ten-thirty but I was tired of fighting the wind, so we put the fishing on hold and drove out to Holmsland's Klit, the barrier island that separates the North Sea from Ringkobing Fiord, the Skjern estuary.

It was only a half-hour drive, but for me it was like going home. Only a few isolated trees, stunted and wind-gnarled, grace Holmsland's beaches, dunes, and marshes. The landscape, the taste of the salt air, the smell of sun on the dry, white sand brought a surge of memories: tramping the Eastham moors with my shotgun and black Lab; waves rolling in from the fearsome blue Atlantic to crash on the Outer Beach; sunny days and storms; the joys, triumphs, and small tragedies of a Cape Cod boyhood.

Spring on the Cape was always an impatient, wishful time. Weeks after the mainland was soft with blossoms and buds, winds off the bleak ocean kept the scrub woods and spartina meadows stark and sparse. A few weeks after Easter, the little pink-and-white mayflowers would creep out from under pine needles and dead oak leaves. Then one day in June the wind would swing around into the southwest, and overnight the scrub oaks and swamp maples leaved out, the marshes turned green, the striped bass began chasing alewives up the rivers, and the hordes of summer people followed close behind. "The old-timers always said that we don't have a real spring," my dad told me. "We just go right from winter into summer."

It is strange how being far from home can sometimes bring you closer to it. But I knew that for Dave, an Iowa farm boy, the scene on Holmsland's was merely a pleasant seascape, not a piece of his heart.

Driving back to Skjern we passed thatch-roofed farmhouses harking back to another century and, at Stauning, a forest of giant's whirligigs churning out wind-generated electricity for the next one.

* * *

That evening I fished the Gundesbol, a sunken trickle of a stream that wound through pastures and cornfields. It varied from ten to fifteen feet wide and was easily wadeable on a firm sand bottom. Because of its narrowness and high, steep dikes—six or seven feet in most places—there was a strange, isolated feel to it, like fishing below ground. I had to be careful getting in and out of the water because of the stinging nettle covering the banks.

There was a small midge hatch, and here and there a few risers. But they proved to be tiny dace. I caught four six-inchers on a Mosquito before moving upstream to a mini-waterfall that tumbled into the first riffle I had seen in Jutland.

Just below the fall, a fish was rising every thirty seconds or so in a little backwater pool. I waited and watched, and it leapt out of the water—a little brown. When I dropped a Coachman in the foam and backwash, the fish socked it and danced around the pool for a minute, jumping like a rainbow, before I brought it in gasping on its side. In the fading light the trout's colors were muted, like a pastel autumn shoreline in a fog. The fish was lightly hooked and shot upstream like a torpedo when I released it.

The afternoon had been warm, and back at the campground the air had that scent of spring—greening grass and new blossoms coming—on the kind of soft wind that brings a vague restlessness, a sense of promise and longing. In the morning we would move on.

* * *

When we drove east from Skjern, marshes and moors fell behind as the land rose to hills and hardwood forests. This was

Viking country. In a field outside Jelling we stopped to view two giant burial mounds, final way stations for untold generations of Norsemen making their journeys to Valhalla. A couple of miles away across town, granite boulders gouged with thousand-year-old runes stood next to crosses in the village churchyard, curiously dissonant pagan punctuation marks in the otherwise Christian terrain.

In the central highlands we stopped to tour Jutland's best-known monument to modern Norse culture—Legoland, in Grindsted. Its plastic-block replicas of Mount Rushmore, the Parthenon, and a cowboy town offered a quirky, whimsical contrast to the ancient bones and stones.

But two of the more curious testaments to the Danish character greeted us farther down the road at Vejle's Saint Nicholas's Church. Visible high up on the north exterior wall of this sturdy brick monument to faith were twenty-three shallow, scooped-out hollows, curiously familiar orbs set amid the architecture of angles and arches.

To the casual tourist they are merely unexplained curiosities. But after consulting a guidebook, the more curious visitor takes a closer look. Only then does the recognition factor come into play: the hemispheric shape, the faint spiderweb cracks. These are human skulls. Local lore says the church's grisly ornamentation was an involuntary donation from twenty-three thieves executed in the early seventeenth century.

An equally gruesome but archaeologically intriguing exhibit dominates the interior of the church: the shriveled, parchment-like body of an Iron-Age woman, displayed under glass in an ornate coffin. Found in a peat bog in 1835, the corpse has been carbon dated to about 500 B.C.

Such artifacts seem easily congruent with the Danes' sunny, easygoing dispositions and curiously lugubrious view of mortality. Not merely dark and brooding like the German *weltanschauung*, but tinged with whimsy in the face of life's absurd conundrums.

"We fat ourself for maggots," Shakespeare's tragic prince observed. I always liked Red Skelton's similar take on things: "You can't take life too seriously," he said when his friend Ozzie Nelson died, "because you never get out of it alive anyway." At St. Nicholas's, Red and Hamlet might both have added: How significant are our petty concerns when we all will be bones and shriveled parchment someday?

A short walk down the cobblestone street from the church, the Sonder River flows pristine and fish-full through downtown. I stopped at the tourist office and bought a map and a permit for the upper Vejle, then joined Dave and a gaggle of tourists on the pedestrian bridge to watch the trout sipping emergers in the center of the business district. There were a lot of trout, though I did not see any big ones, and after the dearth of fish in Skjern I wished fervently that this stretch was not off limits. I consoled myself with the thought that, with the crowd on the bridge, catching one of these trout would be like performing in an arena. And I was buoyed by the license clerk's promise of "wonderful" fishing upriver.

* * *

Patchworks of grainfields and open heath broke up the forest on the road to Vingsted. By the time we got a campsite, the sun was getting low. I rudely left Dave to set up camp by himself and tromped off across the pastures. I knew he forgave fishing fools, and my guilt faded when I got to the river and saw the rise rings.

There were a half-dozen hatches on, and the fly did not seem to matter—Cahill, Coachman, Mosquito, Adams—as long as it was dropped in the fish's feeding lane. I knew it was vanity, but I could not help feeling that I deserved this kind of action after the long winter and the dearth of trout in Skjern. I worked the rod as fast and as long as I could, piling up the numbers like a meat fisherman.

Later, walking back to the campsite in the near-dark, I spotted a flashlight beam on the riverbank and stopped to talk with

Elin and Erik Dreyer, down from Grenaa, in northeast Jutland. Erik held the light while Elin unhooked a fish, then he switched it off. Together we stood at water's edge in the reflected starglow. Both husband and wife were avid fishermen and, like many Danes, had an American connection—his brother lived in Arizona. Both spoke excellent English. They also proudly told of Denmark's Fourth of July celebration, the largest outside the United States.

They were happy at my success and wanted to learn fly fishing sometime. But this night they were having good luck with worms. Seven years before, they had "discovered" the area after Erik read a newspaper article about the Vejle, and they had returned every year since.

"The last five or six years," he said, "it has become one of the good rivers in Denmark." It had also become *their* river, a current of shared memories winding down through the seasons.

The Dreyers were putting back the small trout and had kept only one twelve-inch brown that had bled too much. There were lots of small fish in the Vejle, Erik said, but there were big ones too. "I heard last year they caught a sea trout of ten kilos. So big." He held his hands about two feet apart.

I asked if there was good fishing near Grenaa. Yes, they both said, but it involved mainly salt water. "Last year I got a sea trout of four point six kilos," Elin said. "I was so proud."

When I left the Dreyers they had switched on the flashlight again to release another trout.

* * *

In the morning the chill had put a damper on the hatches. But as the air warmed a few insects began to show, and I had fun fooling the sprightly eight- to ten-inch rainbows that seemed to enjoy dancing across the water in the sunshine.

When the sun got too high and bright, the action slacked off. I moved downstream, to a bend where a stand of sixty-foot beech trees leaned out over the water, putting most of the river in deep shadow. Low-hanging branches made a conventional cast impossible, but I hooked a couple of chunky foot-long browns by flipping out backhand S-casts and floating the fly down in under the trees.

For the previous four days, two or three times a day, I had fought the urge to indulge my anxiety by calling home. Once the worry takes you over, I knew, it can make you a prisoner. Like the people who have to go back into the house five times to make sure they turned off the stove. Finally, at lunchtime I pumped *kroner* into the campground pay phone, vaguely tense until I heard in Libby's cheery "Hello" that all was still well with the world. Both kids were excited to hear they had presents coming.

It took becoming a parent, I knew, to realize how much it was possible to love someone. As children, on the receiving end of that love, we revel early in our growing self-sufficiency. The world, we are sure, will soon be ours to make of it what we will. But before long, as young adults, we are shocked to realize the impossibility of truly controlling our own fate and to face the certainty of our own death. Accepting that is part of growing up, and those who cannot find acceptance never do. But coming to a like realization about our own children is truly terrifying. Strangely, in its pernicious form it can spark wildly disparate aberrations: neurosis, misanthropy, antitheism, and the philosophical suicide described by Camus—religious fanaticism. Skeptics need only read Mark Twain's embittered later works, written after losing his beloved daughters.

That evening, our last in Denmark, I fished a different section of the Vejle, about five miles farther upstream, near the headwaters. Here, newly emerged from an evergreen copse, the river had shrunk to a twelve-foot-wide meadow brook with low, grassy banks. It was a classic spring creek, unassuming but full of promise.

But, as in Skjern, it was a case of the right place but the wrong time. In midafternoon the sun had disappeared behind a low, gray overcast as the day turned cool and blustery. Now, with darkness coming and the temperature headed farther below fifty, there was not an insect to be seen. The wind made the day cold even with a sweater and windbreaker.

I fished stubbornly with dry flies for almost two hours, getting only one hit and seeing two risers. A Danish fisherman I met was not having any better luck with nymphs. When I headed back across the fields and through the woods to the car, the wind was whistling through the treetops.

Back home the next day, I swept up my wife and kids in my arms, and told them tales of Lego mountains, lost Vikings, and the winds of spring.

Later, drifting off to sleep, I cast again for trout in deep, placid waters. I thought of next year, and the next, and what Erik Dreyer had told me that night on the Vejle: "There are lots of streams like this here in Jutland, very beautiful." I knew he was right.

4

Weisser Traun, Deutscher Traun

Chasing Rainbows in Bavaria, June 1990

That's the part I like best: you never know
where a trout stream will lead or where
a hooked trout might haul you.

—Harry Middleton, *On the Spine of Time*

There was a loud hissing in the guides as the fish took off, rocketing out into the fast water. I kept pressure on as the line burned out through my fingers, hoping the tippet would hold. Then I had the trout on the reel, and the drag took over.

For a few seconds the fish stayed deep, ripping off line as it shot downstream. I palmed the reel and the pressure forced it up. At the edge of a riffle the trout exploded out of the river, cartwheeling across the surface and sending up a geyser of water as it fell back. Then the fish shot toward the slack water, angling upstream. I frantically stripped in line to keep it taut.

This was another gleaming Bavarian rainbow, the biggest of the day. From its jump I guessed the fish at nineteen or twenty inches.

I raised the rod higher to increase the pressure, and the trout jumped again, thrashing and shaking its head this time as it splashed down. I regained more line and in a couple of minutes I had forced it in to within about ten feet of my boots. But when the rainbow caught sight of me, it shot downstream once more.

This time the run was shorter. Again I worked the trout back in, and again it took off. My right forearm was aching, but once more I hauled the fish back, painstakingly retrieving the line foot by foot. Now most of the fight was gone from the trout and I eased it toward my hand, rod held high and bent double. The fish made one final lunge, heading for a submerged boulder a few feet away.

I put on even more pressure, straining the leader to its limits. I knew if the trout got under the rock it would break off. The rod tip was nearly touching the water as the fish fought and pulled, only a foot away from the rock. Suddenly the rod sprang back, the fly whizzed past my ear, and the big rainbow was gone.

The sun had disappeared behind the mountains, and only a few minutes remained till dark. There would be no more trout this day. I reeled in the rest of the line and began wading across the river, back to the car. It was the end of a brief but superb interlude on the Deutscher Traun River in Bavaria's Chiemgau region.

Given the choice, most fishermen would rather catch big fish than small ones. In Europe, some of the best places to do this are in the Traun drainage, which lies on both sides of the German–Austrian border. For generations, the area's reputation for consistently producing outsize trout and grayling has attracted anglers from throughout Europe and the world.

Beginning as a glacier-fed trickle along the German–Austrian border, the Deutscher Traun and its tributaries resemble the stony, fast-water rivers of the Rocky-Mountain West. Partly snow-fed, they are swift, clear waters that maintain cool temperatures and consistent levels throughout the summer. These nutrient-rich freestone streams produce big browns and grayling, but the rainbows are the real heavyweights.

Finding rainbows at the end of the autobahn was the goal when Ken and I headed south from Darmstadt on a sweltering, late-June day. For more than a week, Central Europe's weather had been dominated by a stable high-pressure cell that had evolved into a wilting heat wave. The only area getting any relief was the Alps, at the southern edge of the system, where thundershowers brought brief respites.

I was happy to be on the road again with Ken, a retired old salt who had made his way to the navy by way of the Rockies. A onetime F-18 weapons officer who flew missions off carriers in the South China Sea and an ex-bodybuilder (he had once been Mr. Hawaii), Ken was a tender tough guy with more heart than anyone I had ever worked with. We had first hooked up two years earlier on a duck-hunting trip to the Netherlands.

Before that I had seen him around the office—he had arrived about six months prior to our duck hunt—but I did not really know him. Still, on the all-day drive to the marshes and blinds of Kampen an der Ijssel, his stories of a hardscrabble Montana boyhood on the High Plains west of Billings had made my eyes burn. Told in the matter-of-fact manner and rolling cadences of Big Sky Country, they seemed even sadder. For Ken was the product of a family that was not just broken; it was shattered.

His dad had been a small-purse Seattle middleweight with club talent and championship dreams. But his mom had little faith and less patience. When Ken was seven she took off with him and his little sister for Montana, where she married a rancher and a life of isolation; bone-wearying work; bitter-cold, snow-blown winters; and dry, dusty, grasshopper summers.

Ken's stepfather—like his dad, of solid Scandinavian stock—was a good, uncomplicated man who lived the virtues of hard work, uncomplaining at the drudgery and endless days on the range. It was a life of horses, cattle, homegrown vegetables, and the wide prairie sky. "We were dirt poor but we didn't really know it," Ken said.

In the great room of their ranch house was a woodstove that was kept stoked in the cold months. Each night, Ken's stepfather would bank the fire and close the vents all but a crack. In the morning, before first light, he would put on the coffee and revive the fire by adding fresh kindling and tossing a cup of gasoline into the stove. Until the morning when the vapor mix hit critical mass, sparking an explosion that blew out the windows, set his clothes afire, and burned down the house. Ken and his sister jumped out an upstairs window into the snow, alive but also never to be whole again.

For weeks, then months, Ken's stepfather languished in the hospital, his legs burned to charred, oozing hunks of meat. Finally, to save his life, the doctors amputated them at the knees, and he went home in a wheelchair.

Unable or unwilling to run the ranch and care for a crippled husband, Ken's mother bailed out after less than a year. The stepfather went to a care facility, the kids to foster homes. Ken never lived with his sister or mother again.

He spent part of his growing-up time with a Blackfoot family near Hardin, living lean with hand-me-down clothes and few possessions, but learning to love hunting, fishing, camping. In high school Ken was a star athlete, small but scrappy, who carefully cherished the chip on his shoulder and fought at the drop of a hat. "I was always ready," he told me on the way to Kampen. "Just waitin' for somebody to say something." Until Ken was eighteen—when he left for the navy—he wet the bed.

"I used to be so damn embarrassed," he said. "I used to wash my own sheets every day. I didn't want to sleep over to anybody's house. I remember goin' campin' and wakin' up in the mornin' in a wet, cold sleeping bag an' changin' my clothes in the freezin' cold before anybody got up."

More than thirty years later, Ken spoke wistfully of Montana's harsh beauty—horses he had ridden, trout he had caught, deer he had skinned. But he had no plans to move back.

I wondered how he had survived it. The human spirit is huge and indomitable, I knew, but it can be destroyed.

Everyone suffers, and those who are lucky learn from it. Life's most intense experiences, after all, are always either suffering or joy. And everybody's brief interlude on this exquisite blue planet ends at the grave. But those who suffer early and greatly . . . they learn one thing first—and their hearts ache for knowing it: "The idea is very simple," Sherwood Anderson wrote in *Winesburg Ohio,* "so simple that if you are not careful you will forget it. It is this—that everyone in the world is Christ and they are all crucified."

Sharing a freezing duck blind for three days on Lake Ijssel had cemented our friendship. Now, on the way to the Traun, Ken and I were old buddies.

We made the six-hour drive to southern Bavaria in ninety-degree heat. As we cruised along with open windows at seventy to eighty miles an hour, the interior of the car felt like a wind tunnel. Ten miles southeast of Chiemsee, Germany's largest lake, we turned off the Munich–Salzburg autobahn at Siegsdorf, a *Luftkurort* (clean-air spa) that straddled the Weisser Traun River.

Our fishing connection was Rudi Heger, whose family had held the fishing rights on stretches of the Deutscher Traun and its tributaries, the Weisser Traun and the Roter Traun, for a couple of generations. For most of that time angling access was linked with the longtime family business, a guesthouse and café on the

Weisser Traun. I had talked to Rudi on the phone a few weeks before, and he had given me the lowdown on the fishing, mixed with a little history.

In the family tradition, Rudi was groomed to take over the guesthouse and, in furtherance of that plan, sent to study hotel management at the University of California. But when he returned from the Golden State, the plan changed. He decided to build a new business around his first love: fly fishing. Now the guesthouse was closed, the second floor occupied by Traun River Products, a fly-fishing shop and an outlet for wholesale and retail angling supplies. In a few years the company had become renowned throughout Germany for service and high-quality products.

Though Rudi was German, his *weltanschauung* was quintessentially American. He had fished Alaska and the Rockies many times, and during most springs could be found prowling the Keys flats for bonefish, tarpon, and permit.

On his home waters he ran a tight operation, geared toward preserving and perpetuating his beloved Traun. As on many German trout waters, streamer fishing was verboten. Rudi had gone one step farther, requiring barbless hooks. Recently—in a move that verged on heresy within the hidebound German angling community—he had instituted catch-and-release regulations. As far as he knew, it was a first for Germany, where it was considered de rigeur that fish landed be killed, kept, and cooked.

It took Ken and me only a couple of minutes to find Traun River Products. The three-story art-nouveau building on the riverbank next to Siegsdorf's only road bridge was such a good landmark, "Even Mr. Magoo couldn't have missed it," Ken said.

I had looked forward to meeting Rudi in person and was disappointed that, this day, he was out of the office. After obtaining a fishing permit, I picked out some tapered leaders, ten or a dozen local flies (Black-Wing Sedges, Gray Duns, Olives), and a stream thermometer. While I shopped, a half-dozen women took turns answering phones as they bustled among rows of shelves, collecting items and packing them in boxes for the company's thriving mail-order business. When I paid for my permit and gear, we received a map and directions to the streams. Then we drove three miles south to check into our lodgings in the next village, Maria Eck.

When we got out of the car, Ken and I glanced up at the structure on the hillside above the parking lot, then at each other. "Man, you sure this is our hotel?" he asked. "Maybe we took a wrong turn and drove to the prince's palace by mistake."

But there was no mistake. The Kloster Gasthof Maria Eck, a onetime cloister, was more than a hotel. It was an elegant, sumptuously appointed retreat, with gardens and forest paths—unmistakably more spa complex (*Kurzentrum*) than anglers' lodge. It was a bit more than we had expected for about the cost of a Holiday Inn in Cincinnati or Duluth.

We took our time checking in, then rested in our rooms for a half-hour. We ate a leisurely Bavarian dinner of *Spaetzle* and venison ragout on the terrace while waiting for evening and cooler temperatures. I drank a mug of *Helles,* the light, golden beer of southern Germany. It tasted especially good in the heat and I would have had one or two more if I had not been going fishing. Instead, I ordered a bottle of Evian.

Since most trout are not caught under the high sun, we were in no rush. I was sure that once the shadows began lengthening on the river, the fishing would be great. The blazing heat had undoubtedly warmed the water and there were certain to be insect hatches. But toward the end of dinner a few ominous cumulonimbus began approaching from the northwest.

More clouds moved in as I loaded my rod, vest, and boots into the car. By the time we drove five miles west and turned down a gravel road to the river at Traunstein, the sky had turned black with thunderheads. I got into my gear quickly, but as I stepped into the river the wind started to come up and the first raindrops fell. There was a hatch on and I quickly caught a small rainbow, about ten inches. Then came the first flash of lightning. I ignored it and continued fishing. There were many trout rising, dimpling the water between the raindrops. I had a couple of hits but missed them, partly because I had one eye on the brewing weather.

Soon it was upon us—a full-blown thunderstorm with lightning dancing from cloud to cloud, sheets of rain, and violent, squally winds slashing through the trees. If the fishing is good, a thunderstorm presents a problem of conflicting emotions: Take the risk and continue casting, or stop and maybe miss the chance to land that lunker beneath the next rise ring.

Not wanting to make my wife a young widow, I began briskly wading to shore when the jagged fork lightning crackled down to strike the treetops a quarter-mile away.

Ken and I sat a half-hour in the car, until the rain and lightning slacked off, then I went back to fishing. The trout were still rising and I caught another small rainbow, keeping one eye on the flashes in the distance. I had a few more hits but in a little while the storm surged back over us, with torrents of rain and electric-blue flashes streaking across the sky.

We waited in the car another twenty minutes, until it was nearly dark, then drove back to the hotel in a steady downpour. I planned an early start in the morning, but the weather had made me pessimistic about the fishing prospects.

I read in bed for an hour before falling asleep with the sound of the rain still outside the open window and a clear memory of the advice an old-timer had given me about the secret of his longevity: "I've never worried about things I couldn't control."

* * *

At six A.M. on the river, the day was full of promise. Because of the cool, rainy night, there was no insect hatch, but the thin, gray overcast looked as though it might soon lift. I worked the river with several different flies, catching one eight-inch rainbow and yearning for a glimpse of the sun. But around seven-thirty a chilly rain began to fall. Soon it became a steady drizzle and in another hour the valley was socked-in solid. I quit at nine with the rain getting heavier and a white gray mist sinking to the lower meadows on the hillsides.

We thought the weather had closed in for the day and, so, headed back up the valley. The roads were slick with rain and Ken drove carefully. In Siegsdorf we parked beside the bridge and sat in the car, gazing at the rain-pocked river.

After it flowed under Siegsdorf's main street, the Weisser Traun changed character. Over the centuries it had been channelized, straightened, and deepened; its banks lined with riprap. There were trout, I knew, right downtown. But one problem was how to fish for them: the river was too deep to wade, the banks were high, and the rock berm was steep and slippery. Another problem was that streets, cars, people, and buildings do not exactly make an idyllic setting.

"You gonna try it?" Ken asked.

"Nope, guess not," I said.

"Well, let's get out and walk then," Ken said. "Maybe I can get some shots."

"In the pouring rain?"

"Yeah, mood shots."

Right about then, my mood was childishly dire and fretful. All because the weather had spoiled the fishing. But I did get out of the car, and we strolled the tidy, modest shopping district with the rain streaming off our umbrellas. The streets and stores were deserted.

We stopped at the Natural History Museum, mostly to get out of the rain for a while. The place was kind of a one-shot wonder, but it was a pretty big shot: the complete skeleton of a mammoth, found nearby in 1975.

We walked to the train station and then the cemetery. A cemetery in the rain. That was a mood shot, all right, I thought. We strolled leisurely among the graves. I was not really paying attention, just glancing at names and dates on the headstones. Until one caught me up short. It was almost new—the white marble still gleamed—and the name on it was Rudi Heger. The second date engraved in the stone was last year.

"Hey Ken," I said, "come here and look at this."

He walked over, looked, and made a quizzical face. "Huh, weird. What do you make of it?" We both thought for a minute.

"Must be his father," Ken said, "don't you think?"

So Rudi had buried his father a few months before. And I was acting peevish because the rain had ruined my fishing.

At a kiosk near the train station we bought a roast chicken and fries, and walked back to the car. After washing down the food with a liter bottle of Coke, we went for a walk in the *Kurpark,* which bordered the river's right bank, below the bridge. It was a big park, with a half-mile of paths and greensward along the river. The light was too low to see any fish from the bank, but we walked down to a wooden footbridge where, a few weeks before, a friend of a friend had caught a twelve-pound rainbow.

He had pulled it off by using a downstream drift from the bridge, then netting the fish from the riprap. It was an unlikely spot and I might not have believed the story, but I had seen the picture. The fish was shaped like the proverbial football—grossly obese and with a head too small for its girth. I had no doubt it was one of those bread-fed, parkside specimens. After the photo, the friend of a friend had released the big rainbow and we looked for it now. But there were only a few normal-size fish under the bridge.

"See any twelve-pounders down there?" I asked Ken.

"Hell, I barely see any twelve-inchers," he said.

It was still raining, but not as hard. We decided to drive back down the valley, and by the time we reached Traunstein the sky had begun to lighten. We turned down the gravel access road to the big river, and even before the car stopped we could see the rise rings.

There were still a few raindrops, but the sun had begun to burn through. When I walked down to the river there were mayflies and caddis all over and above the water's surface, but the insects in the main hatch were the equivalent of a No. 12 or 14 Caddis, big flies that had set the fish slashing and jumping, frenetic to snatch the bugs in their herky-jerky flight patterns.

I tied on one of Rudi's Black-Wing Sedges, waded out, and caught a chunky, eleven-inch brown on the first cast. For the next couple of hours everything came together. The trout were gorging themselves, the river sparkled in sunlight that streamed down through holes in the clouds, and for a few minutes a faint rainbow appeared in the southeast. Eventually the sky cleared, with a high, bright sun. I lost myself in the river, the rhythm of casting, the summer sky.

Working my way slowly upstream, I cast mainly to risers, but also searched out pockets near the bank and behind rocks or debris.

I used the few Sedges until they were worn out or waterlogged, then caught fish on Adamses and Gray Duns. Most of the fish were rainbows, but I landed a handful of browns and a single nine-inch grayling. One of the rainbows was a deep, handsome sixteen-incher, and I lost two heftier ones close in.

In one spot I worked a gravel bar where the main current had scoured out a deep channel along the streamward edge. Insects, foam, and tiny bits of flotsam had collected along the seam where the swift water ran up against the bar, either barely moving or spinning in tiny eddies. It was a difficult drift, and most times the fly would be torn past and swept down the channel. Or, it would float forlornly, barely moving, over the shallows. Two or three times I snagged leaves or twigs, and had to remove them. But I kept trying because every now and then a snout would barely poke through the surface to suck down a bug, and I thought I saw a couple of big swirls.

Finally I hooked a spunky seven-inch brown that skipped

briefly across the water, then shot past my legs. Close behind was a rainbow as long as my arm that spooked and flared at my feet, shooting back out into the current like a torpedo. For a while after that I wondered what it would have been like to hook and land that fish, and whether it would have counted as fly fishing.

After I walked back to the car to tell Ken, I headed upstream and met two Dutch fishermen on their way down. They were surprised and pleased to meet an American, and one of them reminisced fondly about fishing the Yellowstone. We exchanged notes on the day—he had fished the Deutscher Traun many times and called it "a very good river"—and I told him I was surprised that the rain had not made the water unfishable.

"This is a snow river," he said. "When you have a river that feeds from rain, it gets brown. The only color this river gets is white."

Two hundred yards farther upriver I came upon the river keeper, Alois Blaschke. "*Petri-Heil!*" he said, using the traditional German anglers' greeting. "*Petri-Dank!*" I answered and we stopped to chat. He asked how I had done, then took me to his secret spot.

At midstream, in a very shallow riffle, was a six-foot-high boulder. There was only about six or eight inches of water around the rock, and I might have ignored it and headed for the deeper channel that undercut the brush along the right bank. But Blaschke led me to a spot diagonally upstream where we could see four nice fish hiding in a deep pocket under and half-encircling the boulder on the downstream side.

"Try them," he said. I did, missed one strike, and then lined the fish with a bad cast, sending them flashing in under the rock. We waited five minutes, then Blaschke made a perfect, soft cast and hooked a seventeen-incher that zigzagged over to the channel and jumped twice before he brought it in. After he released the fish, we waded to shore and sat on the bank.

Blaschke explained that being river keeper was a hobby, not

his job, and he had come to it by being friends with Rudi. Because he owned an electronic-components company in Traunstein and another one in Switzerland, he could make use of flextime to be on the river. "I have sometimes the time to go fishing because other people do the work for me," Blaschke said, laughing.

He had begun fly fishing five years ago and had taken it up with a passion. Now he had become an avid proponent of Rudi's no-kill regulations. "This is the best river because of catch-and-release," he said. But to Europeans accustomed to centuries of catch-and-kill, the new approach was not always an easy sell. "It's something people have to learn," he said. "If everybody would take two or three fish every day, in three or four months the river is not empty, but the big fish are gone."

In addition to the controversy within the German angling community, Rudi's experiment had ignited fierce opposition from radical animal-rights groups, who called it torturing fish for pleasure and vowed to stop it. A court test seemed inevitable, and it remained to be seen whether the concept would catch on or be banned.

After saying good-bye to Blaschke, I fished haphazardly back downriver to the car. The afternoon was waning into evening and Ken and I were both hungry, so we drove to an outdoor restaurant–café in Traunstein. The two Dutch fishermen were also there and hailed us when we walked into the courtyard, raising porcelain mugs in greeting. They were already into post-angling mode—laughing, joking, and downing their beers in huge gulps.

It had always puzzled me why most European anglers passed up the best parts of the day—early and late—in favor of socializing and genteel hours astream. But I smiled, knowing I would have the river to myself, and enjoyed my *Jaegerschnitzel*, baby-lettuce salad, and boiled potatoes with a single mug of beer. When we left, the Dutchmen were ordering another round.

Back on the river, the evening was clear and beautiful. The river was mostly in shadow, just a few rays of the sinking sun streaming through the trees, and the air was cooling rapidly. There were still plenty of fish rising, but now they would not touch any of the flies they had been crazy about a couple of hours earlier. After a half-hour of fishing upriver, I had only had two hits. I walked back to the car and sat for a few minutes, discussing tactics with Ken.

Directly across the river was a jumble of huge rocks that looked like promising lies for big fish. But between us and them was fast current in a thirty-foot-wide channel. I picked what I hoped was the best ford and, stepping carefully on the cobble, managed to stay dry getting across, though a couple of times I came within an inch of my boot tops.

I was standing on a narrow gravel bar that split the river into two channels: the wide one I had crossed and a narrower, slower one. The boulders were at the head of the narrow channel, left of the bar facing upriver. I could see fish rising just below them and walked to within thirty feet. Up close I could see that the rocks were even bigger than I had thought. Several were seven or eight feet tall, with two-thirds of their bulk submerged.

The river bubbled through narrow sluices among the boulders, smoothing out behind them into pools four or five feet deep. In the deep water, big fish waited below the gaps, leisurely snatching insects that were practically funneled into their mouths. Other trout cruised the edge of the fast water where it swept past the line of boulders. I softly flicked out a Gray Dun and watched a sixteen-incher float up, look it over, slowly turn away, and sink back down as the fly drifted on past.

I changed flies three times, prompting the same once-over and refusal. Once, three fish rose to the fly and backed off together. They kept sipping naturals, but in the fading light I could not make out the type. Finally, two drowned flies floated by within a foot of my boots. I scooped them up and saw why I was not getting any action. They were big black gnats.

I quickly searched my fly box and found a pattern that was

pretty close, a No. 16. On the first cast a seventeen-inch rainbow smashed it. The fish put up a hard, four-minute battle but, uncharacteristically for a 'bow, did not break the surface. Ken splashed across the river in his street clothes and was getting shots with his zoom lens. I slid the trout across the surface of the water to my hand, taking care to remove the fly gently and quickly.

I asked Ken if he was cold.

"Hell no," he said in his best Gary Cooper voice. "In Montana we never wore any boots."

For the next half-hour, until the light was gone, the action was spectacular. One sixteen-incher I caught jumped five times. When I finally stopped, it was so dark I had to be extra careful wading back across the current because I could not see the bottom.

* * *

I returned to Siegsdorf twice in the years following and both times caught many trout. On one trip, skittering a Royal Wulff past a brush bank on the Deutscher Traun, I landed the fattest brown I had ever seen, an eighteen-incher plump as a carp. The next day, fishing the Weisser Traun under a brilliant midday sun, I caught fish after fish—fifteen to twenty inches—along the shady south shore. The action had not slacked off a bit when I had to leave for home.

5

Split Soul of the Saale

September 1990

I said that the world is absurd, but I was too hasty.
This world in itself is not reasonable, that is all that can be said.
But what is absurd is the confrontation of this irrational and the
wild longing for clarity whose call echoes in the human heart.

—Albert Camus, *The Myth of Sisyphus*

The pool was so overhung with trees it was like a flooded tunnel. Outside this bower, a warm September sun shone on the village of Foerbau, the surrounding forests and fields. But under the thick foliage of the beeches, lindens, and willows it was twilight. I had to squint to make out the rise rings of little trout in the shadows.

For a couple of hours the fishing had been steady and good on the Saale. Not spectacular—six- to ten-inch browns rising consistently to tiny caddis imitations, *Aerschle* (a popular German fly pattern), and Blue-Winged Olives—but pleasingly reliable. Still, perversely, for the last half-hour I had been feeling vaguely dissatisfied.

I glanced down the pool to my brother-in-law, Curt. He was just landing another six-incher and held it up to show me. He is a big man, six feet four inches, and at the time he weighed well over two hundred pounds. The teeny trout looked kind of forlorn held out in front of him.

Curt had stopped over en route to Africa and his job with the Agency for International Development. He had planned his visit partly to see us and partly in the hope that I would fulfill a years-old promise to take him trout fishing in Germany.

Now, standing in the shallow stream, he was an interesting study. With his size and unkempt, reddish beard he looked like a cross between Grizzly Adams and the Emperor Frederick Barbarossa, with a touch of L.L. Bean catalog thrown in. Curt was definitely not a stereotypical button-down diplomat. "He's gotten so big he looks like a bear," my wife had said after he arrived.

He and Libby and the kids and I had squeezed into our Volkswagen Golf in Darmstadt the day before to make what should have been a three-hour drive south and east. But a half-hour south of home, when we turned east at the Heidelberg interchange, the traffic slowed to a crawl on Autobahn A-5. Within a mile it had come to a dead stop. After a few minutes I turned off the engine and got out, joining others ahead of and behind us, people who had left their vehicles to see what had caused the delay.

German traffic jams are legendary. Sometimes it is an accident that turns the speed-limitless *autobahnen* into the world's longest parking lots. Other times it is bad weather or the ubiquitous construction sites. But this time there was no cause in sight, just an unbroken line of stopped cars that stretched into the distance as far as the eye could see.

I got back into the Golf. "I think we'll be here for a while," I said. I was pretty sure I knew what was up. We had even talked about it the day before. We were traveling on a Friday afternoon that marked the start of the State of Hessen's fall school vacation. This traffic jam was simple overload, one of the inevitable facts of life in a country where eighty million people were crammed into an area the size of Wyoming.

After another ten minutes the kids, stuck in their car seats, were getting restless. We all unbuckled and got out of the car to stretch our legs. It was a beautiful autumn afternoon, and there was almost a festive atmosphere among the crowds standing beside their cars or stretching or sitting at the roadside.

Given their congenital penchant for excessive speed, it seemed incongruous for so many forcibly immobilized Germans to be in such good humor, but I had seen it before in similar circumstances. It was as if they welcomed the chance to break out of the mold and become, at least for a while, a mini-community of idlers.

It was another ten minutes before we saw cars up ahead beginning to move. Everyone climbed back in and the traffic proceeded forward, first at walking speed, then a little faster—ten or fifteen miles an hour. We were all hoping that we would soon be up to normal highway speed, but after about a mile—over the crest of the next hill—the traffic began to slow down. For another quarter-mile it was stop-and-go, then it came to a halt again.

Curt and I had planned to fish that evening—normal travel time would have put us on the river about four o'clock—and in my mind I could already feel the press of the cold water against my boots, the bounce of the rod after a strike. But the view out the windshield was about as far as you can get from visions of trout streams.

In another quarter-hour the cars began moving once more.

This time the flow eased along for nearly five miles before it ground to a halt. Again we got out, stretched our legs and backs, and waited.

Over the next couple of hours we went through the same drill several more times. It was getting on toward sunset, and we were still less than thirty miles out of Heidelberg. The traffic report on the car radio said the *Stau* stretched all the way to the Nuernberg interchange, nearly ninety miles. At the rate we were going, we would get there around midnight.

Soon after the traffic started moving again we came to the Heilbronn exit. All hope of fishing that night had long since faded. If we pushed on for several more hours we would not only continue to be frustrated today, but would also be enervated and cranky tomorrow. Our best option was to get off the autobahn and find a hotel for the night.

It was only a couple of miles into Heilbronn. We found a good hotel near the city center and, after checking in, flopped onto our beds in relief. At dinner Curt and I commiserated over several golden goblets of *Pils*. Soon the letdown did not seem so bad, and we all got to sleep early.

* * *

In the morning we hit the road right after breakfast. Traffic was so light on the autobahn it was hard to believe yesterday's nightmare was real, and we reached Nuernberg a little before ten. Then we turned north on A-9.

Until the previous November, A-9 had been one of only two corridors to Berlin from western Germany, an isolated passageway through a captive, hostile land. Now, myriad long-blocked highway links had reopened, up and down the length of the former inner-German border.

In the previous eleven months, millions of *Wessis* (Westies) had made the trek east. And every weekend toylike, plastic, pastel *Trabbis*, spewing blue gray smoke from their two-cycle engines, clogged western roads as *Ossis* (Easties) by the tens of thousands flocked over to visit long-lost relatives or to shop in stores they could only dream of before. The whole situation still seemed strange and new.

An hour north of Nuernberg we turned off the autobahn onto local Route 289. I pulled over and stopped the car. I had received detailed directions over the phone from Bob Williams, an American who lived in the area, and when I scanned the maze of tiny roads spidering the map and noted the dearth of major landmarks, I was glad that I had. I pulled out my notes, which read like instructions for a treasure hunt or a road rally.

I took a hairpin turn in the direction of Schwarzenbach, drove through Bug and Weissdorf, and finally entered Foerbau. There I followed the *Feuerwehr* (Fire Department) signs until I saw a yellow building on the right; I turned into a parking lot, and there was the Saale River. Bob Williams was just making an upstream cast, saw our car, and waved.

Foerbau is what the Germans derisively call a *Kuhdorf* (literally, cow village), one of the numberless undistinguished farming hamlets that dot rural Germany. Many of them are similar: a cluster of brick or half-timbered village farmhouses, many with the living quarters above a barn; a pub or two; sometimes a school or other municipal building; and maybe even a few shops (bakery, butcher shop, grocery store).

Generally, there is not much idyllic or picturesque about such places. Muddy tractor tire tracks mark the streets—which are still occasionally cobblestone—and the scent of manure wafts from stalls and compost piles. Most of these villages have split populations: happy adults and young children on the one hand, and restless teens and young adults desperate to get out on the other.

But after our enervating autobahn adventure of the day before, Foerbau's placid fields and hedgerows looked good to us. We introduced ourselves to Bob and got a fishing report.

"I started out with an *Aerschle* but the last half-hour I've been getting them on Blue-Winged Olives," he said. "I think I've caught six, maybe seven."

The *Aerschle,* a recent invention, was the German fly fisherman's fad fly at the time. It is a simple pattern: a sparse, reddish brown hackle and tail, accented with dabs of blaze orange paint at the base of the tail and sometimes on the head. It matches no particular insect, but it is effective—especially for browns. The fly's converts claim it imitates a female mayfly depositing her eggs. And the name, whimsical slang for "rear end," or "butt," refers to the fluorescent tail dab.

We conferred some more, then, leading the way in his car, Bob took us to Fritz Trautner's tackle shop and fish farm to buy our permits for the Saale—actually the Saechsische Saale, a tributary of the main river.

The permits were good for two sections of water. One was a mile-and-a-half-long stretch just upstream from town. The other started at the parking lot where we had met up with Bob and extended downstream about half a mile. Both were delineated and labeled with landmarks on the mimeographed map that came with the permits.

A half-hour later, Curt and I were geared up and ready to go. "You're sure you have everything?" Libby asked. We checked our vests, hats and fly boxes, and headed for the river. Libby and the kids would explore the area for a couple of hours and return with the car around lunchtime.

We caught fish immediately. There was a little hatch on and the Olives were just the thing.

The Saechsische Saale will never be a Bighorn or a Spey. It is a slow, tepid stream with modest flows in the best of years. Just below Foerbau it is a partly channelized, rock-and-gravel sluice with long, shallow pools and brushy banks.

In an unspoiled setting, the best thing for a trout stream is usually to leave it alone. That is why Montana stopped stocking its rivers. But in a densely populated country like Germany, neglect can mean decline or ruin. All German rivers have been affected by human activity for centuries; some for millennia. They face the usual problems: watershed destruction, streambed alteration, industrial and municipal pollution, highway runoff, animal waste, and leaching of agricultural fertilizers and pesticides. Though massive government expenditures and stringent regulations have ameliorated the most egregious pollution problems, threats to viable fisheries remain in many areas.

A few years before our trip, the upper Saale was all but forgotten by fly fishers. These once-viable trout waters had deteriorated to mainly a chub nursery. It took the dedication and commitment of one man—Peter Silberhorn—to resurrect the river.

Silberhorn was an expert fly fisherman and, by profession, an engineer. He was used to solving problems with math and logic in his work, and had no doubt he could do the same in his avocation. He assumed control of the fishing rights on the upper Saale with one goal in mind: to make the river a showpiece for sound management and conservation practices.

He started with the basics: streambed improvement, the installation of egg boxes, the stocking of fingerlings, bank stabilization, the removal of debris and trash. He put in endless hours on his own and also enlisted volunteers from local fly-fishing clubs. Only a small portion of the effort was mental; most of it was dirty, backbreaking labor.

Under Silberhorn's stewardship, the myriad dimples of rising trout again dotted the upper Saale within a couple of years. For this and for befriending countless American fly fishermen, he received the 1990 Federation of Fly Fishers International Ambassador Award.

For Curt and me, the proof of Silberhorn's success was at the end of our lines—again and again. For more than two hours we had fished the one long, shady pool that lay barely a double-haul cast from the parking lot. The wading was easy—a slender flow spilling down over smooth-worn, baseball-size stones—and in the deep shade the fish kept feeding right through midday.

But now I was getting restless. It was a combination of the semi-darkness and little fish. I found myself seeking out the few tiny patches of sunlight that filtered through the trees and standing in them to cast, searching in vain for a fish over twelve inches.

As Curt eased another six-incher back into the stream, I motioned with my thumb toward the parking lot. We waded back to the bank.

"There's a lot of fish here," Curt said, "but they're all little ones."

"Yeah, I bet we could catch 'em all day long. But I was thinking, maybe we should try it upstream after lunch. What do you think?"

"Yeah, I wouldn't mind. It might be kinda neat. Maybe we could find a few bigger fish."

In a few minutes Libby and the kids drove up.

"How was it, you guys?" she asked.

"Lots of fish," Curt replied.

"Lots of *little* fish," I added. "How was your exploring?"

"Wow, this place is really something," she said. "It's kinda neat but there's not much here except cows and fields and trees."

After a streamside picnic of bread, cheese, and black-currant juice we drove back through the village until we found a road indicated on our fishing map. It was really no more than a dirt cart path that led into open country: rolling pastures with scattered copses and hedgerows. Shortly the road eased up alongside the river, and we pulled over.

"This is a whole different ballgame," I said. "What do you say?"

"Yeah, let's give it a try," Curt answered.

Up here the Saale was a meandering meadow stream. The sandy banks were open, with only occasional clumps of willows or alders. And, in sharp contrast to the caliginous pools below

Foerbau, the river sparkled in a flood of sunlight.

Curt and I got out our gear while the kids tossed rocks at the water. At age five, Travis had a slingshot arm, and most of his throws ended with a splash. But Katrina was not yet three, and most of her pebbles fell short. However, it was not for lack of effort. She would take a tremendous windup, then bring her hand back behind her head and whip her forearm and wrist forward, throwing her whole body into the motion and twisting partway around with the follow-through. Sometimes the stone would fly nearly straight up, landing at her feet, and she would giggle and squeal with delight.

We made plans for Libby to come back and pick us up around five. In the meantime she and the kids would drive east to explore a once-distant land.

* * *

Until ten months earlier, the Saechsische Saale had been a river of two worlds. Springing up above these meadows in the forests of the Waldsteingebirge, it looped and twisted down into Foerbau, on through Weissdorf and Schwarzenbach to Hof, where it dropped its forename as it merged into the main river. Five miles north of Hof, it traced the demarcation line for the world's deadliest border. Then, at Blankenberg, it slipped away to the north into what was once a secret and forbidden universe, a black hole of totalitarianism.

But that malignant reality had imploded under the incessant and obdurate power of a single chant—"Wir sind ein Volk" ("We are one people")—that rang through the autumn gloom in city after city across East Germany. Walls built to last a century had come crashing down.

Like the Thousand-Year Reich before it, the German Democratic Republic had been smashed and tossed onto the scrap heap of history. What remained were millions of ruined lives, a few pathetic apparatchiks, and a handful of useless slogans—these and a legacy of suspicion and fear fueled by the dreaded *Stasi*

(Staatssicherheitsdienst), the secret police. Since the fall of the Wall and the opening of once-secret archives, husbands had learned that their wives had spied on them; congregations that they had been betrayed by their pastors; subordinates that their bosses had denounced them, or vice versa.

Now, towns and villages separated for half a century by a scant few miles of geography but by light years of ideology, which made them as unreachable as Arcturus, were again neighbors.

It was a reminder of the capriciousness of fate that though the place of one's birth alone could not build dreams, it could destroy them. For those who grew up west of the cicatrix of terror that was the inner-German border, life was fulsome and free. But for their cousins on the east side of the concrete, steel, and razor wire, life was consumed by dual hungers: for creature comforts and small material pleasures—from good food to homes, cars, and consumer goods—and for the right to breathe free and travel.

In the end, the hunger for freedom had overcome the fear of prison and death, thereby eliminating totalitarianism's greatest weapon. Risking all, tens of thousands took to the streets, ringing the death knell for the *Bauern und Arbeiter Staat* (Farmers and Workers State).

It was history, but sometimes history has strange personal connections. In the 1970s, before the two-hundred-mile limit, U.S. territorial waters off Cape Cod were thick with Soviet and East German ships. At night, looking seaward from the dunes of the Outer Beach, we could sometimes see so many lights that the fleet looked like a floating city. In those years, after college, I worked as a small-time commercial fisherman, and it was fashionable to denounce these factory fleets, which were reportedly decimating the cod and haddock. It was one of the few times that New England's commercial fishermen, notorious for their misanthropic self-reliance, united in a common cause. Within a few years, the United States had enacted a two-hundred-mile territorial limit, freezing out the fleets of the Eastern Bloc.

I can't recall ever meeting anyone on the Cape who considered the situation from the other perspective but nearly twenty years later, on the island of Ruegen, I met an erstwhile East German seaman who had worked on one of those ships. He was pushing fifty but looked younger, with twinkling eyes and a bushy, black beard.

The fall of the Wall, and the subsequent scrapping of the East German high-seas fleet, had left him high and dry. But his memories of those years were vivid, tinged with poignancy and bitterness. The voyages had been filled with camaraderie and esprit, the catches exceptional, the privileges and pay good by Eastern Bloc standards. Yet it had been a strange interlude. Many times he stood at the rail and gazed at the shore, so near but so unattainable, across the frigid expanse of heartbreak blue.

"We could see the shore, it was so close. But we knew we could never go there," he said. I remember thinking how strange it was that on one of those starlit nights he could have been looking shoreward, toward my home, while I looked seaward, toward his ship.

Now, however, the bad old days were gone and the Saale flowed through free, democratic terrain all the way to its confluence with the Elbe, at Breitenhagen. Already, the era of a divided Germany seemed like the dim memory of a long illness survived, a collective sickness of the soul whose toxins only time could eliminate.

Indeed, after all the initial elation, antagonism between the already prosperous *Wessis* and their poorer *Ossi* cousins was growing. Attitudes were hardening: arrogance and resentment among *Wessis*, a sense of entitlement among *Ossis*. The situation worsened with every uptick of unemployment in the East, every funding demand made on the West. Now it was evident to all Germans that smashing the physical barriers had been the easy part. The ideological and psychological ones would take much longer; some thought at least a generation.

* * *

As Libby and the kids drove off, Curt and I walked upriver to-gether, then split up to pick our spots.

Up here, the Saale had carved out a deeper, narrower channel than below Foerbau. The streambed was soft sand, and when I climbed down the bank I found I had to be careful not to sink so far down as to fill my hip boots. After a few minutes I climbed back up the bank and began casting. Bright sunshine, flowing water, and open countryside made a scene from an angling water-color.

I worked my way upstream, casting to pockets and undercut banks. There was no hatch on and no fish were rising, but I did raise a couple that struck short. I did not waste a lot of time searching out perfect lies but fished steadily, following the maxim that the more you keep your fly on the water the more fish you will catch. Still, despite the perfection of the day, it was tough fishing. After about forty-five minutes I glanced up toward Curt. I got his attention and held out my hands, palms up, in question-ing body language. He just shook his head and headed farther up-stream.

After an hour and a half I had not hooked a fish. I sat down on the bank for five minutes, then walked three hundred yards up-stream to Curt. I was trying to ignore the nagging realization that it had been a mistake to leave the downstream beat. The impetus had been based on whim, not logic. Casting to tiny fish in shallow pools, shady and overhung with foliage, had felt vaguely claustro-phobic.

Now we had wide-open countryside and the sun on our faces—but no fish, big or small. There is a good reason most an-glers head out early or late for trout: it is only seldom that these wariest of fish become active under the midday sun. I knew it, Curt knew it, and still we had been enticed by our own daydreams of brighter waters, bigger fish.

When I came up to Curt he was casting intently.

"Any luck?" I asked.

"Not much. I got one nice grayling, about twelve or thirteen inches."

"Where'd you get him?"

"Back there, near that tree."

It was one of the few shaded spots in view. Curt kept casting. "I just saw a fish rise over on the other side there," he said. "How'd you do?"

"Nothing. Just a couple of hits."

Curt could not get his fish to rise to the fly and finally gave up. We rested and talked strategy for ten minutes.

"We probably should have stayed down by the village," I said. "At least there were plenty of fish there." I was thinking of what Robert Traver wrote in *Trout Madness:* "Fishermen are a perverse and restless lot, constantly poised to migrate to greener pastures, ever helpless recruits for the wild-goose chase."

"Yeah, but we didn't know," he answered. "It was worth a shot to come up here, anyway. I bet we get some more fish later on."

When we split up again, Curt stayed put while I hiked a quarter-mile upriver and began fishing my way down. Finally I caught a little brown, eight or nine inches long, and began feeling more upbeat.

The afternoon was winding down. I lost another trout, then hooked a foot-long grayling in the slack current behind a boulder. I changed direction and walked another few hundred yards upstream, where the river shrank to about ten feet wide. The water did not look productive, and after a couple of dozen casts I headed back down and met Curt near where we had started.

He had caught two more grayling and a trout. "But I made a lot of casts for those three fish," he said. We were tired, hungry and thirsty so we leaned our rods against some bushes and stretched out on the ground.

"That's it for me," I said.

"Yeah, me too. I need a beer."

Twenty minutes later, Libby and the kids drove up. I pushed up my weary bones and got to my feet.

"Hi, Libs. How was it?"

"Well, it was really interesting."

"Where did you guys go?"

"Not very far, really. To this little town just over the border. You wouldn't believe how gray and run-down it all is. There wasn't really anything to do, but it was interesting to see. I can't believe those people had to live like that all those years."

We drove to Foerbau's only guest accommodations, a converted farmhouse and barn across from the butcher shop. The place looked shut up tighter than a drum, and at first I could not raise anybody. But after I pressed the buzzer for the third time, a man in his early thirties answered the door. He eyed us suspiciously at first, but when I explained we needed accommodations he led us inside a dark entryway and up a steep staircase. At the top of the stairs was a giant, open apartment under the eaves of the converted haymow. The only divider walls were around the bathroom, and that had no door.

I said we preferred two rooms and he made an impatient expression. "We have only this," he said. We conferred and decided that, since it was our only choice, we could make do.

When I went downstairs to sign in, I tried to make small talk, but the man's brusque manner and curt replies made it clear he had no interest in conversation. Each question set off a twitch in his right eyebrow, a tic that clearly embarrassed and irritated him.

This guy's personality and attitude played into the prejudicial stereotype of the border region as a dead zone, a place filled with neurotics, losers, and misfits who could not or would not get out. I did find out that he had grown up in the house and ran the pension with his elderly mother. And I learned that we could get breakfast in the morning. But all in all, he seemed about as well-suited for the hospitality industry as your average rattlesnake.

"What did you think of that guy?" I asked Libby and Curt

when I got back upstairs.

"Weird," Libby said.

"Major weird," Curt agreed.

After we carried our luggage upstairs we drove to the sport hall, which had the village's only bar and restaurant. There were five people in the bar, and when we walked in they turned and eyed us as if we might be outlaws. Foerbau was not exactly a tourist Mecca, I knew, and strangers were few and far between.

The restaurant did not start serving meals until six P.M., and we were nearly a half-hour early, so Curt and I ordered half-liter mugs of *Export* beer and toasted the fishing while Libby and the kids sipped soda. The kids found a game room and soon emptied my pockets of one-mark pieces for the pinball machines and video battlefields.

Finally, the place began to fill up, and the waiter brought the menus. Libby and I translated for Curt and the kids. This was *gut-buergerliche Kueche*—homey but hearty fare: *Schnitzel*, roast chicken, boiled salted potatoes with parsley, steamed trout, *Spaet-zle*, French fries, venison goulash, and two kinds of salad—garden (butter lettuce with tomatoes) and cucumber.

The food was not fancy or the dining elegant, but when we finished we were sated and satisfied. By the time we left, there was hardly an empty table or bar stool; music, noise, laughter, and smoke filled the room.

Back in the hayloft the kids fell asleep in a few minutes. The cavernous room with its many dark corners had an eerie feel at night. Libby, Curt, and I joked about our strange host being an ax murderer who planned to bury us in the manure pit or wall us in like the vengeful lunatic in Poe's "The Cask of Amontillado."

But we survived the night, and in the morning the proprietor was correct and cordial. We sat in the breakfast room with sunlight streaming in the windows while he served us coffee, hot chocolate, *Broetchen* with a crock of fresh butter and homemade jam, and one soft-boiled egg apiece. The eggs came in a little wicker basket and were wrapped in a linen-print napkin to keep them warm.

We had to get on the road by early afternoon, but first Curt and I wanted to catch some more trout. We drove back to the stretch of river below the village and, while Libby read and the kids played, we prospected the shady pools. Each of us caught a handful of small fish, and eventually I worked my way down to the weir that marked the lower end of the beat. By then it was time to leave.

On the way home Curt and I returned to an old discussion. His years in Africa—first as a Peace Corps volunteer and finally as an AID official—had left him with a deep scorn for bootstrap philosophers and their right-wing orthodoxies. He had said many times, "Let one of those guys grow up where there's not even enough to eat, no clean drinking water, no schools, no medical care to speak of, and see how far he gets."

I did not have the same experiences but shared his views. The two Germanys offered a classic example: How much hope was there for some poor sap who grew up on the wrong side of the Iron Curtain?

And why was it that the most fervent bootstrap philosophers always seemed to have been born into custom-made boots and had ample help pulling up the straps? One could hope that, like Kafka's hapless civil servant, they might wake up some morning to find themselves metamorphosed into roaches. But, of course, that hope was superfluous. They already were.

Other than solving the universe's metaphysical conundrums, the trip home was uneventful, and when Curt left the next day he said he hoped to get back again soon. I promised that next time, we would go looking for bigger rivers and bigger fish.

6

Angst Amid the Moors

Castles, Kilts, and the Bonnie Clyde, June 1991

O to realize space!
The plenteousness of all, that there are no bounds,
To emerge and be of the sky, of the sun and moon
    and flying clouds, as one with them

—Walt Whitman, "Leaves of Grass"

Certain fly-fishing destinations exist as much in the imagination as in reality: England's chalk streams, where Walton and Berners invented a sport and a perspective; Montana's big rivers—Yellowstone, Blackfoot, Missouri—coursing wild and free as the mythical West. And Scotland, Celtic outland of peat-stained waters and wild, heart-rending moorscapes that haunt anglers' dreams.

"Can you believe it, Norm?" Gus asked. "Scotland. Oh, I love it. It's gonna be wonderful. The Highlands, pints of Guinness, the Hee-Brides."

We were planning the trip for early June and Gus, an old Scotland hand, was psyching me up. We would trace the snaking byways by car, hike the moors, count the castles, hunt for Nessie and the ghost of Bonnie Prince Charlie. And I could squeeze in some fishing.

Over the next weeks I did some research and settled on the River Clyde, just south of Glasgow. After that we would wing it with the fishing.

We left Darmstadt on a balmy, late-spring morning: blue skies and temperatures in the mid-seventies. But two hours north, near Cologne, we drove into dark clouds and a cold rain that stayed with us all the way to Rotterdam.

On the outskirts of the city we turned off the highway and made our way to the port. Like most metropolitan harbor districts, it was ugly with refineries, loading docks, gas and oil tanks, and other industrial facilities.

Waiting in the queue to drive aboard the ferry, we got out and stood around the car, keen with anticipation. Gray stratus—driven before a blustery wind—scudded low overhead, but the rain had stopped and there were ragged holes between the clouds. The ferry was not scheduled to sail for almost two hours, and it was clear that the loading wouldn't start for a while. "I think I'll go into the terminal and see what's up," I said.

Gus had just lit a cigarette. "Okay, I'll stay here with the car," he said.

There was really no more happening inside the terminal than outside, except for one section that had been overrun by a busload of German tourists, mostly middle-aged and elderly women. On the way out I happened to be walking behind three of them—

sturdily built, gray-haired matrons in wool suits, jaws set and striding purposefully toward the exit. Halfway down the corridor, the one in the middle turned first to the companion on her left, then to the friend on the right. Highly indignant, she made her pronouncement on the shore personnel of North Sea Lines: *"Keiner weis bescheid hier. Ueberhaubt keiner weis bescheid."* ("Nobody knows anything around here. Nobody at all knows anything.")

I had to bite my lip to keep from laughing. When I got back to the car and told Gus, he howled and howled until the tears came to his eyes. When he could finally talk again he said, "Oh Norm, that is beautiful. It's just so typically German it's almost unbelievable."

In a little while we boarded the ferry and about an hour later got under way. The sky had begun to clear as the ship wended its way through the maze of shipping channels. In the outer harbor the ferry began to rise and fall on the swells, and then we were in the Channel in a whitecapped sea lashed by a stiff northwest wind. Jackets zipped to our chins, we watched the sun set over choppy waters, then went inside to thaw out and eat dinner. Afterward Gus stopped at the bar, but I went straight to my bunk and fell asleep to the rolling of the ship and the thrumming of the engines.

* * *

In the morning, breakfast in the ship's dining room was loud and crowded. We waited in line for twenty minutes and squeezed our trays onto a nearly full table of strangers. Shortly after we ate, the ship docked in Hull, and a half-hour later we drove off the ferry under blue skies and puffy cumulus.

The port was smaller and shabbier than Rotterdam, and we were soon out of it, passing through a checkerboard countryscape of hedgerow plots: pastures and rolling hay meadows; pale-green spring grainfields rippling in the wind; and mustard yellow rape. Scattered trees—walnuts, oaks, elms—stood out like exclamation points at the roadsides and corners of the plots.

I was glad that Gus was driving. Even in the passenger seat it took me half an hour or more to get beyond the disconcerting feeling that we were careering down the wrong side of the road on Suicide Lane. "See, Norm, nothin' to it. You just have to flip a switch in your mind," Gus said.

We followed the M-62 west, then turned north onto A-1 up through Yorkshire. Here the countryside was less intensively cultivated: fallow fields were grown over with weeds and wildflowers, knolls and swales became hills and hollows. Northwest into Cumbria on A-66 the terrain turned rougher still: heather and gorse, stone walls, and rocky slopes. At Penrith we turned north again, onto M-6; in the far distance to the west were the peaks of the Lake District, clouds piling up over them.

In Carlisle we turned onto M-74 and crossed the line of Hadrian's Wall—built to keep out the fierce Celtic hordes. Ten miles farther on, at Gretna Green, we circled a roundabout, headed north—and left England behind.

"Well, Norm, heeah we ah," Gus said. "Scotland!" He launched into a reprise of his previous Scotland trips: weather, scenery, characters he met along the way. He thought to himself for a minute and then continued.

"I'm gonna tell you something, Norm, that I nevah told anybody. But it's eating away at my brain, an' I know you wouldn't tell anybody." Gus paused for a few seconds.

"You remember that roundabout back there?"

"Yeah, sure."

"Well, when I was heeah the last time, I drove around that thing and there was this girl standin' there with her thumb out. Anyway, I *thought* it was a girl. I couldn't really tell at first because she had on a raincoat with the hood up and blue jeans and boots and a huge backpack. I went around past her and was just gonna turn off up toward Glasgow, but the weather was so terrible and she looked so miserable—it was just pouring down rain like cats and dogs—and I was all by myself.

"So I went around again and stopped. I jumped out and threw her backpack in the trunk and jumped back in—to get out of the rain, you know? When she got in and took off her hood, I saw it *was* a girl. And when she talked I could tell by her accent she was a German girl. So I started talking to her in German, and she was a little bit suspicious at first. Why was I driving an American car and so forth. Until I explained it to her. I asked her where she was going, and she said, '*Irgendwo.*' And I started to laugh. I thought that was just great: 'Somewhere.'"

Gus stopped for a few seconds. I did not know where the story was going, but I hoped it was not in a certain direction. I knew he adored his wife, but sometimes people surprise you. And everyone has secret longings. They can spring from the soul's thinnest soil and require little nurturing.

"You remember that Dave was supposed to go with me on that trip but his mother got sick and he had to fly home?" Gus asked. I said I did.

"Anyways, I was traveling alone. And she didn't have any money. Or hardly any. I think maybe two hundred marks. So I said, why don't we travel together. It was kinda funny, really. This bald-headed old faht and this young girl; she was only twenty-three, still a kid. She wasn't pretty or anything. But she was kind of lively and contrary. I always liked girls like that. Like Marianne." Gus paused again, remembering.

"She had this one expression for everything. '*Das ist ja aetzend!*' ["That's really caustic!"] It didn't matta if something was good or bad. Like a really great view out ovah the North Sea. Or a song on the radio. Or a slow driver on one of those one-lane roads in the Highlands. '*Das ist ja aetzend.*' Everything. I asked her to explain, but she just said, '*Kann ich nicht. Ist nur so.*' ["I can't. That's just the way it is."].

"An' we traveled all ovah. Dundee and Aberdeen an' the Highlands an' all the way up to the Orkney Islands. But everything was very proppa. We nevah slept togetha or anything. We shared the same room, but it was always twin beds. It was strictly on a friendship basis. But if Marianne evah found out, she would just be crazy. She definitely would *not* understand.

"Anyways, we traveled togethah foah nearly a week. When we said good-bye I let her off with her backpack an' we had a big hug and she gave me a kiss on the cheek. We exchanged addresses an' I wished her well. I thought, well I'll nevah hear from her again. But a coupla months later she sent me a postcard from Hamburg. An' ever' now an' then I get a letter from her. At work. I got one just about three weeks ago.

"So that's the story, Norm," Gus said. "My big adventure and non-love affair." He laughed and I laughed along with him, but I knew it was not because either of us thought it was funny.

Each one of us has at some time felt—like Rilke's Malte Laurids Brigge—that, "I am learning to see. I don't know why it is, but everything enters me more deeply and doesn't stop where it once used to." It is this confluence of our yearning for life's essence and the fear of never fully tasting it that sets us searching. To never begin searching signifies an emotional stillbirth; to stop is to commit spiritual suicide.

We continued north through the Borders—the countryside getting more rugged still, rocky slopes and swift rivers—into the Southern Uplands. I had been watching the map, and when we crossed a bridge at Abington I asked Gus to pull over. We got out and walked to the stream bank. This was the Clyde.

"Oh, heah it is," Gus said. "I can see you just countin' the trout already." But there were not many to count in this stretch—a straight, shallow riffle with a modest flow. It was barely twenty feet across and did not look more than eight inches deep anywhere. But I knew that the Clyde flowed on to bigger and better things and that, as in the old song, just around the corner was a rainbow (or brown), not in the sky but in the current.

After Gus had finished a smoke we hit the road again and

soon descended into the Lowlands. This was, a gentler, greener landscape—flatter, with more soil and fewer rocks, the terrain tamed by agriculture.

At Douglas Mill we turned off the highway, and twenty minutes later we were in Carnwath looking for our hotel. When we pulled up in front, it did not seem quite what the brochure had promised. With peeling paint on the trim; small, grimy windows; and the overall appearance of being run-down and soiled, the place looked in need of a good sprucing up. When we went inside, the effect was reinforced. The carpet in the lobby was old and worn, the light fixtures dim or bulbless.

The owner, Marshall Wood, was drinking a beer alone at the small bar off to one side of the lobby, and when we walked in he came over to greet us. He was a big man, six feet four or five inches, and two hundred fifty pounds or more, but because he had a certain defeated look and a soft-spoken, disconsolate manner he did not seem imposing. He checked us in and directed us up the stairs to our rooms, which were small, dark, and in need of paint and wallpaper, as well as a thorough cleaning.

After we finished our inspection, Gus and I met in the hallway to talk over the situation. The accommodations were not ideal, we agreed, but we did not feel like searching for another place. Besides, Marshall had already arranged for us to meet a river bailiff and go fishing on the Clyde. Also, we did not want to hurt the feelings of this big man, who seemed so vulnerable and downhearted. "Anyways, we'll only be sleeping here," Gus pointed out.

After unpacking, we went out for a stroll. With just twenty-five hundred inhabitants, Carnwath was a large village that aspired to be a full-fledged town but seemed unsure how to go about it. In a half-hour we had pretty much covered the main business district—a handful of shops, several pubs, and three inns.

When we got back to our hotel, Marshall was back at the bar, nursing another beer. I could not help but think that he could have better spent his time painting the rooms or replacing the rotting trim out front. We sat down and joined him, talking about the village, and it was not long before he started in on his stock promo speech about the region, touting the fishing, the golf (five courses), and the bargain vacation possibilities.

"You get bed and breakfast in Edinburgh for an astronomical figure. But you go twenty miles outside the city, and you pay half the price."

Gus told Marshall that we planned to go into Edinburgh in a day or two, and that really got him going. It was known as "the rip-off city" he said, a run-down, dangerous place and "the AIDS capital of Europe."

It seems every provincial hamlet lies near a corresponding den of sin and iniquity, a wretched "other place" that serves to remind residents how lucky they are to live where they do. When I was growing up on the Cape, it was Boston. For a fisherman I once met on the Greek island of Alonnysos, it was Athens.

"Man, you really don't like Edinburgh, do you?" Gus asked, laughing.

In a few minutes the door opened, and a little girl about nine or ten came bouncing in. She had curly blonde hair and a mischievous smile.

"Hullo, Daddy," she said, running to Marshall. His eyes lit up as he rose from his stool and swept her up in his arms. After a bear hug, he held her out at arm's length while she giggled, then he put her down gently on his stool and set about making her a sandwich.

Gus and I smiled at each other, pleased to see a more upbeat side to Marshall's irritatingly indolent and angst-ridden personality. His was the downside to the Scottish character, not tragic like the Irish but—at least since the slaughter at Culloden and the Bonnie Prince's flight—sometimes beaten down into near Englishness.

We finished our beers, and shortly a burly bear of a man with a wraparound beard pushed open the door and strode in. He walked over grinning, slapped Marshall on the back, and turned to us. He was as tall as our host but bigger around the middle. And he carried himself in a bigger way.

"These must be your Yanks," he said.

Marshall introduced us to Clive (it rhymed with "hive") Shotton. "Clive knows everything about fishing in these parts," he said.

Clive laughed. "If I knew as much as he says I do, I'd never have a fishless day."

Gus, Clive, and I sat at a table, and Clive made out my permit while giving us the lowdown on the river.

The Clyde begins as an insouciant trickle on the slopes of twenty-three-hundred-foot Queensberry Mountain, northeast of Abington, where Gus and I first spotted it. Within three or four miles it becomes a burbling freestone stream, and by the time it reaches Biggar it has swelled to a smooth-flowing, mature river, meandering through pasture and cropland on its way to Glasgow and the Firth of Clyde. Along its route, the water winds through some of the most beautiful countryside in southern Scotland. In New Lanark, its channel narrows as it roars into a mist-filled gorge to tumble down a series of sandstone steps at the Falls of Clyde.

It is a superb fishery. The river's many tributaries and the region's aquifer-rich substrata assure consistent temperature and water levels, even in times of drought. And the richness of insect life in the Clyde rivals that of the best trout waters.

We could fish now, Clive said, or go meet two of his fishing pals. I was antsy to get on the water—it was already past five P.M.—but I also knew that the angling friendships you make can last a lot longer than the fishing. Our guide made a telephone call, and we drove to an apartment complex at the edge of town. "These blokes'll give you the real lowdown," Clive said. "Especially Bill. He's forgotten more than I'll ever know about the Clyde."

Clive went to a first-floor flat and rang the doorbell. Within seconds the door opened, and we went in to meet Bill Manson and Ferguson Findley. After we shook hands all around, we sat down and Mrs. Manson brought us tea from the kitchen.

Bill and Ferguson had their fly boxes laid out on the coffee table, and as we drank our tea they opened them. One by one they gently lifted out the flies—Cinnamon Sedge, Wee Black, Sand Fly, Light Olive. As Bill and Ferguson held them up—with forefinger and thumb, or balanced in mid-palm—they told of using each one. They described the seasons, times of day, hook size, and they told of the Clyde. The two men spoke of the river, their river, with fervid affection and loyalty, as if it were a woman they loved and could never leave.

"You find blokes that have fished the Clyde for years and that give it a break for a year, even two. But they always come back to it," Clive said.

There are many, more famous Scottish rivers. Names like the Tweed, the Spey, the Tay evoke images of broad pools, private beats, and big fish; of pipe-smoking fishermen in tweeds and deferential gillies standing by to net trophy salmon and sea trout. For some, they also call up nightmare visions of hotel bills and permit fees that would make a member of the royal family break out in a cold sweat.

But the Clyde was different, these men said. For three pounds, anyone could buy a day permit to fish thirty-seven miles of water. "A lot of people call the Clyde 'the working man's river,' " Clive said." And there was a story behind that.

"A hundred and fifty years ago, the Clyde was one of the most prolific salmon rivers in Scotland," Bill began. Then came the industrial revolution and, with it, pollution and dams that destroyed the salmon run. But because nearly all of the pollution was on the lower river, around Glasgow, the trout in the upper reaches were spared. Out of bad luck for the salmon came good fortune for the average fisherman. For the key to the Clyde's accessibility, the men agreed, was that it was not a salmon river. If it were, wealthy outsiders would long since have tried to get control of the fishing rights.

But now, thanks to cleanup efforts and the installation of fish ladders, the salmon had begun to return. It was a fact that evoked mixed feelings among local anglers. At first this was baffling to an outsider—who would not wish for a salmon revival?—but on second thought the dichotomy was clear. On one hand were the glamour and excitement of another game fish—the premier game fish. On the other was the threat of big money moving in.

For these men, salmon fishing held little allure. "Here it's a case of time-shares and Lord So-and-So," Bill said dismissively, going on to explain.

In recent years, fishing rights on some of Scotland's top salmon waters had been sold off in blocks of weeks or months, similar to certain vacation-condominium plans in the United States. Under the arrangement, the purchaser got exclusive access to the water for the same time period each year. The effect was the creation of private reserves for the wealthy. It was not an anomaly, just a new wrinkle in the British angling tradition, which for centuries had tended to restrict the best fishing to people of a certain class and income level.

Bill and Ferguson were tradesmen. Clive was a prison guard. In many parts of Britain these men, priced out of membership in exclusive angling clubs and without friends in the landed gentry, would not be fishing a river such as the Clyde. More than its haunting beauty and top-notch trout fishing, that was what made it so special, inspired such devotion. If the big-name streams were cold, unapproachable, aristocratic grande dames, the Clyde was a country lass, overflowing with joie de vivre and with a smile for everyone.

For nearly fifty years, during the good months, Bill had spent most of his free time on the river. Ferguson had more than forty seasons on the Clyde. Clive, who had moved to Carnwath just eight years before, was the neophyte of the group. "When I first came up, I fished for two years and I couldn't do a damn thing. Then I met Bill," he said. Bill grinned and looked down at the table.

From Bill, Clive learned the water, the right flies, how to tie and when to use them. He learned the techniques—mostly wet flies, fished in pairs or threes, cast downstream on a forty-five-degree diagonal and stripped back slowly. And he learned the tradition, one that Bill had first gleaned from his earliest mentors—"two uncles who were fanatical"—half a century before.

Part of the tradition was the tackle. For though all types of sport fishing were permitted on the Clyde, these men and their brethren felt there was only one. Other anglers might have success with spinning gear, but they wanted no part of it. "It's mechanical fishing, fishing with scrap metal as far as I'm concerned," Bill said.

For him, the long, wispy rods, the looping lines, the wee bits of feather and fur, were not just means to an end. Together with the river and the landscape and the camaraderie and the trout, they *were* the end.

When I asked how the Clyde stacked up against the other, more famous rivers, eyebrows went up all around.

"You mean like the Tweed?" Clive asked, cracking a wry smile. "It's nearly as good a trout water. Nearly." A couple of months before, a ten-pound, eleven-ounce brown had been caught in the Clyde near Crawford, he said. And were there bigger fish? He chuckled knowingly. "Oh there's some whoppers, some beasts."

The day was getting on toward evening, and Clive decided we had better get on the water if we were going to fish. We thanked Mrs. Manson for the tea and said good-bye to Bill and Ferguson. We drove back into the center of Carnwath so Clive could get his car. Then we followed him out into the open countryside, past scattered farms and clusters of houses. Several times we could see the river, and finally we pulled into a dirt road and parked near some railroad tracks. My watch said seven forty-two.

We put on our boots and other gear, and followed the road down under the railroad tracks, through a narrow cattle underpass, and out into a wide, green pasture that sloped toward the river. The field was wet with dew and here and there was trampled muddy with hoofprints where cows, in bovine conformity, had milled about in one spot or trod a single path over and over.

I paused for a few seconds to take in the scene: a flat, nearly treeless landscape with the river flowing through it and the railroad tracks stretching away to the horizon in opposite directions. The orange gold sun, low in the sky and descending toward a line of hills in the far distance, was set off by lines of purple cumulus. The evening was already getting chilly, and I remembered that Marshall had told us it had snowed in the Highlands the night before.

In a few minutes we were at the river and began rigging up. Clive pointed out a gravel bar I could wade to. "If you fish that edge there, it's usually good," he said. He gave a few more pointers about flies and tactics. "Good luck mate," he said, then hiked upriver a hundred yards.

I stepped into the water and began casting. These were the middle reaches of the Clyde. Here the river was about seventy-five feet wide, smooth and deep flowing. The bottom varied from fine, white sand to gravel and, in a few places, to grapefruit-size rocks that were slippery with algae. The current was not fast, and I had no trouble wading, though I had to be careful about the depth.

At first there were few insects, but as the sun sank lower two major hatches got going—a small brown caddis (sedge) and then a pale mayfly Clive had called a yellow sally. The trout began to rise; there weren't many but I saw scattered dimplings here and there. They were not taking artificials—upstream I could see Clive was as fishless as I was—but as usual I got caught up in the scene, the rhythm of casting, mending, and retrieving.

I waded to the head of the bar, dropping the fly over the deep water and letting it drift back to the shallows. I worked the seam at the edge of the bar. I cast across the current to the opposite bank. I tried downstream drifts. Four or five times I switched flies, over and over again putting them right on top of risers. None of it brought a fish to hand. I thought I had two half-hearted hits, but those trout may have been taking naturals near my fly.

In late spring and summer, the Scottish days stretch late into the evening. The sun seems to linger forever on the horizon, setting the river ablaze before it sinks out of sight. Even at ten P.M. the sky gleams silvery and luminescent, backlighting hills and streamside brush.

In the far-north twilight, with the temperature chilling down and the smell of damp pastures filling the air, it was wonderful fishing and lousy catching. When we left at ten-thirty Clive had landed one small trout and I had caught none. As we walked back to the cars he was shaking his head. "Sorry about that, mate," he said. "I just don't understand these fish sometimes. Three nights ago they were mad with hunger."

* * *

Despite Marshall's fulminations, Gus and I had set aside the next morning for Edinburgh. The day was a sunny and breezy, with just a few puffy cumulus dotting the sky. Heading northeast from Carnwath on back roads, we drove through the East Lothian Lowlands—rolling hills, farmhouses, streams bordered by meadows, and only occasional patches of deciduous forest.

Old Scotland hand Gus knew what to expect, but it came as a surprise to me when, after a half-hour's driving, open farm country suddenly became city parks, streets, and blocks of buildings. For Edinburgh is a city with no suburbs. We found a parking lot five blocks from the center and set out on foot.

Edinburgh is not Scotland's largest city. That distinction belongs to Glasgow. But what this gracious, low-key capital lacks in size it makes up for in class.

While Glasgow is a gritty, smokestack town, the throbbing industrial heart of Scotland, Edinburgh is the country's soul, a city where creativity and imagination take precedence over production quotas. Instead of factories, the tone is set by institutions such as the Royal Scottish Academy and the National Gallery. And the biggest event of any year is the Edinburgh Festival, which is actually a collection of festivals that includes the Fringe Festival, the International Film Festival, and the International Jazz Festival. This annual testimonial to the city's cultural richness, started more than a half-century ago, is one of the premier summer events in Europe.

For a first-time visitor, Edinburgh's most striking features are its spaciousness and the well-scrubbed beauty of its neoclassical and art noveau buildings. It is a city of parks and broad boulevards, of greenswards and big trees and Greek revival architecture. Its dominant landmark—grandiose and majestic Edinburgh Castle—towers above the city center like an ancient sentinel.

The architecture and rich cultural tradition earned the city the nickname "Athens of the North."

In search of old Edinburgh, visitors stroll the "Royal Mile" from Castle Rock to the Palace of Holyroodhouse, wending their way among post-medieval dwellings or pausing to observe traditional Scottish crafts (bagpipe and kilt making). But it is Princes Street that embodies the spirit of the modern city: busy but not frenetic, stylish and immaculate, courteous but slightly reserved. The sidewalk scene is kaleidoscopic and Whitmanesque: well-dressed businessmen, beautiful women, old couples in matching tweeds, and map-gawking tourists, from the well-heeled to the backpack set.

"It doesn't seem much like the city Marshall described," I remarked to Gus as we strolled past upscale shops, restaurants, and cafés.

"Marshall's full of crap," Gus said.

At the Balmoral Hotel we nodded to the kilted doorman—complete with tam-o'-shanter—and a little while later stopped in front of what may be the world's most elegant Pizza Hut. We knew we could dine graciously at a half-dozen other places within a few blocks. But we made the news hack's choice of time over pleasure. After a couple of pizza slices washed down with Coke, we made our way back to the car and retraced the route to Lanark.

With its busy streets, its aura of culture and commerce, Edinburgh had been, on the one hand, a mentally energizing interlude. But for all its appeal it was, after all, a bustling city of close to half a million people, and we longed for the wide-open barrens, the lonely landscapes of stream and pasture.

Back at the hotel Marshall was holding down his usual bar stool. He looked over his shoulder and swiveled around when we came in.

"Well, how was the seat of corruption?"

"Not so corrupt after all," Gus answered.

Marshall snorted and turned back to his beer.

We had agreed to meet Clive at three o'clock and since it was already after two, we did not waste much time on small talk. We went to our rooms and got our gear, then headed back to the car and drove to Clive's apartment. He was waiting out front.

"How's it going, fellas?" he asked, sliding into the back seat with his pack and rod case.

"Great," Gus answered. "We left poor Marshall gazing into his beer again, and weeah ready for advensha."

We followed narrow country roads through farmland and pasture, past Biggar and Coulter and Lamington, following the Clyde upstream, to Crawford. There we turned onto a dirt-and-gravel road and crossed a steel bridge. Clive told us to pull over onto the shoulder behind a parked car. "That'll be Ian," he said.

We got out and walked down the bridge embankment to the river. Ian Miller was surveying the water. Clive introduced us, and we shook hands all around. Ian worked for the Scottish National Railroad, we learned, and was river bailiff for the upper Clyde.

"What's she look like today?" Clive asked.

"Pretty good," Ian said. "I see some hatches, and the sun on the water should bring out goodly numbers."

We jointed our rods, pulled on boots and waders, shouldered our gear, and started hiking downriver. Gone were the frontal clouds of the night before. The afternoon was brilliant, the sky heartbreak blue, the river shimmering in the late-spring sun.

* * *

At Crawford, the Clyde is a robust freestone stream, with riffles and rapids and a few long, smooth pools. Mostly it is knee- to hip-deep, but in a few spots the bottom drops out to ten feet or more. In contrast to the cattle pastures and floodplain meadows that border the river downstream, here it is flanked by steep, rocky hills dotted with sheep and evergreens.

As we walked, Ian gave us a rundown on the fishing. Because of a spring drought, the river was down about a foot from its normal June level. This would make the wading easier but the fish more finicky. Still, it should be good. It was the best place he knew of, and he had taken more than a hundred trout from this stretch already that year, he said.

"Do you mean kept or caught?" I asked.

"Kept. Killed and grilled."

My eyebrows went up. Most of my fishing was catch-and-release. I am not a fanatic—fish is one of my favorite foods—but I had not killed that many trout in the past twenty years. "That seems like a lot to take out," I said.

"No, not really," Ian said. "They move back in from downstream. Or up. The river's still full of fish. You'll see." The upper Clyde was his favorite place to be, Ian said. But his dream was to go to New Zealand and fish.

The hard ground made for easy going as we followed the river down, staying back from the bank but watching the water. The sun was high and bright, but there was a spotty rise on. We stopped at a wide curve a third of a mile below the bridge. "We can fish our way up from here," Ian said as we rigged up. "There's a lot of good water. Just be careful you don't step in one of those holes."

We spread out at fifty-yard intervals: me, Ian, then Clive. When I got down into the river, I could see it was full of insect life. Just as Ian had said, the hatches were gearing up under the warming sun.

By the hundreds, caddises, mayflies, stoneflies, and midges struggled to the surface or shore, wriggling out of pupal casings and taking wing. Upstream and down, the trout were sipping, gulping, and slashing. It was not really a rise—much of the action was subsurface, a flash here, a swirl there, all visible only to a careful eye—but it was a feeding turn-on.

With so many hatches, it would not be hard to find a match for one. I put on a caddis imitation and began bouncing it down the riffle, working my way slowly upstream. I was blind-casting and the action was not fast. In twenty minutes I missed a couple of strikes, then hooked and lost a small fish.

Clive gave a shout from downstream and held up a fish, then bent down and eased the trout back into the water. It looked like a rainbow. I saw Ian fight and release two, and finally I landed a fat twelve-inch brown. I held it up for Ian and Clive, and they both gave the thumbs-up sign.

My fly was fouled with slime so I changed it. In the meantime, Ian worked his way up until he was across from me, near the opposite bank. Here the river was wide enough for us to fish across from each other—about thirty feet apart. Ian pointed out good lies, watched for rise rings, and advised me what flies to use and how to get the best drift.

The fish were striking short and I kept missing them. I did manage to hook three but could not land any of them. I began to feel like a klutz.

Ian was fishing only sporadically—concentrating on giving me tips. Still, he caught one small brown and hooked a thrashing two-pound rainbow that shot toward me, cartwheeled, and threw the hook.

I raised a few more fish but could not catch them. Then, too soon, it was time to go. The sun had dipped behind a line of purple clouds, flashing out golden orange rays that transformed the river to burnished copper. Walking back to the car, it was easy to understand Clive's feelings about the Clyde: "I love this damn river," he said. "It's a bonnie river."

* * *

In the morning Gus and I headed north to find the rest of Scotland—up past Edinburgh and Perth to Dunkeld and the valley of the Tay, and farther north still. The landscape began to change again. Gentle hills grew to craggy peaks, and valleys turned to rugged gorges. Grassy meadows and waving fields of grain gave way to heather and gorse and a few scattered broadleaf forests.

There is much water in Scotland, but only one "water of life" (*uisge beatha* in Gaelic)—the country's peat-smoked malt whisky. Just north of the Tay, we detoured from our northerly course to seek out a wee dram.

My firsthand (or first-palate) knowledge of Scotch was spotty, or maybe shot-ty, but a tourist brochure about the Edradour label had piqued my interest. Two assertions in the brochure clinched our decision to make the side trip: One laid claim to Edradour's being the world's smallest distillery; the other to its being one of the best single-malts. Gus, who was better versed in such matters, lit up when I read him the brochure. "Oh, Norm," he said, "just think of it. The best whisky in the world, and weah gonna get paid to drink it. I can hardly stand it. This life is just too hard."

I was still skeptical when we drove up to the facility, an unassuming cluster of buildings nestled in the hills above Pitlochry. But as tour guide Richard Christie wove his tale, I fell under the spell. It was really a love story—told in a lilting burr—of wind-tossed barley dried and smoked over a peat fire, of Highland spring water and oaken casks and scrupulous quality control.

The basic fermentation process took less than a week, Christie explained, but the real secret was the aging process. "We have a saying," he told us. "It takes five or six days to make the whisky, and ten years to drink it."

When we walked past the fermenting vats, the air was thick with the steamy, sweet-sour smell of yeast and mash. I began to feel a dryness in my throat.

We moved on to the storage cellar. "Two percent of the spirits evaporate through the casks each year," Christie said. "We call this the 'angels' share.' "

By the time the tour group finally sat down at the tables in the reception room, most of us had developed a powerful thirst. But not for water.

The clincher in my transformation from doubting Thomas to Edradour believer was the small complimentary glass of amber nectar, slow-burning as a fire of banked coals and smooth as butterscotch. It was as far from generic blended Scottish whisky as Alsatian coq au vin is from Kentucky Fried Chicken. This, Christie informed us, was the true flavor of the Highlands—its soil and water and ancient peat. The taste would have been easy to pursue further. But Gus and I had more ground to cover. Fortified but restrained, we got back on the road.

About ten miles north of Pitlochry, the deciduous forests gave way to evergreens, then dwindled to a few lonely trees on the heather-covered hillsides sloping up to mountain peaks. Some of them wore patches of snow. "Look at that white stuff up there," I said to Gus. "Can you believe summer starts in less than two weeks?"

"Yeah Norm," he laughed, "but summer up here in the Highlands is a little bit different."

This was finally the Scotland of lore and legend, as much a state of mind as a political and geographic entity. For many, it is the real Scotland. The rough-hewn, isolated existence of its farmers, sheepherders, and fishermen is a world away from the genteel urbaneness of Edinburgh, the industrial hum and working-class crush of Glasgow.

The central fact about the Highlands is that, as Gertrude Stein said of the United States, there are more places where there are *not* people than where there *are* people. Hundreds of square miles are virtually untracked wilderness.

But although the Highlands are wild, they are not untouched by the hand of man. The absence of trees that creates the region's spectacular panoramas is partly a result of climate and geology, but also of destructive forestry practices from past centuries—clearcutting for timber and slash-and-burn to create sheep pasture.

Perhaps the Highlands' most striking visual feature is the sky and its incredible play of light: brilliant sunbeams streaming through the smoky gray overcast, cloud shadows racing over mountains and moors, misty veils of showers softening the grays and greens. An ever-present wind sweeping in from the Atlantic and the Irish Sea gives the air a sharpness and clarity rarely seen in overpopulated mainland Europe.

I knew the Highlands had trout water—lots of it: rills, becks, burns, rivers, tarns, and lochs. I could hardly wait to fish them.

In another hour we were in Inverness. After a brief stroll of the downtown, we drove up the River Ness and found a room about twenty minutes outside the city. The next morning we drove back into the downtown.

Inverness is hailed for its rich, if bloody, history and attractions—its namesake castle (on the site of an earlier fortress, where Macbeth worked his vile conspiracy), St. Andrew's Cathedral, a world-class art museum. But its most significant site—five miles from the city center, at Culloden Moor—is more mourned than celebrated. For it was here that the last chance for Scottish independence died a bloody death in April 1746.

The inscription on the stone monument at Culloden says it most eloquently: "the gallant Highlanders who fought for Scotland."

The battle ended nearly nine months of fierce rebellion by the clans under Prince Charles Edward Stuart, "Bonnie Prince Charlie." The Highlanders and their leader, who had returned from French exile to reclaim for his father the British throne taken from his grandfather in 1688, had won victory upon victory, and he came within a whisker of capturing London in December 1745.

But the rebels' fortunes took a downturn, and on April 15 they were tired, hungry, and facing a superior force commanded by the Duke of Cumberland. Hindsight says they fought in the wrong place at the wrong time.

When the battle began in late morning, the Highlanders' fatigue and organizational problems diminished the effectiveness of their fierce broadsword-and-dagger charge. The flat moor provided decisive tactical advantages for the government forces, which were superior in arms and numbers. Artillery (firing grapeshot) and sharpshooters decimated the Highlanders' ranks, causing confusion and disarray. The rebels fought ferociously, but in less than an hour the moor was littered with their dead and dying, and the rest were in full flight.

The terrible slaughter did not end with the battle. The vanquished were pursued without quarter. Wounded and fleeing Highlanders were hunted down and murdered, their bodies mutilated. Bystanders, women, and children were also brutally butchered. The Bonnie Prince evaded a relentless search and made his way to a French ship on the west coast. He died in exile some four decades later, never having set foot in the Highlands again.

In the ensuing months and years, the countryside was laid waste by plundering government troops, and laws were passed to disarm the Scots and eradicate the identity of the High-landers. Kilts and bagpipes were banned, and clan leaders were stripped of their powers. The government made every effort to obliterate the battlefield site. A road was built through the rebel graves. A forest was planted to obscure the moor. But in 1881, stone monuments and a twenty-foot cairn were erected.

After Culloden, I felt more irritated with Marshall, sitting morosely on his barstool back in Carnwath; an oversized loser on a slow track to nowhere. War, oppression, and centuries of wresting an existence from a bleak, inhospitable landscape lashed by some of the harshest weather in Europe had helped mold most Scots into a hardy and independent people. But Marshall was an aberration, indulging his own ennui, wallowing in self-pity. He made me think of that child's ditty: "Yesterday, upon the stair, I met a man who wasn't there."

It was not that I could not empathize with him. Life can break or destroy any of us. But that does not mean we have to give in without a fight. I had seen too many barstool defeatists on Cape Cod (which has the highest alcoholism rate on the East Coast). "Cape Cod fahts," my dad called them. Guys who had bad luck in love, or tough childhoods, or financial setbacks, or just plain hard times, and used them as excuses to feel sorry for themselves and to bemoan their fate from inside a bottle.

Among the most important things I learned from my dad—by example, not by instruction—was never to mistake sensitivity for weakness. But the obverse was also true. Weaklings sometimes hid behind masks of false sensibility. And whining was not existential angst. It was just whining. Real men cry. But they do not snivel.

The extension, of course, was obvious: The kindest, gentlest people are the strongest.

"Life is unfair," John F. Kennedy said. And so it is. But for the strong and tender, it is never futile. They play the cards they are dealt and do not blame the dealer or other people or "fate." They reach out to their friends when they are down, they stick by their families through good times and bad, they go the extra mile for something they believe in. They face up to life's inherent absurdity and confront its inevitable tragedy with grace and fortitude. And in spite of it all—maybe because of it—they can be happy. "Happiness and the absurd are two sons of the same earth," was how Camus put it in *The Myth of Sisyphus*.

* * *

From Culloden we drove southwest on Route 82, along the shore of Loch Ness.

"Keep your eye out for old Nessie," Gus quipped. "If I can just get a photo weah gonna make a million dollahs."

Lying in a verdant valley, bordered by rocky cliffs as well as brilliant green meadows and forested hillsides sloping up from the shoreline, Scotland's most famous loch catches a visitor by surprise. The "monster" whose legend has swept around the world has largely obscured the fact that Loch Ness is a natural wonder unto itself.

Born in the geologic upheavals that wrenched the Northern Highlands away from the rest of Scotland millions of years ago, it boasts impressive dimensions. The lake is twenty-four miles long and varies from one mile to about four miles in width. It averages more than six hundred feet deep and at one point plunges to nearly a thousand. Though Loch Ness is not the largest such body of water in Scotland in terms of surface area—that distinction belongs to Loch Lomond—its volume is unsurpassed in all of Britain. In fact, its more than twenty-six million cubic feet of fresh water is more than all the lakes in England and Wales put together. This fact is cited by Nessie believers confronted with the question of how any "monster" could hide so well for so many years.

Tales of monsters in the loch date back at least to the sixth century and may have originated in Celtic legend. For centuries, locals used a Gaelic term—*Each Uisge,* which means "water horse"—to describe the creatures reputed to inhabit the depths of Loch Ness.

But the modern history of the monster began in May 1933 with an item in the local paper, the *Inverness Courier,* that recounted a sighting by a water baliff. Interest in the "creature" reached near hysteria worldwide in 1934 with the release of a photo by a London physician. It showed what looked like a very large creature with a mostly submerged body; a long, thin neck; and small head raised above the water. The photo immediately gave rise to speculation that the mysterious "monster" was a prehistoric aquatic reptile known as a plesiosaur. (The photo has since been proved to be a hoax.)

Gus and I drove the length of the loch, even stopping at the ruin of Urquhart Castle, which affords a view for miles in both directions. The fact that we saw no monster confirmed my news hack's dubiety. And I felt a little smug after an official at the Loch Ness Monster Exhibition in Drumnadrochit demurred when queried about Nessie. "We're not looking for the media monster anymore," Adrian Shine said. "That isn't what we'd expect to find in the loch these days."

But I was forced to rethink after a more definitive—and contradictory—comment by Alastair MacPherson, tourist director in Inverness. "I believe that many people know and see *something* in the loch," he said. "I have spoken to many sane and sober people who have seen *something.*"

Driving back to the hotel I was surprised to feel gratified. In a time when every square meter of the Earth had been mapped by satellite, and any yuppie with enough cash could climb Everest, it was nice to know there were still a few mysteries.

Gus and I had many plans for the next days, not the least of which for me was more fishing. But that night I came down with a fever, headache, and cough. For the rest of the trip I was little more than a passenger, watching the lochs and rivers and hills and villages flash past the car window. Water, trout water everywhere, nor any drop to fish, I thought, feeling sorry for myself that I was passing it all by.

The day before we headed back to Hull, we checked into the Castle Garry Hotel near Invergarry. An elegant old mansion that had been converted for the tourist trade, the hotel was surrounded by gardens lush with flowering shrubs, huge old trees, and manicured lawns sloping down to Loch Loich. I was still sick as a dog, but I could not stand to leave Scotland without wetting a line one more time. I arranged with the desk clerk to rent a rowboat the next morning.

I got down to the shore before breakfast. The loch was long and narrow, and on the hotel side, the land was nearly flat. But across the lake, mountains rose precipitously out of the peat-stained water.

I fished for about forty minutes, trolling a streamer while I rowed. Mist shrouded the distant peaks. The sky was white, its puffy cumulus broken up by patches of blue. Rain showers periodically spattered the lake, sending tiny floccules rolling across the surface like mercury from a broken thermometer.

I was daydreaming when a good fish hit, nearly pulling my rod over the side. By the time I grabbed it, the fish was off.

When I met Gus at breakfast I was feverish and winded. Afterward, I lay down for an hour before we left.

Back home two days later, the English Channel far off and the Highlands just a memory, the trip felt like unrequited love. I vowed I would return to fish Clive's "bonnie river." And others, until I lost count.

7

The Sun Still Rises

Trout of the Irati, July 1991

The river ran on, no one knew where or why, just as it had in May; from a small stream it flowed into a large river, from the river to the sea, then rose in vapor and returned in rain; and perhaps the very same water he had seen in May was again flowing before his eyes. . . . For what purpose? Why?

—Anton Chekhov, "The Kiss"

The sun comes up late over the peaks above Arive. Just upstream from town, the river swings into a wide curve, spilling over a gravel bar in three braided riffles before reuniting in a long, smooth pool to slip away under the ancient stone bridge.

This chilly summer morning, a heavy gray mist was spilling over the mountains, sweeping down the valley like a sea fog in an onshore blow and raising goose bumps on the back of my neck as I swung around to follow the fly downstream. I turned up the collar of my wool shirt, picked up the line, made two false casts, and laid the Adams down softly on the middle riffle, watching as it bounced downcurrent on tiny wavelets. Up in the village a rooster crowed, its shrill call echoing and re-echoing off the cliffs above the church.

There are surely more spectacular waters, more remote locations. But it is difficult to imagine a more alluring stream than the Irati, the Spanish river made famous by Ernest Hemingway in his 1926 novel *The Sun Also Rises.* Springborn in the western Pyrenees along the Spanish–French border, the Irati winds its way down through a wild, rugged landscape as unspoiled as any in Europe.

This is a region of thick forests and craggy mountains cut by deep, wooded gorges. Orderly, whitewashed villages dot the valleys and high plateaus. Near the villages, kerchiefed women and sun-browned men in *boinas,* the distinctive Basque berets, gather hay in fragrant meadows. In the dooryards of the houses, vegetable gardens spill out over low wood fences.

But the towns are mere specks of civilization amid the vastness of the mountains. The wilderness is the reality. Ibex, chamois, and even brown bears roam the crags and heights. And at the headwaters of the river lies the Irati Forest, one of Europe's last great stands of old-growth beech and oak.

Perhaps no other European angling water flows through the American consciousness with the power of the Irati. Its mystique is as much a part of our mytho-cultural landscape as are Huck Finn's Mississippi and Thoreau's Walden Pond. Many of us who grew up with a love of books and the outdoors have dreamed of sometime visiting the high Basque country, where Jake Barnes and his friend Bill Gorton spent their time hiking, drinking wine, and fishing for big trout amid the solitude of the mountains. Before Hemingway, the Irati belonged to a little corner of Spain. Now it belongs to all of us.

Hemingway was a master of the fishing story as allegory. He grew up hunting and fishing, and both sports remained lifelong passions. But when he wrote about them, they became much more. Sometimes, as in "Big Two-Hearted River," fishing was a healing exercise. In *The Old Man and the Sea*, it became a noble but ultimately futile struggle for unattainable dreams and a small measure of dignity. But always it was more than mere angling. No one wrote as simply and lyrically about the sport until Norman Maclean.

The fishing trip in *The Sun Also Rises* is based loosely on several excursions that Hemingway made to the Irati in the 1920s during the annual Fiesta San Fermín—better known as the Running of the Bulls—in Pamplona. As in the book, the writer and his fellow "lost-generation" expatriates found the area an exhilarating refuge from Pamplona's blazing July heat and the wild carousing of the fiesta. They hiked the mountains, swam in the river, and visited the nearby Monastery of Roncesvalles; but most important of all, they "had good fishing. The nights were cold and the days were hot, and there was always a breeze, even in the heat of the day."

The fish are no longer as big or as plentiful in the Irati. And the dusty trail winding through the mountains is now paved. But little else has changed.

In the gorge upstream from Arive, the lush hardwood forests grow right down to the water's edge. Eagles soar in the thermals, floating above the cliffs and peaks. And the wild brown trout still grow swift and strong in the icy currents. Here, the Irati is a powerful mountain stream, forty to fifty feet across, smooth-flowing and glass-clear. It varies from knee- to waist-deep as it glides over treacherous broken ledge and scattered rocks, occasionally boiling to life in small rapids or gushing through a sluice between two boulders.

Still soiled with the sweat and dust of the plains, I first eased into the current early on a July evening. Like Hemingway and his fictional hero, Jake, Dave and I had traveled up to the Irati Valley from Pamplona. We had spent the morning chasing down the right office to buy a fishing license. When we left the Plaza Castillo around noon, it was so hot the sweat ran down my sides in mini-rivers. Outside the city no wind stirred the grainfields, and the ocher hills were parched and powdery. But in the mountain twilight the gorge was cool and aqueous, green slopes angling up to a deep blue sky. A passing thundershower had soaked the woods, and the air had the damp, clean smell that comes after a mountain rainstorm. Here and there a thin, white mist rose from the river.

A few light-olive mayflies helicoptered up off the surface, but there were too few to spark a rise. Occasionally a small trout leaped dramatically clear of the water to snatch one, falling back with a flat, slapping sound. I fished upstream for about two hours, keeping an eye on the cumulonimbus piling up over the ridges and listening to the distant rumblings to the north. I did not raise a fish, and the light was fading when I hiked back up the steep slope to the car.

By the time we arrived back at the campground in Espinal, the storm had surged back over the mountains from France to come roaring down through the pass at Roncesvalles. Jagged electric blue flashes lit up a landscape savaged by slashing downpours and fierce winds. The tempest continued most of the night, but in the morning the sky had cleared and a fresh breeze was blowing out of the northwest.

* * *

Sunlight was sparkling on wet grass when I crawled out of the tent the next morning. A hundred feet away, a half-dozen kids splashed in the Urrobi, a thin, meandering stream impounded by a stone dam to create a swimming hole. Fortunately, the Irati had not flooded in the night, and among our things the only tangible evidence of the storm was the foot of my sleeping bag, wet where it had hung off the air mattress. I went for a stroll around the campground, and when I came back Dave was smoking his pipe and sitting by the camp stove, waiting for the coffee to boil. With the wind, it was taking a long time. He grinned and motioned me to the other folding stool.

"You know, when you first talked about a camping trip to Spain, I wasn't too keen on it. My wife and I had stayed in a bunch of campsites here. Mostly down south. All of 'em were hot and dusty, and you couldn't find any shade. This is somethin' else."

"I tried to explain it to you. There's a different climate in the mountains."

"I know, but you don't think of this when you think of Spain."

I knew what he meant, and it was just what we needed.

* * *

We had reached this storied stream after four days of highways and heat mirages, a mental cinemascape of countryside and shore from the Rhine to the Bay of Biscay. But always, Oz was the Vascongadas—the Basque provinces—and the high valley of the Irati.

The first morning, as we rolled south down Autobahn 67 from Darmstadt, flat, alluvial plain had given way to the evergreen forests of Rheinland-Pfalz, then to Lorraine's rolling hills and wind-rippled fields of wheat and rye. For the first thirty miles after the French border, traffic was light but steady on the A-4 *autoroute peage*. But after Metz, the highway became virtually deserted. Verdun slipped away behind, then Chalons sur Marne and Riems. Only when the haze and splendid sprawl of Paris loomed in the southwest did the lanes clog with tailgating Renaults and Citroens.

After a fifteen-mile urban gauntlet of noise, congestion, and exhaust fumes, the road and the country opened up again. We swung south onto A-10, down into the green, rural heart of France: grassy knolls and brushy swales and thick woods; villages and wide-stretching farms; and meandering rivers with water plants waving in the current.

The air grew warmer as the highway stretched on down, past Orleans and Blois and Tours. At Chatellerault we left the *autoroute* and, with the sun arcing toward the western horizon, found our way to a campground. We had picked it out of the Michelin Guide, which gave it four stars. But we soon found that the stars were for the amenities, not the setting.

The campground was a huge expanse of summer-dry grass and hedges, with a few spindly poplars and maples interspersed among the hundreds of tent and trailer sites. In one corner, a yellow sand beach sloped down to a small, silty lake. But there were also a snack bar; a gleaming, modern shower and washrooms; an activities center; and tennis courts and playing fields.

Dave and I were thankful that the start of the French August vacation was still more than two weeks away and that only about one out of every ten campsites was occupied. We set up our tent on the brown, flattened grass, got out our folding canvas stools, and relaxed in the evening breeze. Dave was not hungry but I got out the propane stove and heated up a can of chowder. Across the fields, the sun sank below the trees and the few scattered gray-and-white clouds turned orange, then purple. The day was done. We were asleep an hour after dark.

* * *

When we woke in the morning a heavy, gray fog had settled over the countryside. As we were packing up the tent the mist turned to drizzle, then to a gentle rain. We drove for two hours in intermittent rain. But just north of Bourdeaux, the sky lifted and the day turned hot and sunny. The landscape was now ripe grain-fields, vineyards, and chateaux—and, outside Bordeaux, an endless sun-dappled horizon of sunflowers nodding summer yellow in the breeze.

By the time we reached Bayonne, the day was hot and muggy. The air that was rushing through the car windows provided little relief. But as we climbed toward the border, into the Pyrenees foothills, the air turned fresher, the scenery greener. Soon the smell of the ocean was on the breeze as the road wound down to San Sebastian, loveliest of seaside cities. Dave and I drove into the downtown and parked half a block from the shore, near city hall, the onetime grand casino.

Nestled around the curve of its empyrean blue bay and graced with three lovely beaches, San Sebastian was as much seaside park as urban center. Surfers rode the curl up to the edge of the shopping district. Clean-swept streets lined with tamarind and plane trees, classic architecture, and carefully maintained residences and public buildings imparted an understated elegance.

This was a small, compact city of just two hundred thousand residents, with virtually no urban sprawl, and the surrounding green foothills gave it the feel of an outpost amid the countryside. The air was clean and redolent of the sea.

We found no shabby neighborhoods in San Sebastian. And nowhere was there any sign of the despoliation—pollution and industrial detritus—found along the shorelines of most port cities.

Dave and I strolled the banks of the Urumea River, which was neatly channeled between stone walls and bordered by esplanades.

The love of wild rivers is implicit to trout fishing. We are drawn by solitude, by trees and plants and mossy logs, by the play of light and the sound in water purling over ancient stones. Sometimes, for an instant, connected to those quick and numinous creatures that lure us astream, we become part of it—the beauty, the mystery, the magic life force.

But in San Sebastian, the Urumea was no magic river. It was merely moving water employed as a landscape accent: tidy, functional, and carefully conceived. It might as well have been an aqueduct.

We found the tourist office and visited for a half-hour with its longtime director, Rafael Aguirre. He beamed at the chance to share his beloved city with two Americans and began extolling its charms: stunning beaches, healthy sea air, distinctive Basque cuisine; and historic landmarks.

San Sebastian was an ancient city, he said, but the structures were not. "There is a simple explanation for this. In 1813 the city was besieged by the British. This was because it was occupied by the French. And at this time it was completely destroyed."

"But we have many beautiful buildings," Aguirre continued. Had we seen the Miramar Palace, former summer residence of the Spanish royal family? And did we know that nearly a million visitors came to San Sebastian each year? In summer it was the playground of the rich and famous.

Aguirre explained that, because of the city's geography and heritage, San Sebastianers led more active lifestyles than many urban dwellers. The most popular outdoor pastimes were sailing, windsurfing, horseback riding, swimming, and shooting. "Our society is a very *sportif* society," he reiterated.

One of the city's most enduring social traditions, he told us, was its more than one hundred *Sociedades Populares O Gastronomicas,* or clubs dedicated to fine food. These all-male societies, each with forty to eighty members, met twice a week to cook and sample various dishes. Because of San Sebastian's age-old links to the sea, many of the recipes featured fish.

"I would like to invite you to my gastronomy club," Aguirre said. "It is one of the oldest."

I asked when.

"On Thursday, in two days."

Dave and I looked at each other. We had a lot of ground to cover, photos to shoot, and stories to write in those two days. There was no way.

"That's very kind of you," I said, "but we have to leave in the morning."

Aguirre's beaming smile turned to a frown of disappointment. But he gave it one last try. "I can guarantee you that it would be memorable," he said. "Our Basque style of cooking is very special."

We repeated our regrets, shook hands, and said good-bye.

We walked a block to the shore and the promenade that rimmed the bay. The walkway presented a sharp contrast. On our left was the shore boulevard, noisy with traffic and, beyond, the urbane, rococo allure of the Old City. To the right were greenswards with benches, date palms, and an ornate stone balustrade. Ten feet below the railing, on La Concha Beach, bikini-clad bathers strolled the water's edge as the surf thundered onto the strand. Farther out on the blue water, sailboats were lifted on the backs of the swells and eased down again.

We returned to the car through the narrow streets of the Old City, wending our way among flamboyant sandstone-and-stucco, four- and five-story structures crammed with cafés, restaurants, and shops.

We drove about five miles outside the city to the village of Igueldo, which had the area's only campground, and set up our canvas home for the night. We were lucky to get a site because the place was mobbed with the backpack set from central Europe and Scandinavia.

Then we took the winding road up Mount Igeldo. The mountaintop was a garish letdown, dominated by a café/restaurant, mini-amusement park, and hotel. But the tackiness could not mar the vista of the bay and the city of San Sebastian below, aglimmer with the first lights of evening. Down the coast in the other direction, cliffs and green meadows dropped down to the sea.

When we got back to the campground, the music, lights, laughter, and general commotion did not bode well for an early, restful night. But we both fell asleep quickly and slept soundly.

* * *

At seven the next morning, the campground was shrouded in fog and quiet as a funeral: last night's revelers were nowhere to be seen. We ate a hasty breakfast and then hit the road.

The fog burned off on the way to Bilbao but a low, filmy cloud cover remained. It fit the scene when we descended denuded mountainsides to the Basque region's industrial heartland.

Though Bilbao is only an hour's drive west of San Sebastian, they are a world away in outlook and ambience. It would be difficult to find two cities so close geographically and so far apart in other ways. In San Sebastian, gazing out over its bay to the sea beyond, there is a promise of limitless horizons. In Bilbao, squeezed in among factory stacks and scarified hills, the perspective is more mundane.

It was clear at first glance that this was not a carefree resort specializing in selling itself but rather a working-class city that produced things to sell. Things like steel, plastic, lead, and petrochemicals. If San Sebastian was suntan lotion and sand, Bilbao was sweat and industrial grit.

San Sebastian had a compact, decorative quality, but Bilbao was ungainly and plain, bordering on ugly. In the concrete and red-brick facades of its stolid downtown, function trumped form. This was a manufacturing powerhouse of half a million, one of Spain's top steel producers and its biggest port; it was a blighted region of refineries, steel-mill complexes as big as small towns, and giant smokestacks belching sulfurous smoke. The industrial sprawl reached out tentacles for miles, into the hills and down the valleys. Some of the hillsides resembled a moonscape. This, I knew, was what the cheerleaders of laissez-faire capitalism really meant when they proclaimed the inevitability of "progress."

Dave and I drove into the city center and parked near the rail station. A light drizzle was falling, but we got out our umbrellas and started off.

We first looked for a place to buy a city map, surely a cinch on a Saturday at the height of vacation season. But the tourist office was closed, and the two newsstands at the train station had none. We finally found one at El Conte Ingles, the giant department store, but the episode was a tip-off about tourism's minor role in Bilbao.

We strolled the upscale shopping district along the Gran Via de Don Diego Lopez de Hard, then wandered through the Parque de Dona Casilda Iturriza, the moderately attractive but slightly run-down city park. The fountains were not turned on, and the water in them was stagnant and green with algae. Litter was strewn about and children played on unswept walkways gray with dust turning to mud. Here and there a bit of Spanish Victorian flair showed in the downtown area, but in general the city seemed strikingly downbeat after San Sebastian.

We headed for the footbridge that crossed over the Nervion River to the Old City. On the map, the Nervion was auspiciously blue, but close up it was as filthy, sad, and violated as Florence's Arno. Gazing down into the sinuous, stagnant, smutty brown estuary, garbage-lined and bespeaking industrial might, made me feel as dreary as the day. It sharpened the longing for mountains and clear, fast water.

We crossed over to the east bank of the river and climbed the hill to the Begona district. Its medieval/early-Renaissance flavor was a relief after the new town's relentlessly bleak industrial modernism. From the heights near the Santiago Cathedral, we saw a very different city from the one we had observed at street level. Like a flawed beauty best viewed from a distance, the Nervion River stretched out below, and the sea of red-tile roofs receding into the distance had a certain charm. Even the industrial haze only seemed to soften and enhance the scene.

An hour later, back on the coastal highway, we were relieved to leave Bilbao in the rearview mirror. Traffic was heavy, the day hot and muggy. We consulted our campground guide and began planning our stopover for the night. The guidebook showed a half-dozen campgrounds strung out along the coast over twenty-five or thirty miles. But what we assumed would be a routine travel task turned out to be a futile, frustrating, five-hour search that involved winding over back roads, into towns, up hills, and down valleys.

We saw campgrounds packed so tightly that the manager would have needed a shoehorn to squeeze in another tent or pop-up camper. These places were located along the highway, near beaches, in honky-tonk tourist towns. One, in Sonona, sat outside the walls of a massive prison. But everywhere the signs said the same thing: *Completo* (Full).

Around nine P.M. we finally gave up on camping. We backtracked and found a small *hostel* in Gama, just off the coast highway.

* * *

In the morning we ate a hasty breakfast of coffee and rolls, then headed southeast. Dave and I were both anxious to escape the tourist-infested coast. I drove, and for the first couple of miles I had to turn on the wipers because of a heavy, gray mist. Shortly, though, it thinned to fog, and then the sun burned through. By the time we reached Llodio the day was hot and dry, with a Delft sky.

At Vitoria we got off the four-lane highway and headed east, roughly following the course of the Rio Arakil. The valley was compact, squeezed between the Sierrra de Urquilla range in the north and the Sierra de Urbasa in the south. Dusty, gray villages dotted rolling hills and far-stretching farmland—a patchwork of grain and potato fields plowed into the red, stony soil. Aluminum irrigation pipes, flashing silver in the sun, carried water from the river to walking sprinklers that soaked the russet earth in giant circles. At certain sun angles, rainbows hung briefly in the spray, fading as the droplets settled onto the crops.

At Irurtzun, where the Rio Arakil merged with the Rio Larraun and swung south, we came upon a celebration. Dave and I got out of the car and followed four giant cloth figures that were dancing and swaying to a handful of flute players and one drummer. It was the third Sunday in July, and we had blundered into the village's Fiesta San Martin.

Dave got out his camera and began shooting, but when the procession reached the village square, stern-faced men began gesturing for him to stop. He lowered the camera so it hung from the strap around his neck, and the men relaxed. Young people and old were dancing in the center of the square. Off to one side were kiosks with food, wine, soft drinks, and trinkets.

We watched the dancing for five minutes, then worked our way over toward the kiosks. Dave raised his camera nonchalantly and the shutter clicked, the motor drive whirred. In fifteen seconds, one of the previous objectors was after him with a broom. Finally it dawned on us that we were the only outsiders. This was a private occasion, not a tourist event. Dave lowered the camera again and held out his hands, palms up, while backing away from the broom in his face.

We retreated to a shady side street at the edge of the square and watched the celebration for a few minutes more before returning to the car.

In another half-hour we were strolling across the mosaics of Pamplona's Plaza del Castillo. The afternoon was hot and dry, with no wind stirring. The plaza was lined with cafés and outdoor tables under broad umbrellas. We sat down at one and ordered bottles of mineral water. It was too hot for anything else, except maybe beer, but I knew if I drank one in the midday heat it would make me groggy and would likely give me a headache later.

"No bulls this trip," Dave said.

"Nope," I answered. Because of scheduling problems at the office, we were a week too late for San Fermin. A week late and a wineskin short, I thought.

We struck up a conversation with a young woman at the next table. She was sorry we had missed the fiesta. She had grown up in Pamplona, and the celebration was in her blood. "San Fermin is a party that is in the street. It is for the old people and the young people, the rich people and the poor people," she said. During the school year, she studied in London, but in summer she returned to her beloved hometown amid the arid plains of central Navarre.

What she loved most about Pamplona was its friendliness. Many cities—London being a prime example, she said—were cold and impersonal. They fostered alienation and isolation. Not Pamplona. "If someone is alone here, it is no trouble to meet people," she told us.

For visitors and natives alike, the central square was an informal social club, she explained. Many a new friendship or romance began across a table on the Plaza del Castillo. "Idoya," she said when we held out our hands and introduced ourselves, "Idoya Zorriillar. A good Basque name."

We said good-bye and walked four blocks to the fifteenth-century Gothic cathedral. Behind the church a path led to part of the medieval bulwark that once enclosed the city, and from the top of the wall we took in the view out across the Arga Valley, to the foothills of the Pyrenees and the high peaks beyond.

Like all of Spain, Pamplona has a stormy history. It began as a Basque settlement in pre-Christian times and was variously conquered and occupied by Romans, Visigoths, Moors, and French. According to popular legend, the city was named for the Roman general Pompey, who camped on the bluff with his legions in the winter of 75–74 B.C.

We walked back to the square, then through the tangled streets of the old town, which was packed with postcard and trinket shops, and along the Paseo Ernest Hemingway. "I guess that's part of what Faulkner was talking about," I said as we gazed at the street sign.

"What do you mean?" Dave asked.

"Making a 'scratch on the face of immortality.' That's what he said writers were aiming for."

"Yeah, I guess both those guys made pretty big scratches."

After a stop at the Plaza de Toros and the empty bullring, it was time to go. We drove about five miles out of the city to a campground near Eusa. Sited on a barren bluff, the place was clean and spacious. It had a fine view out over the dry plains to the mountains, but there was hardly a tree to be found. The ground was hard and dusty, with here and there a tuft of dried grass.

After we set up the tent, we cooked some soup over the stove and watched the sky turn colors until dark.

*   *   *

In the morning we packed up early and headed into Pamplona to get my fishing license. We got caught in rush-hour traffic, and the city was already baking in the July sun when we parked near the tourist bureau. They had no licenses but sent us to a government office where they *thought* we could get one. We drove about twelve blocks to a nondescript building where we were given yet another address. We were both shaking our heads by the time we got to the Gobierno de Ordenacion del Territoris, Vivienta Y Medio Ambiente on Calle de Alhondiga. As I waited in line at the barred window, I was prepared for another runaround. But when I said, "*Licencias de Pesca,*" the clerk answered, "*Si, pasaporte.*"

Five minutes later I handed over seven hundred fifty pesetas and sighed with relief. We were finally on our way. Dave and I were tired of cities, their pavement and impressive buildings and relentless commerce. Tired of hectic highways and tourist havens and the news hack's crammed daily docket of interviews, photo shoots, and legwork, which had left us enervated and cranky.

But as the road out of Pamplona climbed into the foothills, our mood evolved with the countryside. Wheat fields changed from straw to pale green, and a few wooded patches began to appear on the slopes. A light breeze stirred the leaves on the trees, and the heat was not as intense. Just before Espinal we came into a region of thickly wooded hillsides and high, green mountains. After the high temperatures and dust of the plains, it felt like another country. The Germans have a word for this type of landscape: *Augenweide.* Roughly translated, it means a restful meadow for the eyes.

As we came down through the hills from Burguette and Garralda, our first glimpse of the Irati was of a thin, shining ribbon twining through the green valley. Straddled by a stone bridge, with cliffs and mountains towering above, it was a scene to break your heart.

* * *

The Vascongadas is a world apart. Comprised of the three Basque Provinces—Alava, Vizcaya, and Guipuzcoa, as well as part of Navarre—this region of northwest Spain has some of the country's friendliest people, most spectacular scenery, and most interesting history and traditions.

The Basque people have long intrigued historians and ethnographers. An air of mystery shrouds their origins, and their language is unrelated to any other known tongue. Some authorities have linked them to Stone Age inhabitants of the western Pyrenees. Others have claimed their ancestors were Celts or the lost citizens of Atlantis. But the truth remains obscure. What is known is that the Basques are a hardy and fiercely independent people who have inhabited the western Pyrenees for thousands of years. Despite subjugation by myriad conquerors, they have stubbornly clung to their traditions and their language.

Throughout their history, the Basques have enjoyed various degrees of autonomy. The high point was the Basque kingdom of Navarre, with its capital in Pamplona, which flourished from the mid-tenth century until it was conquered by Castille in 1521.

During the Spanish Civil War, the Basque region was granted semi-independence by the Republican government. This came to an abrupt end in 1939 with the victory of Generalissimo Francisco Franco's fascist forces and the subsequent brutal suppression of the Basque language and culture.

But some Basques never accepted incorporation into Spain. Since 1968 the outlawed separatist group ETA had periodically mounted terror campaigns against Spanish officials and institutions. In our wanderings Dave and I had seen spotty evidence of the separatist fever incubating in the Vascongadas. Here and there ETA graffiti scarred highway overpasses and public buildings. Outside Guardia Civil headquarters in Bilbao, young men in flak jackets carrying automatic weapons had stood guard with wary, watchful eyes.

Much of the Vascongadas is a cordilleran wilderness. It is a landscape that has profoundly shaped the spirit of its people, fostering self-reliance and solitary livelihoods: sheep herding, farming, logging, handicrafts. At its southern edge, where the stony foothills of the Pyrenees slope down to the Ebro River Valley, it is a region of small towns set amid fields and vineyards. This is arid country, made fruitful by sprinklers and irrigation ditches.

But the true Basque country is to the north, in the forested hills and mountains of the western Pyrenees. Because of its nearness to the coast, clouds and moisture sweep in from the Atlantic and the Bay of Biscay to spill over the mountaintops in great, rolling billows. Watered in winter by snows and in summer by frequent thunderstorms—and with its mountain peaks shrouded in mist—it is a region of lush forests, verdant meadows, and rushing streams.

But the reach of the moist ocean breezes is limited. Twenty miles east of the Irati, in the Roncal Valley, the countryside dries out. Beeches and oaks yield to moisture-conserving black pines. Instead of grass and damp humus, the forest floor is littered with dry, brown needles.

The clean, well-kept villages with their gleaming stuccoed houses stand in sharp contrast to the dusty gray-stone towns of the plains. Here the people are cheerful, relaxed, and resolutely independent. Strangers are invariably greeted with a "Hola" and a smile. Even the very old are tanned and robust, a result of lifetimes of exercise and outdoor living.

One day, with hand gestures and miserable pocket-dictionary

Spanish, I tried a conversation with three local anglers in Arive. They were watching a small trout holding in the current among the weeds beneath the bridge. One of the fishermen, an old man with rolled-down hip boots and no teeth, mimed the fluid casting motion of a fly rod to indicate the best way to fish the river. Upstream, he motioned, were *"muchas Truchas grande"* ("many big trout"). Recently, one had been caught that weighed *"dos kilos"* (two kilograms). Downstream, he was not so sure about. The youngest of the group, a dark-haired man of about forty, shrugged his shoulders and stuck out his right arm, waggling his hand with the palm down to indicate the fishing was an iffy proposition.

* * *

A half-mile above the big curve in Arive, the Irati emerged from its deep, twisting gorge to spill down through a broad, gentle stretch that could have been laid out with a transit. Here the river was a lively freestone stream, bubbling and splashing over smooth-worn rocks. Along the edges, brushy willows overhung swift-flowing channels and a little farther back, poplars swayed in the wind. I could see this stretch from the bridge pool.

I wound the line back onto the reel and waded upstream from the bridge, squeezing the leader against the cork grip while the fly dangled free on the last three or four inches of tippet. When I had gone about fifty yards, I stopped in midcurrent and clipped off the Adams, hooking it into the wool patch on my vest. Since there was no rise on, I tied on an attractor, a big yellow Grizzly Wulff, and began casting to the pockets and lies. I had the river to myself and slipped into an early-morning reverie about friends, family, life's vicissitudes.

After dropping me off and getting a few shots of the bridge in the early mist, Dave had headed out in the car on his own to shoot other landmarks. Then he would putter around the campsite for a while before coming to get me for lunch. Dave was easygoing and levelheaded, and we had had some great assignments together. He was not a fisherman, but he loved camping and freely shared his gear.

More than a decade earlier, Dave and his flight attendant wife had quit their jobs in Miami and set off on a honeymoon camping trip across Europe. Afterward, they vowed to return, and within a year Dave had landed the job in Darmstadt. Their dream had become reality. Less than a month later he found his wife drowned in a hotel bathtub at the Frankfurt Airport. Exhausted and sick with a cold after a grueling transatlantic flight, she had climbed into the hot water and passed out, the victim of a rare medical phenomenon. Like many people who have suffered a great loss when young, Dave was gentle and pensive.

As the morning wore on, the sun burned through the mist periodically, and the streamside meadows came alive with bees, butterflies, and grasshoppers. I switched to a hopper imitation and continued working my way upstream. The flowing river, the scents of the summer meadows, and the bird calls evoked other mornings on the water. And my dad. All the early mornings with my dad.

Mist and trout rising on a Cape Cod kettle-hole pond. Bluefish tearing through a school of sand eels on a flood tide as the burnt orange disk of the sun edged up over the horizon. The whistle of duck wings low overhead before they swung around to splash down among the decoys.

As I fished the Irati that day, my own son was six, soon to start first grade; my little girl was three. What would I give them? What would the collection of shared memories for their mental scrapbooks look like? I hoped as rich and variegated as mine, though I would try to spare them a few.

I remembered how suddenly and inconsolably I had cried in school one day in the third grade. The pretty young teacher, Miss Reynolds, tried to comfort me and asked what was wrong. Finally, through sobs, I told her about the nightmare. Since my mom had left five years before, my little brother and I had lived with a series of families while my dad struggled to get a new business going. A couple of months before, he had finally been able to rent a cottage for the three of us, and we were a family again. But the little-boy fear that something might happen to take it away was deep in my psyche. He was all we had, and I had dreamt that he died.

I missed him now, on the river, wished he were here. But for him Europe was the view from inside a half-track as he and a couple of million buddies smashed Hitler's *Wehrmacht* back to Berlin. Bombed-out cities, hunger, mud, freezing cold, and death. No vacation slides of tourist sites and lissome lasses.

My first Irati trout was a surprise. The morning was waning and I had been fishing on automatic pilot for an hour or more, casting by rote and switching flies occasionally, just for a change. Finally I put on a big old gaudy Royal Coachman, a No. 12. To match-the-hatch purists it looks like a stuffed rooster, but it had broken fishless spells for me from the Yellowstone to the Weisser Traun.

On the fourth cast I dropped the Coachman in close to a tangle of willows, and a sprightly eight-incher darted out to smack it a couple of inches from the branches that trailed in the current. I was daydreaming but set the hook by reflex. The little fish splashed and tugged gamely, but in half a minute was gulping air on its side in the shallows, its gleaming pastel spots brilliant against the gray white sand. I quickly unhooked the trout and eased it back into the water; it shot away downstream like a torpedo.

Despite a windbreaker, vest, and wool shirt, I was chilled from standing in the cold water, and I stayed on the sandbar a few minutes to warm up. The sun had not yet redeemed its pledge, and mist was still blowing down the valley.

I smiled, thinking of my wife and kids, still warm in their beds at her parents' house in Connecticut. The time was a little after five A.M. there. It would be another two hours before they got up and going. The kids would head for the family room to turn on cartoons. Libby and her mom would start breakfast and begin to plan their day. In a week I would join them.

I hoped they were doing lots of fun things—movies, museums, the beach—and that the pain had eased some. Seven months before, Libby's only sister had been killed in a car crash the week before Christmas. Ceci was twenty-three.

At fourteen, Libby's mom had lost her mother. Now, almost half a century later, one of her daughters had been torn from her with the same savage suddenness. With the inexorable random absurdity of fate, her loss had come full circle. Sometimes tragedy seems to stalk certain people, or families. But that is merely perception. If we live long enough, life will keep its promise of sorrow to us all.

Facing upriver, my gaze rose toward the high, green valleys and meadows around Roncesvalles. According to legend, it was near the pass there that Roland, of *Chanson* fame, was killed in the eighth century when Basques and Saracens, angered at the dismantling of Pamplona's fortifications, slaughtered the rear guard of Charlemagne's army. Later, the monastery was a way station for tens of thousands of pilgrims traversing the pass on their way to the shrine at Santiago de Compostela.

The cloister's spare, understated Romanesque church would seem quaint beside the great cathedrals—Cologne, St. Peter's, Strasbourg, St. Mark's. But its builders must have sensed that here the edifice was not paramount. Mornings, when the sun climbs up over the spine of the Pyrenees, the milky white, east-facing windows behind the altar come ablaze with the fierce incandescence of million-watt bulbs. The loveliest corner of the complex is the small courtyard and fountain at the crypt of King Sancho el Fuerte, eighth king of Navarre, who died April 7, 1234.

I caught one more little trout before Dave showed up and we headed back to the campsite. Packaged soup, cheese, and canned meat on crusty white bread taste excellent when you are famished from half a day of outdoor exercise. After lunch, we washed our aluminum mess kits in the campground's soapstone sink as the last shreds of mountain mist blew away, leaving only the high, blue Pyrenean sky. We napped on our sleeping bags in the sun for another hour before heading upriver.

There is a fine paved road that roughly parallels the Irati, winding up from Arive through the gorge into the mountains. On a busy day, two cars may pass over the road in an hour, and—in theory at least—it provides good access to the river. The reality is another matter. In the gorge, the slopes are in places so steep and overgrown with beech, walnut, and mountain ash that getting down to the river is nearly impossible. Once you do get down, you may find it a special challenge to get back out when you are done fishing.

But swallowed up in the gorge, with the Irati surging against your boots and swallows dipping and weaving overhead, thoughts of future complications slip away downstream. There is only the moment, and it is now and forever. The fish are there; they have always been there. So have the mountains, and the forest. And you are part of them, just as they are part of you.

It was all there in Hemingway's masterpiece, an undercurrent that bulged beneath the surface story like the upwelling from a spring. There was Pamplona, with its crazy, drunken fiesta and the tangled web of relationships that changed from moment to moment. And there was the Irati, cool and clean and ever-flowing.

The quote from Ecclesiastes set the tone for the book: Lovers and friends may desert or betray you, tragedies may tear apart the fabric of your life, but "the earth abideth forever." And may the trout of the Irati still be finning in the current long after you and I and all those we love or despise are gone.

The late afternoon sun was angled overhead, etching the valley in sunlight and shadow. Big yellow mayflies began emerging on the river, along with a few tiny black caddises. On the smooth-flowing water, the rings of rising fish rippled the reflected sky. Casting to the dimples, I hooked and lost three trout and caught a couple more, keeping one chunky eleven-incher for dinner.

Later, back at the campsite, I poached it over the camp stove with a sliced onion and the hearty Navarre red wine. I ate the fish in the gathering darkness, with the cold mist rolling back in through the campground. The flesh was delicious and peach-colored, and the sauce tasted like trout-wine soup.

8

Altweibersommer on the Eder

October 1991

When the blackbird flew out of sight,
It marked the edge
Of one of many circles.

—Wallace Stevens, "Thirteen Ways
of Looking at a Blackbird"

Of the German seasons, *Altweibersommer* is the most affect-
ing. Spring is lovelier and more longed for. And summer, at its
best, is radiant and bountiful. Fall is a time of winding down.
Winter can be fierce or, more likely, merely deadening. But,

perhaps because of its brevity and unpredictability—it occurs only intermittently—*Altweibersommer* is a precious gift.

Of course, it is not a true season, in the meteorological sense. The literal translation is "Old Wives' Summer," and it is analogous to our Indian summer. But there are subtle differences. The best word to describe it is a German one: *eigenartig*, meaning both peculiar and special. *Altweibersommer* comes after the first frosts. In parks and boulevards, the leaves on the plane trees have begun to shrivel and drop. The beer gardens have closed, and the first gray-fog days of autumn have worked their melancholy way on the spirit.

Then one morning, as unexpected as a butterfly in winter, it is there: golden sunshine and heartbreak-blue sky, shirtsleeve warm. It may last only a few days. Or linger for weeks.

The year I fished the Eder, fall came early. For weeks the mornings were dominated by the pea-soup Rhine-Valley fogs. Sometimes the sun never broke through, and they lasted all day. Combined with speed and aggressive drivers, they caused huge rush-hour pileups on the Wiesbaden–Frankfurt autobahn, several times turning the superhighway into a vast junkyard and deadly parking lot. The naturally fatalistic Germans seemed even more so. Dismal weather and death-by-car dominated the nightly news.

One Wednesday I got a call from my buddy Berris, known to his friends by his nickname, "Bear," who lived about an hour and a half away. He was planning a weekend outing on the Eder with his fly-fishing club. It would be both a fishing trip and a German-American friendship fest.

"Some of our German friends have told us the grayling have really been schooling up," Bear said. "They've invited us to fish their club waters for the day." It was a great chance to get onto a stretch of stream that was closed to outsiders, he explained. It did not seem much like fishing weather, but I thought the trip might change the mood, and I was looking forward to fishing with Bear.

Leaving my wife and kids warm in their beds, I headed out in the early autumn chill on Saturday before sunup and drove north up the autobahn. A little over an hour later I pulled into a parking lot in Giessen. Bear was waiting beside his car, and we wasted no time loading his gear and getting back on the road. The coppery orb of the sun was edging up over the north Hessen hills as we turned onto the autobahn entry ramp.

"It looks like it's going to be a beautiful morning," Bear said.

"Yes it does," I chimed in. The day was already off to an auspicious start.

We drove northwest, toward the Westerwald, sometimes talking about families, friends, and fishing, sometimes just sharing the silence and the ride. After about an hour, we pulled into a guesthouse parking lot and met up with the others. We were four Germans and three Americans: Rudi, Peter, Heinrich, and Heinrich's wife, Hiltrud; Bear, David, and me.

We drove in a caravan to the home of the club president, where the Germans obtained day permits for their American guests. Under the rules of the club, each German member was allowed to purchase one guest permit on a given day. The maximum was three in a calendar year. This meant, of course, that each of us Americans was receiving a special gift.

When we were finished, the club president sent us off with a *"Petri-Heil!" "Petri-Dank!"* We responded in near unison.

Duly licensed and as properly documented (*legal und ordnungsgemaess*) as any good, orderly German, we got back into the cars and drove a couple of miles to the Eder. We turned down a gravel road and followed it for about a quarter-mile, then pulled into a turnout a hundred feet from the water.

It was still early in the day, not yet nine. While we geared up, Bear explained the tactics: small, sparse-hackle flies and light tippets. We would start by splitting into several groups, taking different stretches of the river. After that it was a matter of courtesy and common sense.

"Let's fish together." Bear said to me.

He and I had been friends for a little more than three years. Bear had begun the friendship with a letter after reading one of my fly-fishing features. Ours had been first an epistolary, then a telephonic relationship. When we finally met in person, it seemed like a long-deferred inevitability.

Bear, I had come to know, was one of those rare people who, by their nature, affect the world around them in only positive ways. Like the current in a deep-flowing river, his influence was placid but profound.

An army chaplain and ordained Baptist minister, he was one of those truly religious people who do not wear their devoutness on their sleeves or use it to reproach others. Bear's vision was far-seeing and affirmative. The central themes of his life were faith, family, and fly fishing. For him they were linked and led ineluctably to other things: service to humanity, building bridges to friendship, and reverence for nature. He was the only man I knew who actually spoke of fly fishing's "spiritual aspect." And when he said it, the phrase was natural and fitting. You felt he had earned the right to say it.

Growing up in Fayetteville, Arkansas, Bear had spent his early days "cane-pole fishing or taking a hand line and running a crawdad under a rock." But at thirteen he had made a discovery that led to an epiphany of sorts.

"I started reading magazines—*Outdoor Life, Field and Stream*—and they talked about another technique of fishing that we had never practiced. That was fly fishing. I found it so interesting that you could take feathers and all these things that you could find out in the farm fields, and you could make your own lures, your own bait, and you could fool the fish."

Bear sent away for a Montgomery Ward fiberglass fly rod and walked down to nearby Clear Creek. The perch and bass that smashed his tiny popping bugs made him an instant convert.

Since then he had fished from the Pacific Northwest to Pennsylvania, from Czechoslovakia to Norway, and many places in between. He had caught king salmon in Alaska, grayling in Bavaria; he had explored the Catskills with Joan Wulff and the Danube with Theo Matschewsky—one of Europe's most notable fly fishers; and he had imparted his love and knowledge of fly fishing to myriad disciples, from kindergartners to pensioners.

Part of the reason for Bear's wandering ways was the peripatetic army life. "It sure does give you some great opportunities to fish," he had told me last year. It also provided other opportunities. He had spent the previous winter living out of a tent near the Saudi Arabia–Kuwait border, far from the trout streams he loved. Operation Desert Storm had taken him to what Iraqi dictator Saddam Hussein had threatened would be "the mother of all wars."

But even war could not stop Bear's fly fishing. In the evenings, when the sun dropped low over the sweltering sands, he would remove his four-piece Sage 6-weight rod from its desert-camouflage case and spin loops in the air over the desert, aiming his cast to the imaginary rainbow beyond the next dune. He had brought back a photo of a fellow fly fisher casting from an M-60 tank, and another of himself casting hopefully into the Red Sea.

For Bear, camaraderie, ethics, and conservation were as important to the sport as catching fish. Having founded two German Federation of Fly Fishers clubs, encouraged the startup of others as far away as Czechoslovakia, and worked tirelessly for stream preservation and the catch-and-release ethic, he was well known in European fly-fishing circles.

We had talked much about fishing and other things. We had tied flies, and watched videos, and cast on the lawn at club meetings. But we had never fished together before. But today, because of Bear, I was standing a roll cast from one of Europe's storied streams.

The Eder is a modest but auspiciously lambent river. Springing out of the steep hills and evergreen forests of the *Rothaargebirge* (literally, Red-haired Mountains), it ambles down through the north Hessen countryside, which is best described in German—*eine liebliche Landschaft*. That is, not wild and untrammeled but lovely, pastoral: hilltop conifer thickets declining to hardwood glades; farm-and-orchard valleys; pocket-size, tile-roofed towns.

It is a Grimm brothers landscape (Jakob and Wilhelm's hometown, Kassel, is just downstream), fraught with the *ur*-German concept of nature: mystical, animistic, and inward-looking.

The Eder itself is not a spectacular stream of falls, rapids, and mountain torrents. But it is a well-watered, carefully nurtured resource, long renowned as an angler's treasure. Locals still recount tales of the post-World War II days, when Winston Churchill waded its riffles and pools.

As we walked to the stream a smoky haze was still on the hills, but with the climbing sun it was thinning fast. We had ventured less than a hundred yards from the car when Bear stopped. "Norm, I think I see a pretty good spot right here," he said.

It was a medium-size pool, with a couple of large rocks visible at the tail and, upstream, a wider section that extended about fifty feet in one smooth stretch to a shallow riffle at the head. The current surged around the rocks, but it looked as if there was a protected pocket between them and, likely, other rocks below the surface. On our side were the road and open meadow, but trees and brush overhung the far bank, shading most of the pocket.

Bear reached into his fly box and handed me a tiny bluish gray creation with barely enough hackle to keep it afloat. I tied it on and he attached its twin to his own tippet. We walked near the edge of the bank while he gave me tips. I should wade in below the rocks and cast upstream to the pocket. "There should be some grayling right in there," he said.

"Where are you going to fish?"

"I'm your guide," he said. "I've had good fishing here before. I'd like to watch you catch some."

I followed his instructions and on the fourth or fifth cast, the fly disappeared in a splash. I was fast to a thrashing grayling. It headed up into the pool, then shot down, and I was so excited I horsed it in to the bank, a fat fourteen-incher. Bear took a picture and sent me back out.

I hooked another fish, a little smaller, not bothering to wade to shore but bringing it to hand. Before releasing it in midstream, I held it up to show Bear, and he nodded and smiled.

I kept casting to the same spot, every few casts raising or hooking a fish. There were a few small mayflies on the water but no real hatch. The river was low and clear from lack of rain, and sometimes I could see the flash of the fish just before they struck. In twenty minutes I had landed four grayling, lost just as many, and missed a half-dozen strikes. The whole time, Bear sat on the bank smiling and watching. Finally I waded to shore.

"When the grayling are schooling like this, sometimes they'll just keep feeding," he said. "You hardly have to move at all."

He wanted me to keep fishing, but I refused to hog it all. "I want to see you catch some," I said. "Maybe I'll learn something."

Bear waded out to virtually the same spot. His casting was fluid and effortless, the stripping and mending flawless. His back cast never dropped, and his forward cast landed as softly as a rose petal. During the drift, the line never bulged, the fly never dragged. In less than a minute he caught a fish, then quickly took two more before the bite finally stopped.

"Isn't it glorious?" he said as he climbed out of the river. "A beautiful day, great friends, and fine fishing."

The haze had burned away to a perfect *Altweibersommer* day. Sunshine filled the valley, highlighting the few bright splashes of color—amber gold beeches, crimson maples—on the green hill-sides. After weeks of pensive, hopeless gray the sky was a yearning and brilliant blue.

For the next couple of hours we worked our way upstream, fishing close enough to observe but not disturb each other. Bear continued to defer to me: the best spots, the easiest approaches, quick advice on the right fly to switch to when the action slacked off.

A little before one, we walked back to the cars to meet up with the others for lunch. The weather and the fishing had put everybody in a festive mood. No one could know how long *Altweibersommer* would last, but we all knew to make the most of it.

Bear, David, and I had brought sandwiches and sodas, but the Germans were laying on a spread like a Cezanne or Manet painting. Hiltrud shook out two big blankets, spread them on the grass, and set a wicker picnic basket in the middle. She lifted its lid and brought out slivered cucumbers, three kinds of cheese, pâté, black bread, and a veritable charcuterie of sausage meats. She arranged the comestibles and containers on the blankets, then sat down cross-legged.

Leaning against the car with my bologna and mayonnaise on white bread, I felt like a beggar at a banquet.

Heinrich retrieved three cloth sacks from his trunk and carried them over, clinking, to set beside the basket. Then he sat down and pulled out a half-dozen dark-brown bottles of beer, two bottles of *Blauer Burgunder* wine, and a liter bottle of mineral water. With a shiny silver opener—the kind with two levers and half gears—he deftly extracted the cork from one of the wine bottles. He reached into another sack and came out with a handful of glasses—the little, three-ounce ones used at wine tastings, each embossed with the name and logo of the vineyard. Laughing, he passed them around and filled them generously.

"Come on," Heinrich said, motioning with his wineglass to the three Americans hanging around like the bride's ex-boyfriends at a wedding.

Thinking it a polite formality, I said thanks, but noted that we had brought our own lunches.

"Come on, he repeated. You don't want to offend us, do you?"

"He's right," Bear said, smiling, "They invited us."

It finally dawned on me: Yes, of course; they had invited us. For the Germans fishing was not just an outdoor pastime; it was also a social occasion, and I should have known they would be gracious hosts. I had lived eleven years in Germany, I spoke the language fluently, my wife and I had many friends. I knew that when friends "invited" you to dine out with them (*"wir moechten euch einladen"*), it meant they were treating and took it for granted that you would accept. To decline or insist on going Dutch was a *Beleidigung*, a faux pas. But my fishing experience with Germans was minimal. I was unsure where social etiquette and angling etiquette merged and diverged.

Bear, David, and I tossed our lunch bags into the cars and squeezed onto the blankets among the others and the food and drink. I drank one glass of wine, but I knew if I had any more at midday I would end up with a headache. Still, the beer bottles were sweating in the sun so I felt obliged to empty one. It was cool but not cold, and it tasted especially good with the black bread and sausage meat.

When the meal was winding down, Hiltrud reached into the basket and passed out squares of dark chocolate, then apple slices. I lay on my back, hands behind my head, and the big meal, the warm sun made me feel like taking a nap. But when the others stretched, groaned, and started cleaning up I joined in. After another ten minutes we headed back to the Eder.

This time Bear and I walked farther upriver. I thought about how all morning he had given me the best chances. Then I thought about what he did as a career: counseling for broken marriages; chastisement for abusers and support for victims; guidance for troubled teens; comfort and compassion for widows and orphans, for the lonely and the sick at heart far from home, for the terminally ill, the infirm of body and soul. He was psychiatrist, social worker, and spiritual healer. Not for a great deal of money. Not for power. Not for fame. For what, then?

We all like to think of ourselves as good people. But there is good and there is better. For most of us, compassion is feeling sorry for those less fortunate, wishing it were otherwise. But for Bear it meant always giving of himself. He was happily married, devoted to his wife and two boys. But he had also dedicated his life to God and to his other, *our* other family: the human family.

To me, he was like a river whose flow is continuously diverted to water parched fields far from its banks. Eventually, it seemed, the demand must empty the stream. But there was no sign of it in Bear. Grace and love flowed from wellsprings deep within, feeding currents of compassion and caring that never ran dry. For Bear, loving God and his fellow man was not a goal for life. It was life.

I envied him his faith. As a boy I, too, had been a devout Baptist. But in hindsight it was a devoutness of another sort, induced and overshadowed by fear. The way our minister presented it, being "saved" seemed like a kind of insurance policy against eternal damnation. But it did not make the fear go away, only shifted its focus. Many nights I lay awake, haunted by the child's fear that parents, siblings, friends might face the hellfire I had escaped.

There had been no epiphany, no tragic or shockingly absurd twist of fate that changed my mind. Just a gradual eroding of convictions.

I consulted my minister about the universal conundrums that trouble thoughtful, introspective teenagers. If God created the universe, what was there before? How could God be both one being and three. If He was all-powerful and all-knowing why did he allow terrible things to happen? How could there be any free will if, even before creating Adam and Eve, He had known everything that would happen forever after? The pastor's answers were always platitudes or quotes from Scripture, flawlessly recited but vague and unsatisfactory to an inquiring young mind.

One night when I was fourteen, the Catholic church in our town burned down. My best friend was Catholic, and he and I rode our bikes there as soon as we heard about it the next morning. A crowd had gathered to watch the fire department hose down the smoldering ruins, and a lot of the people looked as ashen as the gutted building. But there, on the edge of the police cordon, was my Baptist pastor, smiling and taking pictures. When he saw me, he called me over and made a sly remark about how he bet that with the insurance money they would rebuild it better than before. Sometimes these things have a way of happening, he said, when the building gets old and needs a lot of repairs. He gave me a wink as I walked away.

Another time, while giving us a ride home from Wednesday-night Bible study, this pastor explained why he always waited until the kids were in their houses before driving away. His old neighborhood in New York had been beset by major crime problems. One night, a girl who had been dropped off was dragged from her doorway and raped "by a big black man."

"They" caused a lot of problems, he explained. He had friends in the NYPD who said you couldn't knock "them" out with a nightstick. "Their skulls are a lot thicker than ours, you know," said our pastor. "That's why they're such good boxers."

Kids' minds will turn all kinds of contortions to prevent them from judging the adults in their lives. This was also the time of the freedom marches down South, when the pictures on our TV belied the history lessons I had learned about "one nation under God" and "all men are created equal."

I thought about these things long and hard, and it made me sad and depressed. Jesus had preached love and understanding. How could the purposes of a merciful and loving God be served by a racist bigot? Gradually I drifted away from the church, and by the time the pastor died a few years later I was a believer in the rightness of sex, love, poetry, and folk music, and the random indifference of the universe.

*   *   *

The afternoon was warm and placid, and sunshine filled the valley. It was one of those golden days you remember in the depths of winter.

Bear and I got back on the river in a long, shallow stretch. We started about a hundred feet from each other but gradually fished our way apart. Bear was working upstream, while I began fishing crosscurrent and downstream. The grayling were still biting, though not as ravenously as in the morning. I could see that Bear was catching more fish than I was—four for three, or maybe five for four. He had told me that most of the fish in the Eder would be grayling, but I was beginning to wonder if the river's storied trout had gone south with the birds—until I put on a Humpy and caught a seven-inch brown.

Already the sun was arcing down toward the hills, putting the far shore and a third of the river in shadow. Many people do not realize that Germany lies on the same latitude as Newfoundland. Now, in late October, with the diurnal ceding ever more to the nocturnal, the long, dark winter nights were coming fast. The endless silver-sky evenings of midsummer were a distant dream.

Soon the whole river was in shadow. The air was cooling fast, and I was glad I had not taken off my shirt in the midday warmth. I had changed to a Coachman, still fishing a downstream drift through a riffle, when I felt a sudden jolt. The fish jumped, raced crosscurrent, and jumped again. I realized it was a rainbow. Just for the sheer joy of it, I took my time landing the fish. When it slipped into my hand I grasped it gently, lifting the trout free of the water so I could remove the fly without stooping. Just over sixteen inches, the rainbow was brilliant pink and silver even in the fading light.

"Well, it looks like you're a better fisherman than the rest of us."

I turned to see Bear and Peter standing in the gravel road, grinning, some fifty feet away.

"Hold it up and let us see it," Bear said. I did, briefly, then pushed out the point of the hook and bent down to put the fish back into the water. It scooted away over the shallow riffle, leaving a tiny wake.

We fished for another twenty minutes—I caught one more grayling—before strolling back to the cars in the gathering dusk. I had landed fifteen fish, all but two of them grayling. The others had also landed many grayling. But my rainbow was the fish of the day.

When we had pulled off boots and waders, broken down rods, and put them back in their cases, we drove to a guesthouse a couple of miles downriver. It was nearly dark when we arrived. We all had a hearty meal and exchanged fish tales. The others were staying over, but Bear and I had to get home. Because I was driving, I had to toast our success with mineral water while the others quaffed beers. The goblets of golden, foam-capped *Pils* looked awfully tasty, but I stuck by my vow never to drink and drive. It made no difference to Bear—he drank no alcohol—but he also did not judge.

We got up to go after about a half-hour.

"*Petri-Heil!*" the others said.

"*Petri-Dank!*" we replied.

On the ride back, Bear and I were pretty quiet. We were both tired and did not feel the need to talk much. The day on the water together had been enough.

After I dropped him off, riding down the autobahn in the dark car I replayed the day in my mind. *Altweibersommer* would surely end soon. Just as surely, the flannel gray German winter would follow on its heels. The sun-spangled stream full of grayling would be a mere memory. Then I corrected myself. Not mere. There was nothing mere about memories. Together with anticipation, they made up much of life.

I thought some more about Bear. The better I got to know him, the more affected I was by his personality. I wished I could be like him but knew I never would. I had too many foibles and failings, too much doubt and ingrained agnosticism. But I hoped that one day I could be more like him. Less selfish, less prideful, more devoted to people and causes beyond myself. With more reverence for life's great mysteries and little joys.

To Bear, those things came naturally, an outgrowth of his personality and a merciful and loving faith. But I would have to work at them. I promised myself I would.

9

Frost on the Fulda

December 1991

*Die Liebe steht dem Tode entgegen, nur sie, nicht die
Vernunft, is staerker als er.**

—Thomas Mann, *Der Zauberberg* (*The Magic Mountain*)

We all know that some of our most vivid and enduring angling
memories have barely tenuous connections to catching fish. And
one place can have many associations. For me this is especially
true of the Fulda River, named for the central German city
through which it flows.

---

* *Love stands opposed to death, only love, not reason, is stronger than death.*

I first went to Fulda aboard a U.S. Army Blackhawk helicopter, accompanying four other journalists on a tour of the murderous no-man's land that was then the East German border. After landing at an army airfield outside the city, we rode in a van to the headquarters of the Eleventh Armored Cavalry Regiment for a reception and briefing. Our host was a young captain who had attended West Point but could have come from central casting. He was handsome, athletic, and earnest in outlining his unit's role in the event of a massive Soviet invasion from the east.

In central Germany, the attempted breakthrough point would likely be the Fulda Gap, a wide pass through the Rhoen Mountains, twelve miles east of the city. It was common knowledge, the captain said, that the Warsaw Pact had an overwhelming numerical advantage in tanks, artillery, and troops. But if an attack came, the Americans would smash it with professionalism, esprit de corps, and superior equipment and planning. The young officer's confidence and command of strategic details made a convincing impression, even on five hard-bitten news hacks.

After the briefing we reboarded the van for a ride across the city and then through spring green fields. Finally the driver pulled into a dirt road at the edge of a forest, where a half-track was waiting to take us the final mile through thickets of fir and spruce.

The border outpost, manned by a handful of troops, was a couple of hundred yards from the steel-mesh fence—supported by concrete posts and ribboned along the top with concertina wire. It snaked over hills and down gullies as far as the eye could see, roughly north and south. Highlighted by the barren strip along the eastern side, it made an ugly gash through the verdant landscape

We climbed the observation tower and looked across to East Germany, where the guards in their tower were looking at us. Then we turned the binoculars, and the duty sergeant pointed out the swale where, a few years before, a young man had tried to escape to the West. He had been shot by the East Germans and was left to bleed to death while tangled in the fence.

"Every now and then he would try to move," the sergeant said. "They could hear him moan."

The American squad had wanted to rescue the young man but were ordered not to. It might create an incident, they were told. All they could do was watch him die, and it took most of the day, some six hours.

When we squeezed back into the clanking half-track, it felt as if we were leaving the GIs out on the edge of the world. And while flying back I had many thoughts about Fulda; none of them had to do with fishing.

The next year, sharing a weekend getaway with a German girlfriend, I saw Fulda from a different angle. We took an afternoon for a mini-tour: castle, cathedral, city hall, marketplace, and the *Phasanerie*, a onetime hunting lodge with formal gardens from the days of the Landgrave. Like most small German cities, Fulda was attractive, pedestrian friendly, and meticulously preserved. The only disquieting aspect was the too-tranquil backwater ambience—and implied threat—shared by other border towns (Wolfsburg, Bayreuth, Goettingen) that had been arbitrarily cut off from half of the compass rose.

Fulda was worth the trip, but we got almost as big a kick out of a village ten miles south: Lieblos an der Strasse (Loveless on the Street). I pulled over when I saw the sign, and we took pictures of each other standing next to it, laughing. I remember thinking (though I kept it to myself) that the town's name was a pretty good description of our relationship, which had begun with a bang of passion but was winding down to a whimper of indifference. We still had fun together and would finish as friends, but the days of lovers' infatuation were ending.

Nearly ten years later I was researching fishing spots close to home when my friend Bear told me about a stream an hour northeast of Frankfurt: the Fulda. The trout were few and far between, he said, but it was full of grayling.

By the time I got around to planning a day on the river, trout season had been over for more than two months. But grayling were fair game until the end of the year. My buddy Dave B. stopped by the house around seven on a cold, dark December Sunday morning, and I was glad to let him drive.

As we headed north on the autobahn there was no glorious sunrise, just a pale strip that began to show along the eastern horizon and spread across the sky, turning it from charcoal to lead. I think both of us were wishing we had stayed in bed, and we did not talk much for the first hour. But as we got closer to the river we shook off our drowsiness and began to get keyed up about fishing.

Just outside Fulda we met up with Robert, George, and Karl, the two Americans and one German who would show us the lay of the river. They also had our permits, which cost five dollars each. We followed their car through nearly deserted city streets and out onto state Route 27.

Sundays are always quiet in Germany, but because of the weather and the season it was even quieter than usual. This was *Zweiter Advent,* the second of the four Sundays leading up to Christmas. Throughout the country Advent is a hushed, holy season, a time of joy and devoutness; of office parties and Christmas markets filled with toys and trinkets, *Gluehwein,* and candied almonds; of pensive reflection on the year past; and cherished family ties.

A couple of miles south of the city we turned onto a tiny, paved strip that switchbacked through fallow brown fields to the village of Welkers. When we pulled into the church parking lot we had not passed another car since leaving Route 27. And no one was out walking.

Another friend, Jim, pulled in behind us. We put on our gear standing by the cars in the bitter chill, and I wondered again why

I had left my warm bed. The drive had brought us only seventy-five miles north and a couple of hundred feet higher in altitude, but that was enough to make us feel as if we had left in the fall and arrived in the winter. Everything was frosted—trees, grass, bare ground—and ice fog hung in the valley. The air was so still, not a breath of wind stirring or a sound coming from anywhere, that we spoke in whispers without thinking about it.

"Hey," George said, aloud, "its after nine. We ain't gotta worry about wakin' up the town." We all laughed and after that tried to talk in normal tones, but we still found ourselves lowering our voices.

When everybody was outfitted we talked tactics, deciding to split into two groups. Karl, George, and Robert would fish downstream from the village. Dave, Jim, and I would fish upstream. Given the weather, nymphs were the only logical fly choice. "Beadheads," George said. "Always kill 'em here with Beadheads."

We exchanged the German angler's good luck salutation (muted), "*Petri-Heil!*," "*Petri-Dank!*," and headed for the stream. I looked back to watch the other three as they clomped out of the parking lot and across the road. Bundled up in heavy clothes and waddling in waders, they looked like three fat men out for a stroll. I imagine we looked just as dashing.

As we walked to the river, the white-frozen grass crunched beneath our feet, unnaturally loud amid the dead silence of the village Sabbath. Jim stopped at the first pool, but Dave and I headed farther upriver, staying back from the bank so as not to spook the fish.

About fifty yards above Jim, right at the water's edge, we came upon a large frozen spider web, perfectly glazed with ice from the fog. Stretched between alder bushes, it was nearly two feet across. This was not a simple net but one of those intricate geometric patterns once offered as proof that there is a God. Even in the December gloom, the strands gleamed like crystal lacework. There was no reason for the web to be there a couple of weeks before Christmas, and the spider was nowhere to be seen.

"Hey, that's pretty neat," Dave said. He went ahead another thirty feet and started to cast, but I just kept staring at the spider web from different angles. I could have kicked myself for not bringing a camera. Finally I walked past Dave and stepped into the river. I was bundled up as warmly as anyone, but quickly I could feel the cold through my boots. The water was the color of very weak tea.

At Welkers, the Fulda meanders through meadows and pastures, down through the village, and past the old mill, finally flowing under the autobahn and on toward its namesake city. It is a small stream, nowhere more than twenty feet across and fishable in hip boots, though there are a few pools over wader depth. On most stretches the current is slow and smooth-flowing, the bottom mainly sand. But here and there the water speeds up, riffling over gravel bars and rounded stones.

Though bordered by open land, the banks are intermittently thick with alders and willows, making a classic ten o'clock–two o'-clock cast often difficult or impossible. With Beadheads, a roll cast or a little backhand flip was our best option. Not pretty, but practical.

No wind came up as we fished, and the ice fog hung above the river and meadows. It did not take long for the damp cold to seep beneath the layers of clothing. And when I reached down into the water to free the fly from a snag, the shock went all the way to my shoulder. The year was winding down to the winter solstice. In the cycle of seasons, this was the time of dying. My family and I knew it too well. In two weeks would come the terrible anniversary of Ceci's death.

Life, of course, is a search for meaning amid chaos, a struggle to accept our own mortality. We try to make sense of the capriciousness of existence and its inevitable end. But all young people's deaths are senseless.

A few months before Libby's sister was killed, she had taken her first real job: teaching fifth graders in a small-town New Hampshire school. The kids loved her and she loved them back. Full of élan vital and the thrill of a limitless future known only to the young, she had barely reached the end of the beginning: twenty-three.

There had been an ice storm in the night, but Ceci was a good and careful driver. That morning, she left early to give herself an extra margin. Ten minutes later came the call that school was canceled because of dangerous road conditions. But it was an eternity too late for Ceci. On a hill slick with black ice, her Plymouth had skidded across the centerline and slammed head-on into an oncoming BMW. And Christmas, once pure joy, would never be the same for our family again.

The year was a cycle. After the decline of fall, the death of winter, came the rebirth of spring, the flowering of summer. And life was supposed to be a cycle. But not for Ceci. And not for the East German kid who died tangled in concertina wire a few miles away. For them it was cut short, barely a quarter-turn. For me the cycle continued. I had a profession that gave satisfaction as well as salary; a loving wife I had seen through serious illness; and, due to great medicine and good fortune, two beautiful kids. Now the beginning of the middle was past.

Downstream, Dave looked as if he had a fish on. I had felt a couple of taps, but they might have been rocks. I made another cast and watched it drop short. When I checked the rod I saw that the guides had grown ringlets of ice; the tip-top was barely big enough for the line to pass through. One at a time I squeezed them between my fingers to melt the ice, then went back to fishing.

The parking lot was nearly full now, people were filing into the church, and the bells began to peal. This was how to drive out the death grip. The early German tribes had their pagan winter festivals to banish the evil spirits and placate the gods. The transition to the Christ Mass had been smooth, offering hope and redemption in this killingest of killing seasons. And the *Tannen-baum*, symbol of life eternal and ever green, had become part of it.

Dave walked up and stopped beside me, puffing into cupped hands. "Man, it's cold. My fingers aren't working right."

"Mine either. Any fish?" I asked.

"Nope. Nothin'."

"I thought I saw you with one on."

"That was a dead branch. You get any?"

"Nothing. Any sign of the other guys?"

"Nope. They're probably way down near the autobahn by now."

We fished upstream for another hour and a half, leapfrogging each other by thirty yards at a time. The river narrowed down and shallowed out; the banks got thicker with brush and trees. I waded one long stretch that was only three or four yards wide and mostly calf-deep. Just before we walked back to the car for lunch, I hooked a fish under the bushes along the right bank. It got off.

Now the churchgoers were gone, and again our cars were the only ones in the lot. Jim was sitting in his, eating a sandwich. He was thinking of heading home.

"Not yet, man," Dave said. "You just drove all the way up here."

"Yeah," I agreed, "We'll head downstream after lunch."

Twenty minutes later, when we walked to the village and crossed the road, we found that the river had a different structure. Where it passed the old mill, it had been channeled into a deep, straight-sided sluice, but after that it widened out. There were more gaps in the bank-side brush than was the case upstream, and we spread out to look for the openings. The hanging fog had finally lifted, but there was still no hint of sun.

I stopped at a wide curve where a huge maple leaned across the river from the opposite bank, while Dave and Jim continued on downstream. The tree side of the river was a shallow, rocky riffle, but on my side—the outside of the curve—the current had carved out a yard-deep channel. There were even a few deeper pockets, tangled with roots and driftwood, where it washed in under the bank.

I flipped out my Beadhead and let it bounce down the channel, following it with the rod tip. Then I did it again. And again.

On the fourth or fifth cast, the line stopped. I set the hook and felt a hard strike. The rod started bouncing and the fish took off for the undercut bank. It almost got in among the roots, but I horsed it out. It then shot across the riffle and downstream, dorsal fin flaring. After a minute or so I brought it to hand, a thick-shouldered grayling of about fifteen inches.

After I extracted the hook, the fish rested in my hand, gills working, for several seconds. I did not toss it out but held it gently, just below the surface, while the pain from the icy water shot up my arm. The fish was a flash of numinous beauty amid the dead landscape. Even the browns and grays of this sunless day could not extinguish its silver-and-shimmering-rainbow brilliance. Finally it squirted away into the current, leaving only the scent of thyme.

I bounced the nymph down the channel again and got another hard strike, but this time I had the fish on for only a few seconds. My guides were iced up once more, and I took a break to clear them. I knew grayling sometimes hung in pods, so I stepped back from the water to find Dave, then gave him a shout and a wave.

"You have some good luck?" he asked after he had walked up.

"Yeah, I got a nice one. Why don't you try a drift down through this channel."

I moved down to the pool twenty yards below, and in a minute or so Dave gave a shout.

"Got one!"

I walked back and watched him land a fish that looked like a twin to mine.

"I had two hits first but I missed 'em," he said.

"Yeah, I bet there's a school in here."

Dave caught another, smaller, grayling, then called me back up and I landed a ten-incher. After that, the action stopped and we moved farther downriver. A half-hour later we met up with George, Karl, and Robert on their way back. George lifted a grayling that looked to be about fourteen inches.

"This one's dinner," he said, chuckling. "How'd you guys do?"

"We got a couple."

"We got half a dozen apiece."

"How far down?"

Robert chimed in. "About halfway down to the autobahn. Where the brush grows in real thick." They headed for the cars while Dave and I continued downstream, crunching across the still-frozen meadow.

"You think they're bullshitting us?" Dave asked.

"I don't know, do you?"

"Hard to say. George can be kind of a blowhard. But the other guys are pretty straight."

Fishing downriver we caught nothing, and after another half-hour we were chilled to the bone. As we walked back, the early darkness was coming, and in the village the lighted windows of the houses glowed yellow against the deepening gray. In two weeks the winter solstice would be here, Christmas close on its heels. Then the corner would be turned, the days would begin to get longer, minutely at first and then making bigger gains into the greening spring. Until the year turned another corner in June, inevitably to circle back to the season of dying.

* * *

Dave and I returned to the Fulda on a warm, blue-sky afternoon the following September. The green meadows were just beginning to take on a hint of gold, and yellow green leaves fluttered down from the willows, landing softly on the water and spinning down in the current.

We had the river to ourselves, there were many hatches, and

we caught grayling continuously on dry flies; it did not seem to matter which ones. We finally quit with darkness coming and the evening chill turning our breath to white puffs. I kept the last fish of the day—a fat thirteen-incher—and when I cleaned it later at home the grayling's stomach was full of a virtual entomologist's collection: mayflies, mosquitoes, moths, earwigs, and even a few beetles.

10

The Jihlava and the Svratka

Intimations of Mortality, June 1992

He saw his face reflected in the quietly moving water, and there
was something in this reflection that reminded him of something
he had forgotten and when he reflected on it, he remembered.

—Hermann Hesse, *Siddhartha*

Milos Zelinka followed the drift of the fly, waiting, waiting as
it floated down to where the fish had risen. Two, three, four feet
and it was there. Then came the splash; he lifted the rod tip and
was fast to the trout.

He battled the fish for one or two minutes, losing and regaining line, then worked it closer, finally lifting the rod tip high and

reaching down to grip the trout behind the gills. He removed the fly from its jaw, then quickly dispatched it with a sharp blow to the skull and slipped it, still quivering, into the creel with the two others. It was a fine June afternoon on the Jihlava.

Along with my buddy Dave C., I had come to Czechoslovakia's Moravia region to chase its trout and meet the man who loved and nurtured them. This was my first time in Moravia, an area of rolling hills, farms, and forests dotted with sleepy towns and villages.

Many of them seemed interchangeable: A church and a small green. Stucco-and-brick houses, many shabby and run-down, surrounded by lush, overgrown lawns and gardens. Rosebushes and shrubs spilled over into neighbors' yards, and everywhere were fruit trees—not carefully coddled showpieces but big, old gnarly ones growing wild and free.

Life was simpler out here, two to three hours' drive beyond the crowds of Prague. Because cars were still scarce—a new Skoda cost two to three years' salary—the roads were peaceful and nearly empty. People walked, rode bikes, or took trains and buses. High-stepping farm horses clip-clopped down the main streets, pulling wooden wagons.

There was much poverty, the legacy of four decades of communist economic disasters. But it was a poverty with dignity. There was none of the Third World squalor and hopelessness.

Here and there we had encountered incongruous monuments to socialist central planning, principally sprawling factories with towering smokestacks. Shoehorned rudely into pastoral valleys, they were as out of place as a pro wrestler at a garden party. Since the fall of the Berlin Wall two and a half years before, most of them had become industrial fossils, their outdated technology and products hopelessly incapable of competing in a free market.

For more than five decades, the lives of Moravia's residents were circumscribed by the hard realities of politics and economics. For Zelinka, a hydrobiologist at the University of Brno, it meant that some things were simply not possible. But this day he focused on casting to trout in the clear Jihlava. The past was far downstream.

Dave and I had arrived in Moravia three days before after an all-day drive from Darmstadt. The first stop was Nedvedice, a town of eighteen hundred, northwest of Brno on the Svratka River. It was after eight-thirty P.M. when we checked into the Hotel Atelier, across the street from the village church.

After carrying our gear to our rooms, we headed for the hotel restaurant, where owner Bokuslav Krcil and his wife, Helena, served us a dinner of garden salad, rice, and chicken breasts stuffed with apple. It all tasted homegrown, and the chicken had a sweet, nutty, faintly herbal flavor. I thought it probably had spent its life free-ranging a side yard for insects and grasses instead of gorging on corn in a screen-floored warehouse. With a bottle of German beer added in, my meal came to just under seventy kroner, about two dollars and fifty cents.

After we paid the check, Krcil—a shy, amiable man in his mid fifties—brought a bottle of Russian vodka to our table, and we toasted each other with shots. Dave wanted to stay for another beer or two but the eleven and a half hours of driving had finished me. I went upstairs and fell asleep in about ten minutes.

The next morning, at breakfast, we met Milos Zelinka Jr., a thin, angular man of around forty. Sporting unkempt hair and a bushy mustache, he seemed to be perpetually smoking or lighting or stubbing out a cigarette. Though the younger Milos spoke little English, his German was passable. During the meal we began to get acquainted, and we talked about the fishing. I tried to keep my eyebrows from going up when he ordered a beer while Dave and I sipped coffee and ate our eggs, bread, and jam.

Milos Jr. was a water chemist for the city of Brno and, though unmarried, had two sons, fifteen and ten. Following in his father's bootsteps, he was a lifelong fly fisher as well as a competitive caster. The high point of his casting was 1977, when he was

European champion. "I have silver and bronze medals, too," he said. "Two or three." Today we would fish the Svratka, his favorite river because of its grayling. "Not really big, but many," he said. He would show me how to catch them.

After breakfast we loaded the gear into our car and drove about four miles down the valley, where we pulled into a dirt road and parked near the river, behind a stand of willows. I got out, stretched, and strolled to the streamside.

Here the Svratka was a lively freestone stream, thirty to sixty feet wide. Most of it looked wadeable—shallow riffles and gravel bars—but here and there were deeper pools and pockets. The banks, overgrown with grass, nettles, and Queen Anne's lace, sloped up at the farther margins to lush hillsides thick with gooseberry, ash, birch, spruce, pine, maple, chestnut, and oak.

When I returned to the car, we donned our gear and pieced together our rods, then walked down and waded into the river. Milos had on a gold bead-head nymph, but I tied on an Adams. I almost always started with dry flies. It was an aesthetic preference, but sometimes when—even fishless—I stuck with them stubbornly and against all logic, it bordered on obsessive-compulsive behavior.

There was no hatch on yet, but conditions looked auspicious. It was a late-spring morning replete with the promise of summer. The sun, already high and warm, incandescent yellow white in the hazy blue sky, sparkled on the moving water and hung suspended over the green hills. It was T-shirt weather.

Milos Jr. started fishing downstream and I headed up. Within a minute he had a fish on. I kept casting but turned to watch as he released it, a small grayling. A couple of minutes later he hooked another. And it continued. While I fished dry flies upstream in the best British gentleman's tradition, Milos caught the fish.

Wielding his 5-weight like a treasure hunter's metal detector, he probed riffles, pockets, and pools with a short line and a sensitive hand. Though bright and gleaming, the treasures he descried were not lifeless stones and alloys, but quick and enigmatic creatures.

Like the river, the morning flowed on peaceful and unhurried. I finally got a hit on a Royal Wulff, then caught a ten-inch grayling. When I relented and put on a Beadhead, I had three or four bumps, missing the fish each time, before I hooked and landed another grayling. But I quickly became bored with "sinker fishing." A few small mayflies began to show on the water, and I switched back to dries. I finally landed a nine-inch rainbow before we stopped for lunch.

As we ate our sandwiches, I asked Milos Jr. how many fish he had caught. He thought a minute: "Probably twenty or twenty-five," he said. Most were grayling, beauteous and capricious creatures he never tired of. Trout were okay, but grayling had always been his favorite fish. "Anyway," he said, "Trout are easier to catch." I smiled to myself, thinking that the pronouncement would come as a surprise to most trout devotees. I had pursued these "easy" fish over the better part of two continents and had yet to prove his axiom.

Milos Jr. loved nymphing, calling it the "most efficient" method. He had certainly proved that to me. But, though I was not any kind of purist, I had my doubts as to whether efficiency was the paramount consideration in angling. He smoked a cigarette between bites of sandwich, and after lunch he smoked another. Then we packed up the car and headed back upriver.

While Dave drove, Milos Jr. gave us a talking tour of the valley, and I translated from the German. In most places the road followed close along the river, and I kept one eye out for fishing spots. There were a few towns and villages along the route but no outstanding landmarks. That is, until we reached the twelve-mile-long reservoir and two-hundred-foot-high, bottom-release dam that in 1957 transformed the Svratka from a lukewarm chub water holding a handful of salmonids to a first-rate trout and grayling fishery. We drove up a slanting access road, parked at the top of the dam, and gazed out across the water and the hills of the Bohemian–Moravian heights.

I knew we were close to the Czech–Slovak border and asked Milos Jr. what he thought of the disagreement that was then threatening to split the two republics. It did not bother him, he said. In fact, it was probably good because, while the Czechs were quickly becoming more Western, the Slovaks were clinging to the old ways.

"In Slovakia there are only communists. It is bad, very bad," he said.

We drove back down the valley, stopping several times to survey the river. "Good here," Milos Jr. said at one place, "but maybe not today." Here and there I noticed trees with numbers on them along the roadside. I asked Milos Jr. about them and he explained that they were fruit trees. Because they were on public land, people could pay a nominal fee for the right to harvest the fruit from a particular tree. Most of them were plum trees, Milos Jr. said, and the fruit was usually not eaten fresh but made into *slivovitz*, the region's fiery plum brandy.

Five miles north of Nedvedice, he directed Dave to slow down and turn right. We crossed a narrow bridge over the Svratka, then followed a dirt road that curved around to the left, toward a cluster of houses and outbuildings. We pulled over and parked on the grass, about thirty feet from the stream.

"This village is called Korouzne," Milos Jr. said, nodding toward the houses that edged up close to the riverbank. It was a scene of pastoral tranquility: calf-high grass and vegetable gardens and flowering shrubs and fruit trees and, surrounding it all, a lush green forest. The only sounds came from the flowing river and a few scattered chickens clucking and scratching in the yards.

We geared up and Milos Jr. talked tactics. He would use nymphs, of course. He opened his fly box and pointed out three or four that he favored for the area. Then we split up. Gritting my teeth, I tied on a March Brown and started fishing. The air was absolutely still, and to the west a line of thunderheads was building.

First I worked some riffled water upstream from the village. When I raised no fish I switched to a Hare's Ear and moved farther up. I had a bump or two but did not hook up. I tried a Beadhead. Still nothing. I walked back down and met Milos Jr., puffing on his ever-present cigarette. The sun was getting low, beginning to slip behind the thunderheads, which now obscured a third of the sky. I asked what he had caught and he held up one finger, shaking his head.

"Bad, very bad. The weather is bad," he said, indicating the approaching storm.

Milos Jr. asked if I wanted to leave. I shook my head and we headed off in opposite directions again. I was tired of dredging the river with nymphs and, anyway, they were producing nothing. I might as well not catch anything on dry flies.

I tied on a Parachute Blue Dun and began working a long pool right in front of the houses. In a couple of minutes I turned to see a small boy watching me. He wore a faded flannel shirt rolled up to the elbows, blue jeans, and dirty sneakers. He looked about six or seven. He did not say anything but just stood watching with his hands in his pockets—not smiling or frowning, but with a neutral expression on his face.

A minute later I saw a splash, my fly disappeared, and I set the hook. When I lifted the fish, a six-inch brown, from the water I turned to show the boy. He grinned and nodded, watched me release the trout, then turned and hurried away.

The whole sky had turned black. An old woman in a print dress came along the bank herding a gaggle of goslings. They were about the size of full-grown mallards but still mostly covered in gray down. The young geese could not yet honk, only peep. The woman carried a long stick, and if they started to stray she thrust it out and forced them back to the path. With their squeaky vocalizations, Prussian officers' walk, and Charles de Gaulle hauteur—breasts outthrust and bills in the air—they seemed pompous and comical.

I caught two more browns, then paused to de-slime and dry the fly. I did not notice any hatch, but I had obviously hit on something the fish wanted. Over the next fifteen minutes I caught five more. I felt the first raindrops but kept on fishing. The rain never became a downpour, just a steady shower with big drops that pocked the water, and it lasted only three or four minutes. Through it, the fish kept biting and they continued after it stopped. Finally I snapped off the fly with a whip-cracking back cast that made me wince.

I searched my fly box for another Parachute Blue Dun but knew there was none. Finally I tied on a Mosquito. I fished another twenty minutes but caught only one more trout. That made thirteen. All were browns between six and eleven inches. I had lost a handful of others and at least one grayling. Not too shabby for "bad, very bad" conditions, I thought.

When I walked back to the car and met Milos Jr., he initially seemed perplexed and skeptical, for he had caught only two more fish after the first one. But then he grinned and slapped me on the back. He asked which fly I had used and nodded when I told him. "That was the right one, today," he said. "That sure was the right one."

* * *

The next morning, Sunday, I woke to the church bell pealing and a rooster crowing outside the hotel window. When I sat up in bed I could see people walking to church. They came down the street in small groups or couples or singly—the men and boys in suits, most of the women and girls in bright dresses—stopping in front of the church's double doors to smile and chat in the sunshine before filing in together for the service. A few of the old women, bent and slowed with age, wore the traditional black folk costume that signified mourning. Some looked as if they had worn it for decades.

When Milos Jr. arrived, around nine, I asked him if the country was still religious after fifty years of state-sanctioned atheism. He was not sure but thought "about half" the people attended church regularly. He was not one of them.

When Dave came downstairs we hit the road. The fishing was on hold for a day while we went looking for Moravia.

First we drove up to Nedvedice's most famous landmark, Pjernstein Castle. Hewn out of a limestone ridge two miles outside town and nestled among towering chestnuts, lindens, and maples, this *ur*-Gothic relic (thirteenth-century) harks back to feudal wars and ancient legends. Like all castles—monuments to a bygone age—Pjernstein is at once impressive and timeworn, instructive and irrelevant. After we paid the entrance fee, Jana Rusnakova, the teenage tour guide, led us through the castle's various halls and chambers—from the Oath Room to the Hall of Knights—giving a running commentary of fact and fancy.

Much of it was tales of archaic concepts—knighthood and chivalry and the divine right of the ruling classes—among a long-dead aristocracy. But the best story was the legend of the irreverent servant girl who, as punishment from God, was doomed never to find peace in life or death. It was said that her ghost haunted the castle still.

Back outside, we were yanked abruptly from the romantic past back into the reality of post-communist Czechoslovakia. Outside a filthy, stinking pissoir stood a girl selling tiny strips of gray, crinkly toilet paper/hand towels for one krone each.

From the castle we drove south and a half-hour later, in Tisnov, we entered the *Porta Coeli* (Heaven's Gate) convent and monastery. At first glance, the name could have been taken as ironic. All around were signs of neglect and decay. On the exterior walls, huge areas of stucco had crumbled off to expose bare brick.

Most of the windows in the outbuildings were smashed or losing their glazing, and the courtyard was overgrown with weeds.

Though parts of the complex were undergoing renovation, it had obviously gone many years unoccupied by either nuns or monks. But two years ago that had changed, said our guide, eighteen-year-old Milena Barkova. The first Cistercian nuns in nearly half a century had moved in, transferred down from Denmark by church officials. Ten more were coming, she said.

When I asked if the cloister had been expropriated by the Communists, she hesitated and gave a quizzical look. "I think so," she said. "I'm not sure." It was a refrain familiar throughout Eastern Europe: people well-versed in the ancient past but "not sure" of their own recent history because much of it had been brutally suppressed.

From Porta Coeli we strolled a couple of blocks to downtown Tisnov. This day, most of the town center was taken up by a fair, with carnival booths, rides, games, and food-and-drink kiosks. Behind the fairgrounds was a long, sprawling factory, shuttered and quiet on this Sunday. I asked Milos Jr. what was made there, and he explained that the place was a combination paper mill and cardboard factory. This surprised me. The paper-mill towns I had seen in New England, the South, and the Northwest had all been made unmistakable by their stench and the fouled waterways they bordered. Tisnov, on the banks of the near-pristine Svratka, had neither trait.

I told this to Milos Jr., and he swelled with pride. There had been pollution from the factory in the past, he said. Nothing as extreme as what I described, but still enough to reduce the water quality downstream. Two years earlier, however, a new treatment plant had gone into service, and now there were trout and grayling all the way down to Brno. He himself had caught his biggest trout, a four-pound brown, in downtown Brno last year. And the water was still improving.

"One year, then the water is clean. Now, very good," he said.

I did not respond and must have seemed pretty dense, so he continued his explanation. "That's my job. I check the water from these factories." The laws were clear and tough, he said. Polluters must clean up or face severe penalties.

When I asked if this was a recent development he said no, it was a longtime policy resulting from a basic reality: The people of the region were willing to fight for clean air and water, and to prevent despoliation of the land. This did not jibe with the demonization of Eastern Bloc countries as benighted backwaters ruled by dirty-industry apartchiks ravaging the environment in the name of progress for their "workers' democracies."

Americans tend to assume that we invented the concept of environmentalism. And, of course, I had seen more than a few ecological disaster areas in eastern Europe, especially in East Germany. But I thought of some of my New England home rivers—the Narragansett, the Taunton, the Merrimack, the Androscoggin—for centuries virtual demesnes of the polluters and dam builders.

I remembered how angry my dad had become one time as we drove up to his camp in the mountains of western Maine when I was twelve. When we crossed the putrid brown Androscoggin at Turner's Falls, I asked him why the river could not be cleaned up. Why was the International Paper mill upstream at Rumford allowed to pour its filth into the river and fill the valley with the sickening stench from its smokestack?

"Because the people need the jobs," he said. "And those bastards [the mill owners] always threaten to move out if anybody tries to make them clean up their mess." My father was a calm, taciturn man and I had never heard him talk like that. In the years after, whenever we crossed the bridge at Turner's Falls I remembered it.

Now, one ocean and half a continent away, I was a visitor in a poor but proud land, standing beside the clear Svratka. Here, the memory of the Androscoggin, opaque and frothy with toxic foam, made me ashamed for my homeland and its dogma of transcendence. We were not the supreme environmentalists. We could learn a few things from other peoples.

When we got back on the road, the conversation turned to fishing. I asked Milos Jr. what his favorite flies were. He laughed and, between puffs on his cigarette, prevaricated like a politician: "If the mayflies are hatching it's a Mayfly, if the sedges are hatching it's a Sedge." But finally he admitted that if there was no hatch, his favorite all-around dry fly was a Mosquito. The Ritz and the Freshwater Shrimp topped his list of nymphs.

I wished we were fishing, but instead we followed the twisting back roads northeast of Brno to the Punkva Cave. Milos Jr. had assured us it was worth a side trip, and he was right. Gouged out of the three-hundred-fifty-million-year-old limestone of the Moravian Karst by the river of the same name, the site offered an unusual spelunking experience: an underground cruise.

Outside the cave mouth the June afternoon was hot, but by the time the electric launch glided into the second underground chamber, all twenty-four passengers were pulling up their collars and wrapping their arms around themselves; the temperature was forty-four degrees. This was what "the chill of the grave" means, I thought. No matter how hot it got outside, the air was always cold down here. When the guide said the water temperature was thirty-nine degrees year round, I asked Milos Jr. if the Punkva was a good trout river. "Yes, down the valley," he said, but he had never fished it.

We rode the boat through narrow passageways, where the gunwales nearly scraped the walls and the ceiling was close overhead. And we passed through cathedral-like chambers of eighty feet or more across. One of the cave's whimsical features was a stalactite-stalagmite pair named "Romeo and Juliet." Over tens of thousands of years, these formations—measuring ten feet and five feet, respectively—had inched closer and closer, growing down from the ceiling and up from the floor of the cave. But because of a change in water seepage they had stopped only a foot apart, "like two lovers who will never come together," our guide said.

The cave was dimly lit but the water was as clear as a saint's conscience, and I watched for fish the half-mile in and back out again. As far as I could tell there were none, but they could have been cruising the depths. The bottom was visible in only a few places, and the guide announced that one pool was 125 feet deep.

I had not realized that I was uneasy during the cruise, but when the boat glided back out into the sunlight I felt myself relax. I was not usually claustrophobic, but the subterranean cold and darkness had seemed ominous and foreboding, and I was glad to be out of them.

We had timed our visit well. The cave was a huge tourist attraction, and when Milos Jr. and I walked back to the car, the parking lot was packed. In addition to the many Czech vehicles, there were scores with French, German, Dutch, or Austrian plates. On one side was a line of tour buses.

As we drove back down the valley, I was glad to leave. I knew that the Austerlitz battlefield—where in 1805 Napoleon crushed the Russian and Austrian armies—was nearby, but I'd had my fill of sightseeing. I was looking forward to tomorrow: fishing the Jihlava with Milos Sr.

* * *

Milos Sr. was very different from his son. Soft-spoken and impeccably groomed, he had a refined quality that was undiminished by his clothes: a flannel shirt and a faded, threadbare fishing vest. At sixty-seven, he looked ten years younger. Like his son's, his English was iffy. But unlike Milos Jr., he spoke German like a native.

After introductions we sat together in the hotel dining room to plan out the day. He asked about my friend Bear, whom he had fished with the previous fall. At that time, Bear—long a driving force in the Federation of Fly Fishers—had signed up the

180-member Moravian Fly Fishing Club as the first FFF group in Eastern Europe. The whole club was grateful, Milos Sr. told me. After decades of isolation, Czech fishermen were eager for contacts in the West. "Please thank him again for us," Milos said. "He did it, practically. We did not know how."

The elder Milos also hoped the FFF connection would help engender a new ethic. Traditionally, local anglers kept and ate the fish they caught, within the limits of the regulations. The year before, more than twenty-three thousand had been taken from the Svratka. "We want to change that so the fishermen, the people, think of it as a sport," he said. The FFF, with its catch-and-release philosophy, could play a major role in the change.

A retired professor at Masaryk University in Brno, Milos Sr. had followed an interesting route to his life's work. Born in Setin to a fishing family, he had received his first fly rod at the age of seven. It was love at first cast, and out of his passion for angling sprang a love of flowing waters and the creatures that inhabit them. Eventually, an avocation became a course of study and, finally, a career—as a hydrobiologist and member of the university's Natural Sciences faculty.

"I was a fly fisherman before I was a hydrobiologist," he said. "My hobby led me to my profession." And he was not alone. Of seven colleagues in his department, three were fly fishermen. The popularity of fishing, especially fly fishing, Milos explained, was a major factor in Moravia's environmentalist tradition. "In Brno alone there are over a thousand fly fishermen and over fourteen thousand sport anglers," he said.

The sun was getting high and we were all eager to get on the water. Dave and I checked out of our rooms and loaded the car. The next two nights we would sleep beside the Jihlava. With Milos leading the way in his Skoda, we drove south for about forty minutes, following tiny, twisting byways until finally, outside Mohelno, we climbed a hill, then descended in switchback curves into a deep valley. We turned left onto a gravel road that was soon beside the river and that ended at a streamside meadow bordered by thick woods. At the edge of the trees was a wooden outhouse. This was the national-forest campground.

At the hotel Milos Sr. had seemed subdued and reticent but now he was in his element. When I said his vest looked as if it could hold a lot of equipment, he glanced down and laughed. "It drives my wife crazy," he said. "She sews new vests and sells them, and she keeps after me to take one of the new ones. Mine is falling apart and I have to keep asking her to fix it." The olive canvas was worn and badly faded, and he opened it up to show where it had frayed and been re-sewn at the corners.

We sat down in the grass for a few minutes, and he got out his flies, a collection of tiny, sparse-hackle patterns—Mosquitoes, Sedges, Adamses, Flying Ants—most in muted colors. They were beautifully tied but so small—down to No. 20s—and so sparse that I was immediately skeptical. But Milos Sr. soon convinced me. The flies were the result of a lifetime of discovery in and around the streams he loved: the Jihlava, the Svratka, the Dyje. Like his personality, the patterns were subtle and understated.

His favorite, he said, was the *graue Eintagsfliege* (Gray Mayfly), a hook-and-feather imitation of *Baetis rhodaui*, the region's most common aquatic insect. He held one in the palm of his hand, pointing to the translucent, smoky gray wings, clipped in a precise, plump-teardrop shape. "Pigeon feather," he said. In Czechoslovakia, few people had money for expensive tying materials, he explained. They learned to make do with what they could get.

I handed him my fly box and he poked around with his index finger, nodding at a few patterns, making a quizzical expression at others, and shaking his head at many. He was especially dismissive of the attractors: Royal Coachman, Yellow Wulff, Humpy, and a couple of other large, colorful creations. For Milos was a purist. He had spent more than half a century learning the myriad life forms that filled trout's stomachs and creating patterns as close as possible to the real creatures. Anyway, he said, these "flashy, exotic flies," would not work on his rivers.

One oft-repeated maxim says you never really know a man until you've seen him drunk and seen him cry. Maybe that is so, maybe not, but sharing a duck blind and wading a stream with somebody are right up there. We walked to the river and waded in.

Near Mohelno the Jihlava is a medium-large river, sixty to ninety feet wide. The bottom is mainly gravel and smooth stones, but here and there are patches of fine, white sand.

We started out in Milos Sr.'s favorite pool, a long, smooth section that was calf- to thigh-deep. At first we fished side by side, watching for rises and using a downstream drift. He had two hits but missed them. Then he hooked his first trout. I moved away to give him room while he played the fish. After he tucked it away into the creel, I stayed back to watch.

I knew that for many years Milos Sr. had coached the Czech national fly-casting team. Both his son and wife had become European champions under his tutelage, and as I watched him it was easy to see why.

Motionless and serene, he watched for five, ten, seconds. Fifty feet downstream, a tiny circle rippled the silver film. He swept the rod tip back to two o'clock, forward to ten, then back again to two, speeding up the line with a downward pull at each stop, shooting it out with effortlessness and fluidity on both the forward and back casts. As Milos Sr. stood in midstream, the water up around his thighs, curve and bend of rod and line soon became part of one continuous motion of ever-expanding loops, finally lengthening out into a flat, straight line that settled softly on the water.

When it landed, the fly barely touched the edge of the expanding rings. Then it was pulled inexorably downcurrent, the leader bisecting the circlets until, just before the tip touched the center, Milos Sr. picked it up and began the rhythmic pattern anew.

As I began casting again, I hooked and lost a small fish while my companion was landing his second. We worked our way downstream, and I finally caught a chunky, spunky ten-inch brown. "*Guter Fisch,*" he said, "Good fish."

Then the rise slacked off, and for a half-hour even Milos Sr. could not raise a fish. Finally he hooked his third, the last trout in his self-imposed limit. When he eased it into the creel, the sun was high overhead. "Shall we eat now? (*'Wollen wir jetzt essen?'*)" he asked.

Stretched out in the summer-green meadow, with the river flowing by a few feet away, we shared a box lunch, and Milos Sr. spoke of his lifelong love affair with "his" streams—the Jihlava, the Svratka, the Dyje. He had fished them, studied them, and fought to keep them clean and free. When he spoke of them, it was with reverence, in a language that was part science, part poetry.

His favorite, he said, was the Jihlava, whose richness of aquatic life—average concentrations of eight thousand small creatures (the mayflies alone numbered fifteen hundred) per square meter—supported the thriving populations of trout and grayling. In turn, these insects, crustaceans, worms, and mollusks indicated an abundance of microscopic organisms—both plant and animal—that served as their food sources.

"We did some very good studies," he said.

Milos Sr. spoke of the wild, unspoiled countryside, its forests and fields teeming with wildlife, from red stags and roe deer to wild boar, hawks, grouse, and myriad songbirds. Just downstream, he said, motioning with his hand, the Jihlava flowed into a steep-sided valley that was virtual wilderness. The next paved road was seven miles farther down.

He pulled out three brown beer bottles, extracted his jackknife from a vest pocket, and folded out the opener. The bottles were beaded with moisture, and I could almost taste the beer. But, ever mindful of the inevitable headache that would follow, I declined.

He shrugged, opening two and passing one to Dave.

Talk turned to fishing. Unlike his son, who preferred grayling, Milos Sr. was a devoted trout fisherman. "Brown trout," he emphasized. "No rainbows. I don't like them." For him, the brown was part of Moravia's wild heritage, while the rainbow was merely a foreign interloper. When he used the word "trout" he meant browns.

"Trout are territorial fish," he said. "They need space. If another fish comes, they are driven away or go away on their own. Rainbows are aggressive. Grayling are *very* aggressive. They hang in schools and drive away the trout. The trout really suffer."

I asked his favorite angling method. He was not a fanatic, he said, but he almost always fished on top. "My son is an expert with the nymph," he said. "But I prefer dry-fly fishing."

The conversation turned to his life. How was it living under communism, I wondered, and how was life now?

Milos Sr. hesitated a moment, gave a thoughtful look before answering. Since the rending of the Iron Curtain, some things had changed, others had not. "By us it was not like in the other Eastern Bloc countries. We always had enough," he said. But there were other issues besides the availability of food and basic consumer goods. The whole system—based on a set of well-intentioned but fundamentally unworkable ideas that went terribly wrong—was corrupt, based as much on power and privilege as any feudal society.

As an academic, he had made a little less money than a bus driver. "Well-paid were the police, the politicians, the factory bosses. But these were all Communists," he said. "It was impossible to get [these jobs] if you were not in the Party. . . . The main prerequisite was being in the Party. For everything."

For Milos Sr., this was a betrayal of conscience that he refused—repeatedly—to commit, and that meant that he could never reach the pinnacle of his profession. In the Czech university system, with its three levels of professor—assistant, docent, and full professor—only party members reached the top rank. But he was spared the worst retribution—dismissal and prison—because he had been a hero of the World War II anti-Nazi resistance. "I was never arrested . . . nothing like that," he said. But the apartchiks had other methods.

"For example, when my son wanted to go to *Gymnasium* [high school], that was very hard." In the end, Milos Jr. was able to attend the college-preparatory institution he wanted, but only because the director—a former student of his father's—defied the communist authorities.

During his last twelve years at the university, Milos Sr. went without a salary hike. "To get a pay raise, you also had to be in the Party." He said. But there were other compensations. "For me the work wasn't work," he told me. "It was fun, a hobby too." He loved it all: the research, the teaching, and the solidarity among colleagues. "In my department . . . there were not any Communists," he said.

Milos Sr. had retired three years earlier, just before the tide of democracy swept through the Eastern Bloc, but he still occasionally lectured at the university.

Of course there were things about his life he wished had been different. Travel was one. He would love to have fished for trout in New Zealand, British Columbia, Montana. At one time, the Iron Curtain made that impossible. Now it was the cost. He and his wife lived on a monthly pension of less than $200 a month.

But Milos Sr. was not one to waste energy lamenting lost opportunities. "I'm already too old for it," he said. He spoke of his life's circumscriptions with no recrimination. He knew that the dashed hopes, the lost chances were shared by tens of millions of people. And he was a rare individual among the many: an upright, principled man who, though cheated by fate, had not become bitter.

"Our children—or the next generation—will have it better," he said. In the meantime, he had the cold, flowing waters of the Jihlava. And the trout.

Finished with eating, we headed back to the river. Milos Sr. searched out a shallow ford a little below the campground and waded across. I followed. On the other side we followed a narrow, muddy path that snaked downriver behind a tangled wall of streamside brush. About a hundred yards farther along, the brush disappeared, the river opened up, and we stood on a grassy bank at the edge of a long, broad stretch that curved down to the right. On the opposite bank a half-dozen small cabins with metal roofs were scattered in a meadow. The hay was new-mown and raked into piles, and the sweet scent of it filled the air.

"Here, one fishes better upstream," Milos Sr. said. He pointed out the many small riffles and tossed in a stick to show that the current was swifter than up by the campground. Then he grabbed the end of his leader and snipped off the Gray Mayfly, returning it to his fly box and taking out a dark-brown caddis imitation. "Here are many sedges," he proclaimed, "not so many mayflies."

While he tied on the new fly, I walked another hundred feet downstream, then entered the water and began casting. Here the river was too deep to wade the middle, but along the bank it was mostly shallow, with plenty of room for a back cast.

I had on a Light Cahill, but after half a dozen casts I switched to a Deer-Hair Sedge. Milos was already releasing a fish. Soon I hooked one also, battling it upstream, then down. When I got the trout in close, I could see it was a brown—fat and thick-shouldered, but not long. Maybe thirteen inches. As I was reaching for the fish, rod raised high, it thrashed the water once and popped the tippet about four inches above the fly.

For the next couple of hours we cast to a few risers, worked the shoreline, and blind-drifted the riffles. Because the sun was high and bright, the action was slow. Milos caught three more fish, but I could not seem to land one. I missed a half-dozen strikes, briefly hooked and lost another handful of trout, and had one almost in my hand when the hook pulled out. Fishing with a champion, I was looking like a klutz.

The time was a little after four o'clock when we hiked back upstream and reforded the river to the campground.

It was time to say good-bye. Milos Sr. shook our hands and wished us luck. After he drove away, Dave and I unloaded our gear: propane stove, cooler, canned goods, folding chairs. We set up the tent and afterward, while Dave gathered rocks for a fire ring, I lay on the cool grass under the westering sun, hands clasped beneath my head, gazing into the blue void. I dozed off and on but never fell into a real sleep. When I got up, the tree shadows had lengthened and the air was cooling. I put on a wool shirt under my vest and ambled back to the river.

I started in the big pool but there was not much doing, so I began working my way upriver. Soon the tree shadows merged into each other, then the sun dipped below the hilltops and most of the valley came into shadow. I still had not hooked a fish, so I decided to change my luck. I waded across and climbed out on the far bank, hiking up and watching the water. I walked about a quarter-mile, spotting a few dimplers, but there was no rise.

Now the sky was pale with the high, silver light of summer evenings in northern latitudes. Reflected in the water, it gave the river a silver gray sheen, like a foggy mirror. I heard a splash, then another, and glanced toward the far bank in time to see the ripples. I bet it's caddis, I thought. As I was tying on one of Milos's Deer-Hair Sedges, there were three more splashes.

At midday, the river's chill, felt through nylon waders, had been a welcome relief. But when I entered the water this time it made me shiver. In the fast-fading light I could see my breath.

Casting to risers, I had two quick hits, then caught an eight-incher. I hooked two more and lost them. The trout were feeding in splashy, slashing rises, sometimes seeming to slap the fly without taking it. Again and again I missed strikes. Finally the timing was right, the rod doubled over, and after three jumps I landed a foot-long brown.

I had become chilled while standing up to my crotch in the water, and as I walked back I was glad to see the glow of a fire. At the campground, the first thing I did was pull off my waders and toast the back of my legs for ten minutes, listening to the summer-night sounds and the river burbling nearby. Then I cleaned the fish and fried it in butter. In the heat and yellow glow of the campfire, the sweet, flaky flesh had an extra tang.

*　　*　　*

When I woke in the morning, the grass was wet with dew and sunlight was just beginning to filter into the valley. I made a few casts before breakfast but rose no fish. When Dave got up we chowed down with scrambled eggs and beans.

About two hundred feet from our tent, at the foot of the meadow, a boulder the size of a dump truck edged up to the river. The current swept up against it, swirling in little eddies along its flat face before rushing on down. While I was scrubbing the pans I noticed a water ouzel, one of nature's more curious creatures, tending a mud-and-twig nest stuck to the boulder's face about six feet above the water. Periodically it fluttered from its nest to a rock in midstream, bobbing nervously before stepping into the water. Half a minute or more later it would emerge a few feet upstream, stretching out its neck and swallowing a worm or insect larva plucked from the streambed.

When I returned with the clean cookware, Dave had finished stowing the food. "Found a tick on me," he said. "There must be a lot of them in this grass."

I did not pay much attention to the comment. As kids rambling Cape Cod's woods, fields and marshes, my brother and I had coped with these tiny, blood-sucking arachnids every summer. We picked them off us, off our cats, and off our Labrador retriever, Mauki. We stuck them with pins, burned them with matches and dropped them into jars of kerosene. Some of the ones we picked off Mauki were swollen with blood and as big as grapes. They were no big deal, just another minor nuisance, like the deerflies, the mosquitoes, and the gnats that, if the wind was calm, ate us up when we walked the marshes for stripers. The gnats were the worst. "Damn things have buck teeth," my dad used to say.

With the sun climbing, we forded the Jihlava and hiked downstream. After we passed the broad, open stretch that Milos Sr. and I had fished the day before, the path swerved away from the river. Entering wooded bottomland, it crossed over a concrete sluiceway on a couple of planks, then followed the diverted flow to a run-down mill. The diversion gate was closed and the mill wheel—immobile on its rusty axle—hung from the side of the building like a useless appendage. The trickle of water in the sluiceway flowed on past to spill back into the river on the left side of the mill.

I checked out the river access both up- and downstream. On the right bank, where we stood, huge old lindens and oaks grew right down to the river's edge, overhanging a series of large pools. But across the river the streamside terrain was more open: intermittent sandy banks, brush, and grassy swales. I stepped into the water and hugged the edge, walking upstream until I found a spot where I could cross. With only hip boots on, Dave stood no chance and headed back.

Here the Jihlava was tranquil and smooth-flowing, more chalk stream than freestone torrent. Passing through the pools it made several lazy curves before straightening out and resuming its true identity two hundred yards down, in a series of braided riffles.

I sat on the bank watching and waiting, allowing the fish and the silt I had stirred up to settle down. When I stood up, I put on my polarized sunglasses, and in a few minutes I began to spot trout. They were good-sized fish, aqueous and streamlined in the current, leisurely feeding and holding in the flow. Most of them were in the shade near the far bank. I picked out an eighteen-incher and drifted an Adams over it. No take. I tried again with the same result, then again, but the fish eased down and away into the shadows. I cast to another, fifteen or sixteen inches. It rose to inspect the fly, sank back, and ignored it.

Finally I hooked and landed an eleven-inch brown, releasing it quickly. Near the far bank I spotted another fish, finning lazily and taking its ease behind a bike-tire-sized rock. When the Adams floated past the boulder, the fish snatched it and took off in a rush. It fought like a good-size trout, stripping out line and momentarily giving me second thoughts about the tippet. But when I landed it and pulled out the tape, the fish was barely over a foot long. Still, thick-bodied and deep, it would nicely fill the frying pan.

I slipped my Swiss Army knife out of its case and was about to smack the fish on top of its skull. Then I looked at it again: a copper belly, brilliant spots, the beginnings of a hook jaw, the depthless black of its eye. I relented and stooped down to ease it into a little backwater, held it by the tail and pushed it back and forth until the trout revived and held itself upright with no effort. When I released it, the fish swam out slowly about ten feet and turned up-current, holding there behind a small rock for a minute and a half or two minutes. Then it angled across the river and passed out of sight.

I sat for a minute and thought how lucky I was to be fishing on the Jihlava. And in so many other places: the languid, marsh-winding streams of Jutland, the legendary Traun, the Wiesent with its giant mayfly hatch, the bonnie Clyde. And best of all, the wild-rushing freshets and cuckoo-song evenings of the High Pyrenees.

With most of them I felt as Aldo Leopold wrote in *A Sand County Almanac:* "What was big was not the trout, but the chance. What was full was not my creel, but my memory."

Out in the shady pool I could see more trout drifting in the gentle flow. I knew I could probably catch some. But I wanted a change—call it a riverine version of "the grass is always greener" syndrome. I wanted sunlight and fast water.

A quarter-mile down, the river curved around to the left before entering a gorge with cliffs squeezing in on both sides. Here the Jihlava became deeper and swifter, churning and splashing over boulders and upthrust ledges. On the right bank the cliffs rose straight out of the river, and the current washed up against the sheer rock face in wavelets, swirling down in eddies and foam. But along the left bank, where I was, a sandy path snaked between the water and the cliffs.

Facing down-current I could make a diagonal cross-stream cast and, shortstopping the line to drop the leader in an S-curve, bounce the fly along the cliffs for a few feet of free float before I had to pick it up and cast again. I fished for five minutes like that but had no hits.

Up till then I had been faithfully using Milos Sr.'s flies. These near-perfect imitations of the Jihlava's natural insect life inspired confidence, especially after I watched his success with them. But now I was having heretical thoughts. I looked at the bouncing wavelets, the deep water, and the swift current, clipped off the No. 18 gray-winged mayfly, and tied on a Coachman. Not a little one, but a big, bright, high-floating showboat of a fly—a No. 10—one of the "flashy, exotic" flies that Milos disparaged.

On the first cast, the Coachman disappeared in a splash, and a thirteen- or fourteen-inch brown jumped, took off downstream, jumped again, and threw the hook. Over the next hour I hooked five more fish but could not land any of them. When the action stopped under the noonday sun, I began hiking back.

Just below the campground, next to the massive boulder, I spotted a good-sized fish cruising a pocket of slack water. Twice I floated the Coachman down over the pocket with no response, but on the third cast a six-inch trout shot out of the shadows and grabbed the fly.

After lunch Dave and I drove into Brno. We stopped once, in Cebin, to view the glorious ten-foot statue of a Soviet soldier sporting a bouquet on his Kalashnikov and looking noble and resolute with a flowing cape. I wondered what it must have been like not only to live under the heel of an oppressor, but also to be forced to honor him with monuments. And now that the occupation was over, did it all seem like an unreal, half-century-long nightmare?

In Brno we strolled around the center and loaded up on supplies in the open-air market at Zelny trh. Manned by a mix of babushkas, young mini-capitalists and robust farm couples, it featured everything from eggs to eight-tracks.

Like a once-beautiful woman who has seen hard times, Brno had the slightly worn, down-at-the-heels look of other Eastern European cities. Immaculate cobblestone streets and a historic center hinted at faded glory and gave a glimmer of hope that the city would regain its splendor.

We strolled the downtown for an hour and a half, pausing for cake and coffee at an outdoor cafe. Dave wanted to stretch out the *Kaffeepause* but I was impatient to get back on the river and we left a little after 4 o'clock.

* * *

The sun was already behind the hills when I waded into the Jihlava upriver from the campground. This time I had on long underwear beneath my dungarees and it did not feel so cold. The river again had the gloss of faintly tarnished silver but this time it was tinged pastel pink with the day's afterglow.

There was a hatch on—light olives—and the fish were feeding steadily. Occasionally one jumped clear of the water in pursuit of a darting ephemera. I had an hour of fast action, landing four browns and missing or losing a dozen others, before darkness obscured the rise.

Back at the camp, sitting beside a blazing fire with the stars coming out, the river plashing and purling close by and a night chill settling over the valley, I remembered part of the conversation I had with Milos the day before. Though he despised the de jure atheism of the communists, he was not religious in the conventional sense. "My church is nature," he said, "all this."

It was a worthy creed, I thought, with a long line of exemplary and diverse adherents that included my fellow Bay Stater Thoreau, Teddy Roosevelt, Aldo Leopold, John Muir, and Edward Abbey.

The next day, we packed up early for the grueling all-day drive back to Darmstadt. Twice we got stuck in traffic jams: once on the highway outside Prague and once in downtown. The area under my right arm felt swollen and sore the whole trip, and when I got home late that night and undressed to get into the shower, Libby pointed to the right side of my chest and said with disgust, "Yuck! What's that?"

I looked down and saw the reason for my sore armpit: It was a tick, embedded in the pectoral muscle and ringed by a bright red circle that felt warm to the touch. The soreness was from a lymph gland that had swollen to the size of a walnut.

I ripped out the tick and, at Libby's insistence, went to the emergency room at the local hospital. There the physician gave me two tablets of doxycycline and told me to go to our family doctor to get a prescription for two weeks' worth of the antibiotic. He could not write me a prescription, he explained, because German hospital regulations forbade it.

I spent the next few days in bed with fever, aches, chills, and a pounding headache that made it impossible to read. But when I went to our family doctor, he pooh-poohed the emergency-room physician's concern, gave me a few day's worth of another antibiotic—amoxicillin—and sent me on my way.

After a week or so I felt a little better. I was not my old self—I felt tired all the time and was occasionally achy and out of sorts—but I was too busy to think about it much. I had a young family, I was working at a full-time profession, and in my free time

I was renovating our house and planning to build three others out behind our barn to jump us up out of the paycheck-to-mortgage-payment syndrome.

In hindsight, I can see that I was full of hubris about myself and was cavalier about health risks. Though I worried constantly about my wife and kids, I felt myself immortal. After all, sicknesses you got over, injuries healed, and good health could be taken for granted.

I was in good shape—the prime of my life, really. I hiked and camped all over Europe, skied the glacier in Zermatt many summers, shot chamois in the Alps, pheasants in Yugoslavia, and geese on the frigid Baltic. I flew planes on two continents, rode a bike and swam to keep fit, and traveled over half the world in pursuit of my profession. I was sure that was the way my life would always be. What reason did I have for concern?

11

An Alpine Idyll

or God, Trout, and Vietnam, July 1992

Rock, and snow peaks all around, the sky, and great birds and black rivers—what words are there to seize such ringing splendor?

—Peter Matthiessen, *The Snow Leopard*

It was raining upriver. The precipitation had started in the late afternoon with black clouds piling up over the Totes Gebirge and the glaciers of the Dachstein massif. For a couple of hours the sound of distant thunder had rumbled down through the mountains. Now the water in the river was starting to rise. Not much yet, an inch or an inch and a half maybe, but enough to show on the bank.

I made a short cast up and across, dropping the Adams in close to the willow branches that swayed in the current. It drifted less than six inches before disappearing in a geyser of water. Instantly the line came taut and the reel began to sing.

The fish rocketed upstream, but after about fifteen yards seemed to tire of fighting the drag and the swelling current. It thrashed around on the surface for a few seconds, then made a surge across the river. I put on more pressure, and it dropped back a few feet, then shot off downstream into a heavy riffle. I swung around to follow and stopped it about twenty yards away, my rod and line pulsing with the current and the trout.

Carefully I forced the fish back upriver, easing it a foot or two at a time against the force of the water. It stayed in the main current, ignoring for some reason the brushy shore where the 5X tippet might easily have snagged and snapped. When the trout was ten feet below me, its back and tail breaking the surface, I could see that it was a big brown, thick-set and hefty. Twenty, maybe twenty-two inches.

I eased the fish closer, the rod bouncing as the trout churned and splashed. Carefully I reached around my back for the net, stretching it toward the shaking head. Seeing the mesh, the fish made a sudden lunge back downstream, ripping out another ten feet of line. As I began to force it back, the fish thrashed its tail and the fly came zinging past my ear, catching in a willow branch above my head.

That was the one Karl had promised, I knew. Still, I felt no great disappointment about the fish. Only a sense of loss that now, with the river rising and darkness coming fast, a four-day summer quest across Austria's Salzkammergut was nearly at an end.

It had started in Bad Ischl, an elegant old spa town twenty-five miles east of Salzburg, when two friends and I pulled up to the Hotel Stadt Salzburg a little after seven o'clock on a July evening. Famished after a seven-hour drive from central Germany, we quickly checked in and headed for the hotel's courtyard café, where owner Walter Stadtler and guide Karl Reisenbichler greeted us with grins, raised beer glasses, and a hearty "*Servus.*"

Stadtler, who took over the third-generation family hotel from his father, was a jovial host and a fly-fishing fanatic. One of the changes he had made was expanding the hotel's angling horizons. He now offered fishing packages on more than fifty miles of water throughout the Salzkammergut, a region of towering mountains, lakes, rivers, and postcard villages, an area that includes parts of the Steiermark, Oberoesterreich, and Salzburg provinces. A brief trip three years before had whetted my appetite, and this time I wanted to sample the whole feast.

My traveling companions, army chaplain Wilford "Willy" Widgin and pediatrician Nick Giovanni, had signed on for the trip after hearing my tales of many fish and fast waters. Though we were acquainted through mutual friends, this would be our first time fishing together. On the phone, Reisenbichler had assured me that conditions were ideal: The main snowmelt was over, the rivers were low and clear, and the hatches many and varied.

We ate dinner under a linden tree while I caught up on what was new with Karl and Walter. The café lamps had not yet been turned on and the courtyard was in the soft shadow of pre-twilight, when the sun has slipped behind the mountains but the valley is suffused with light from the Alpine sky. A few cumulonimbus loomed over the ridge across the river, and by the time we finished eating they had started to rumble.

The beer was foamy and delicious, and the meal of venison strips in mushroom cream sauce over *Spaetzle* was even better. But we were itchy to get on the water, so we donned waders and vests at curbside, assembled rods, and strolled across the street to the Ischler Ache. On the way we met a German angler heading back to the hotel, and I asked him how the fishing was. He was abrupt, almost rude: "*Sie verschwenden Ihre Zeit, es kommt ein Gewitter.*"

("You're wasting your time, a thunderstorm is coming.")

I chuckled and told him we would try it anyway. One of the things I learned during fifteen years on the Continent is that Europeans bring a different set of expectations to the angling experience. Most of my American buddies prefer to fish as long and as hard as they can. But Europeans tend to pursue fly fishing as an extension of the genteel life: dressing stylishly, staying dry and presentable, dining well at a reasonable hour, and, afterward, reflecting on the day in congenial company.

The Ischler Ache was Walter's house river. Curving in around the southwestern edge of Bad Ischl, it flowed past the hotel to its confluence with the Traun a block from downtown. It is a comfortable river to fish, not too big or too fast, and so clear over its bright bed that in the smooth water you can spot fish from the road in all but the deepest pools.

By the time we waded into the river, the first few raindrops were pocking the water. But so were the rise rings of many trout. We spread out at fifty-yard intervals and started fishing. There were at least four hatches coming off the water—caddisses and mayflies. A No. 14 Deer-Hair Sedge looked to be a pretty good match for the dominant hatch, and my third cast seemed to confirm that. I cast to a rise, and a twelve-inch brown sucked the fly under. The fish jumped once when it felt the prick of the hook but then went deep. I gave the trout its head, savoring the first fish of the trip. As I was releasing it I noted its pale, bright underside, a close match for the chalk-and-sand streambed.

Within a few minutes the sky blackened and the wind went still. Now there were fish rising everywhere. I missed a couple, then hooked a twin of the first in a seam of current near the opposite bank. As I was fighting the fish, a rush of wind swept down the valley, and the rain began to pour down, setting a million floccules dancing across the surface of the river. Thirty seconds later came a simultaneous flash and crash overhead.

I released the fish and ducked in under an overhanging bush, hoping the shower would be brief. But in ten minutes my hair was dripping, my shirt soaked. I waded back across the river and walked to the hotel with Nick and Willy, who had been smart enough to put on rain jackets. We drank one more beer each in the dining room, and I could not resist telling the German how good the fishing had been. Then I headed upstairs for a hot shower.

* * *

The next morning, Karl met us at the hotel for breakfast, and we loaded our gear into his RV. The day did not look promising, for we left Bad Ischl in a steady downpour with gray black clouds and shrouds of white mist obscuring the mountains. But as we drove north out of the Hoellengebirge the weather began to lift. By the time we turned down a dirt road alongside the River Alm, there was a high, Alpine blue sky with a few puffy cumulus.

Karl acted as if he had known it all along. "*Die Gewitter haengen in den Bergen*" ('The thunderstorms hang in the mountains')," he said, and moved on to more immediate concerns: flies and tactics for the Alm.

The section we were on, a three-mile stretch near Morchdorf, was controlled by a nearby Franciscan monastery. Because the monks believed in keeping the angling pressure low, we would be the only fishermen on the water. Here the Alm is a clear, smooth-flowing river, seventy-five to ninety feet wide. Slipping down a streambed of yellow rocks, gravel, and sand it takes on the illusion of a honey gold tinge, like a vintage Spaetlese Morio-Muskat wine. Alders, maples, ashes, and willows thicket the banks, here and there trailing branches in the current. Most places are wade-able, though a couple of the bigger pools go past chest deep.

Because of the Alm's exceptional clarity, Karl favored sparse-hackle dries—Blue Dun, Cahill, Mosquito—or sometimes a Pheasant Tail or gold-ribbed Hare's Ear fished in the film. We geared up in the morning sunshine and strolled down the road, really no more than a cart path, picking our sections. Karl sent us off with the traditional, "*Petri-Heil!*"

The sun was soon high and incandescent white, perfect for sunbathing but less than ideal for stalking twilight-loving trout. Fortunately, the Alm is a prolific grayling river, and *Thymallus thymallus* are much less light-shy than trout. On the Alm, grayling are reliable feeders most times of the day. In low light—early and late or under an overcast sky—they can be voracious.

Fishing a seven-foot, 6X leader, I caught grayling in the smooth mid-current, bouncing a fly down the riffles and in the dappled shadows under the brush. In a little over two hours I landed eight, from eight to fourteen inches, hooked and lost a handful, and missed another dozen strikes.

Trading fish stories over lunch, we learned that we had raised similar numbers of grayling. Willy had also caught a small rainbow, and Nick took two. Eating *Fleischwurst* on Bauernbrot in the shade of Karl's camper, the three of us began to get better acquainted. On the ride down from Germany we had exchanged bare-bones life stories.

Willy, a South Carolina country boy and Baptist minister, had been in the army for twenty-six years. He had signed up for the chaplain corps upon graduating from Wake Forest Seminary in 1967 and, after joining a Ranger unit, he had been sent to Vietnam. Since then he had seen a number of duty stations throughout the United States and Germany. Because he was a passionate fly fisherman, his favorite posting was Alaska, and he tried to stay there.

"Request for extension of tour" was the military term for it. Once, Willy's request was granted and he got two more years. But the services are known to discourage "homesteading"—staying on one base for several tours of duty. The second time Willy asked for an extension he got back a denial and a terse note: "Chaplain, you'll have to find another place to fish."

He laughed now, telling the story. "They figured out my secret," he said.

Nick had been born in the Bronx to Sicilian immigrant parents but grew up in New Jersey. After getting his undergraduate degree at CUNY he had gone to medical school in Bologna, Italy, returning to Brooklyn for his pediatrics residency. Because of his urban childhood he had come late to fishing, first tagging along with army buddies. Eight years before our trip, he had started with reservoir bass. But now he was hooked on fly fishing and trout. And country music played loud.

I briefly recounted my boyhood with spinning rod and a shotgun, my years on the beaches, estuaries, and kettle-hole ponds of Cape Cod.

"Sounds like a pretty good childhood," Nick said.

I told, also, of my congenital wanderlust and described how I had sought out Europe for the news hack's life of deadlines and one-day immortality.

Willy finished another bite of his sandwich and posed a question. "Norm, now are you a religious person?"

"Not in a formal sense. I'm an agnostic. Or a backslid Baptist. Whichever way you look at it. I don't know that there is a God, but I don't know that there isn't, either."

"Well, what made you turn away from it?"

"Nothing, really. I guess I just changed."

"What about you, Nick?" asked Willy.

"I guess I'm an agnostic, too."

"Were you raised up a Catholic?"

"Sure, like every good Italian kid. But you know what I say now? Don't come to me with all these rituals and crap. Show me, prove it to me."

"And what do you think about all this?" Willy made a sweeping, circular motion with the crust of his sandwich, gesturing at the trees, the sky, the river. "Where did it come from?"

"Geology, evolution, we don't know it all."

"Do you think we will sometime?"

"I doubt it. I don't know," said Nick

After lunch the hot summer afternoon turned hotter. There was virtually no wind, and in the thin Alpine air the sun was relentless. My nylon waders gave me a comfort advantage over Willy and Nick in their neoprene, but still I had to keep seeking out shady stretches along the banks. A half-dozen times I took off my hat and bent over to soak my head in the current, straightening up fast to let the cold water trickle down my neck and back.

When we met back at the camper I had caught four more grayling, the biggest about ten inches, and two small rainbows. Nick had done a little better, Willy a little worse. All of us were exhausted from the heat. The only event of note had been Willy's encounter with some young Austrians. "I came around a bend and there was a guy lying buck naked on the edge of the bank. I didn't know what the polite thing to do was, so I just kept on fishing. And darned if there wasn't a guy and a girl around the next bend. She was pretty nice-looking, too," he said, chuckling.

After cooling down with soft drinks, Willy walked back to the river. Ten minutes later he was back with the tale of a huge brown that had smashed his Hendrickson as he dapped it in under the willows. "I knew there had to be a big fish there. I didn't have five feet of line out. But he scared the devil out of me, and I broke him off when I set the hook."

Back on the road, we headed east into the mountains, and an hour later we crossed the glacial blue Steyr River, wild and roiling as it roared down out of the Totes Gebirge (the name means Dead Mountains). Just before sunset we pulled into the village of Kastellbell-Tschauss, which consisted of a handful of dairy farms, a tiny church—and Gasthof Winkler.

Gasthof Winkler was a country guesthouse-style hotel, featuring a timbered dining room with fireplace, immaculate rooms, hearty entrees, and old-fashioned *gemuetlichkeit*. We would dine well, sleep on feather pillows, and in the morning celebrate the Fourth of July by fishing the Teichl.

* * *

The tree shadows were long and there was still a mountain chill in the air when we began putting on our gear at streamside. Now Nick and Willy were glad for their neoprene, and we all got out our long underwear. Hopping around in the cold with goose bumps, white legs, and bony knees, we were not exactly *Playgirl* centerfold candidates.

"You know, it's a good thing we've got wives," Willy said. "We're not much to look at, are we?"

The Teichl is a swift, powerful, but not large river with a great variety of riverine habitat—riffles, rapids, deep pools, long gravel bars, and pocket water. In its remotest stretch it enters a deep-cut canyon, where cliffs quickly climb to a hundred feet. Here and there, huge boulders of conglomerate split the current, and for several miles the only access is via a narrow path that follows the river.

We hiked in together, splitting off at various places along the bank; first Nick, then Willy. It was almost nine A.M. but most of the sunlight that reached the canyon floor and the river had to filter through the branches of tall firs and larches.

I kept going and the path began climbing—ten, twenty, and finally forty feet above the river. I stopped and stepped to the edge to peer down. Here the Teichl was deep and smooth-flowing, dotted with boulders and blowdowns. A flicker of movement caught my eye; then I saw the rise ring. I put on my polarized sunglasses and kept watching. A minute later, in a deep boulder pocket, a big trout floated effortlessly to the surface, tipped up to sip an insect in the film, and slowly sank back down. Behind other rocks and logs there were more fish, all feeding leisurely and undisturbed.

It took me ten minutes to hike ahead and down, then wade upstream to within casting range. The bottom was soft with silt that made for difficult wading. There was no real hatch, but I saw a few winged ants and tied on a No. 14 Royal Coachman. Because the water was within a few inches of my wader tops I had to cast with my arm high, and I spooked a big trout with a sloppy cast. But I waded a little farther, flipped the Coachman in behind another mossy boulder, saw the splash, heard the smack, and came up fast to a fish. It shot off for a submerged log, but I forced it back and a few minutes later landed and released it, a chunky thirteen-inch brown with big, brilliant spots.

The fishable area was small. Most of the pockets were angler-proof. The bottom was too soft and the river ran swift and deep right up against the face of the cliff. But I did get one more trout on the Coachman, a fat fourteen-incher that I kept for dinner.

Downriver the wading was easier, cobbles and gravel and—in many places—water that was waist deep or less. But I caught only one more fish before lunch, a skinny six-inch brown that seemed to think it was a rainbow and jumped twice.

The day had warmed nicely and I was sweating by the time I hiked back to the camper. Nick and Willy had already stripped down to remove their long johns, and I did the same. They had caught a handful of rainbows and browns, but no big fish. After relaxing for an hour over lunch, we headed deeper into the canyon.

About a mile and a half in, the Teichl surged out of a tight curve and flattened out over a long, shallow pool. While midday slipped away into late afternoon, we fished leisurely and carefully, with not another human in sight. There was no sound but the river and a high wind in the trees. It was hard to believe that this was Europe, one of the world's most urbanized regions. We all caught fish—grayling, rainbows, and browns. Most were not large, but I did land a deep-bellied sixteen-inch grayling that fought like a big brown.

In the late afternoon, the sky closed in and it began to drizzle.

We continued fishing in the rain for a little while but soon gave it up and made the trek back out. Later, at the hotel, the first golden beer looked even more delicious than usual. Until then, Willy had drunk only soda, so the rest of us were surprised when he ordered wine. He caught our looks and offered an explanation.

"You know, when I was young I used to be a lot more fire and brimstone. But my views have relaxed. I guess I don't see things quite so black and white any more. I find a glass of wine now and then can be pretty enjoyable."

We clinked our glasses with "*Prost*" and "*Petri-Heil!*" downing big drafts and holding up our glasses afterward in the German and Austrian way to show we had not taken timid sips but had drunk heartily to each other.

During dinner we carried on three- and four-way conversations, with me serving as interpreter between Karl and Willy and Nick. Nick was frustrated because he spoke another language but it was not the one needed.

"Damn, I wish I could use my Italian."

Willy was curious about Nick's route into medicine and, finally, the army. "Nick," he said, "how did you come to go to medical school in Italy?"

Nick took a puff of his pipe, tilted his head and said, "There was this thing called the draft. And I had a low draft number."

"So you did that instead of becoming a grunt?"

"Or a corpse." Nobody said anything, and Nick took a drink of his beer.

"Maybe I'm doing a little more now. I don't know," he said. I had known Nick only briefly and while he wasn't in the office, but he had a calm about him that made me think he was a good pediatrician.

"What about you, Norm, were you ever in the service?"

"No. I had a high number."

Like many a college kid, I had sat glued to the radio the night of the first draft lottery, and the strangeness of it—of the times—remained vivid. It was the absurd validation of the cliché that your life depends on chance. My best buddy, with a low number, earnestly weighing the pros and cons of Canada and the Green Berets. Losing track of him until a letter four years later told me that he had been wounded on a Special Forces recon mission but was now "A-OK, no scar outside the bathing-suit area." And the question so many of us, in our youth, did not ask ourselves and now could never answer.

"You know, I'll never forget Vietnam," Willy said. "One time we were on patrol and we got caught in an ambush. The NVA was shooting at us, and we were shooting back at them. And between us was a farmer, out there in the rice paddies with a water buffalo, plowing. And when the shooting started, he took a stick and he tapped that water buffalo on the back of his legs to make him get down, and they both crouched down in the rice paddy. And when it stopped, he got back up and started plowing again."

"All I could think was, here's a guy caught between two ideologies and he doesn't care about either one. He just wants to plow his rice fields."

The talk turned back to fishing, and Karl voiced his disappointment that none of us had yet caught a trophy fish. "Monday I want everybody to catch a big fish. I guarantee you that," he said. Monday we would fish the legendary Traun.

* * *

In the morning, after breakfast, we headed southwest into the snow-capped peaks of the Totes Gebirge. Willy and Nick tied flies while Karl drove along twisting mountain roads to the loveliest of the Traun's tributaries. They made slow progress, but the fact that they could do it at all was a tribute to Karl's driving and the RV's excellent suspension. I merely watched, knowing that if I tried it I would be carsick within five minutes.

At Kainisch, the Oedenseer Traun is really two rivers. Emerging from an alder swamp as a web of brooklets, it quickly twines together into a meandering meadow stream, a watercress rill with undercut, sandy banks and pocket-size pools. But below the village it becomes a lively freestone stream with rocky, forested slopes slanting up from its margins.

We started fishing the upstream section in a light rain that soon lifted to reveal mist-veiled mountains and patches of blue. Periodically, the tinkle of cowbells drifted across from the green hillside meadows that sloped up to gray-stone mountainsides and, far above, blue white ice fields.

I followed the winding channel up toward the alders, fishing a number of dry flies with no success. But when I switched to short-lining a Beadhead, in this case a brown-and-yellow mayfly nymph, I caught a six-inch brook trout. In Maine this would have been natural, but in the Alps it seemed exotic. Rainbows have been widely introduced throughout Europe, but brookies are found in only a few places.

In parts of the German-speaking countries, things can get confusing. The German word for the native brown trout, *Bach-forelle,* translates literally as brook trout. The mistake appears frequently on English-language brochures in Germany, Austria, and Switzerland, and occasionally in other countries. The German word for our North American brook trout is *Bachsaibling,* literally brook char. Americans hoping to find brookies on the Continent set themselves up for disappointment if they do not get the distinction clear.

I fished on down the river, landing a small brown and losing a fish that wrapped the leader around a tree root. I had another six or eight hits but missed them. Finally I found a bathtub-size pool that had been scoured out around a boulder. I could see a half-dozen trout circling and foraging, and I carefully lowered the Beadhead, jigging it up and down with little more than the leader out.

It was almost like dunking a worm in a sunfish pond. Three of the fish shot toward the fly, and a fifteen-inch rainbow made it first. The resulting commotion quickly emptied the pool and when I released the fish, it scooted in under the rock.

But in four or five minutes, it reappeared with two others. A few minutes later three more trout swam back into view. I dropped the Beadhead in again, and another good rainbow shot up after it but turned in a flash and disappeared back down. After that I did not try for these fish any more but instead watched them like specimens in an open-air aquarium.

In the afternoon we moved downstream. Karl wanted to fish with me, so we hiked about a quarter-mile below Willy and Nick. Here was swift water with many footstool-size rocks.

"Behind every one there is a fish," Karl said. He looked through my fly box and picked out a big Grizzly Wulff, a No. 10, with a fluorescent green body. It had been a long-ignored gift, one from a boxful of beautiful, meticulously tied flies given to me by Bear before my Scotland trip.

I thought Karl's comment about the rocks was just enthusiasm, but when I started fishing it turned out to be true. I would drop the fly just in front of a rock, strip in line while it was sucked downstream and into the slack water. A fish hit the Wulff almost every time. Sometimes the take would be a sipping; at other times, a minor explosion.

If I did not strip fast enough, I missed the strike because of slack in the line. More than a few times I struck too hard and fast, yanking the fly out of the trout's mouth. But I also hooked fish. Many fish. Brookies, browns, and rainbows. Several times I had to de-slime and dry the fly, then apply more floatant, but it kept producing. After a while, the Wulff began to show a little wear, but the thread was still tight, the hackle stiff and upright.

Finally I lost the fly to a ten-inch brookie that didn't like the feel of a hand closing around its middle. I put on another Grizzly Wulff, this one a store-bought version with a canary yellow body, and went back to fishing. I don't know whether it was because, like Dumbo, I believed I had lost the "magic feather" or because the fish stopped feeding or because the foxfire green Wulff really was the one and only perfect fly for that time and river, but the action came to almost a dead stop.

In one pool Karl spotted a big rainbow feeding and had me cast to it. The fish looked the fly over twice, then sulked. I switched flies and gave it a rest. On the next pass, the story was the same: a rise, a look, then a turn-away. At Karl's urging—he wanted me to catch a big fish—I switched flies two more times but finally gave up.

In a little while it began to rain. I caught one more trout and while Karl was taking a picture he slipped, filling one of his boots and dunking my camera. When the rain began to come down harder, we headed for the camper.

Coming down out of the Totes Gebirge, the rain was a steady drizzle, clouds obscuring the view from the pass at Bad Aussee. Willy and Nick had given up on the scenery again, clamped their fly-tying vises to the RV's table, and begun debating patterns. But we soon drove down out of the weather and along the shore of the Halstaetter See. The lake was smooth and gray, with here and there a wisp of mist drifting across.

On the lake's south shore lies the tourist town of Hallstatt, which the nineteenth-century German explorer Alexander von Humboldt called "the most beautiful lakeside town in the world." Still picture-postcard pretty and studiedly quaint, it is a pocket-sized gem squeezed between the lake and the Salzberg (literally, Salt Mountain), the peak that towers above.

A waterfall tumbles into the center of town, where it is trans-formed into a fast-rushing stream in a channel of paving stones. Around the market square, flowers and vines trail down from balconies, and evergreens cling to the mountainside above the rooftops.

Along the shore, guesthouses and cafés provide tableside panoramas of the lake and the snow-capped peaks of the Salzkam-mergut.

With about eleven hundred inhabitants and fewer than four hundred houses, Hallstatt enjoys a renown far out of proportion to its size. This is partly because of its fame as a vacation spot but more the result of the 1846 discovery of an ancient Celtic grave-yard on the Salzberg. The archaeological treasures found there were so extensive that it remains the most important Early Iron Age site in Europe. The name Hallstatt Culture is now applied to the entire epoch, from about 1000 B.C. to 500 B.C., and a museum offers visitors a peek into the past.

Perhaps more fascinating than its history and beauty is the town's curiously practical attitude toward death. In the graveyard adjacent to the tiny Catholic church, the few dozen burial mounds are neat and well tended, each one marked by a simple cross. Most of these are wooden, but there are a few iron ones. None of them is very old. For though death may be forever, space limitations in Hallstatt mean burial is not.

The proof is in the *Beinhaus,* or charnel house, at the rear of the graveyard. Stacked neatly on wooden shelves lining three walls of the building are hundreds of gleaming white skulls. The names and the dates of birth and death are carefully lettered on most, and many are decorated with miniature paintings: Maltese crosses, roses, ivy. Arranged in family groups, the skulls document local genealogies over many generations. The other bones—femurs, tibias, fibulas, and so on—are stacked on the floor up to the bot-tom shelf.

Farther down the valley, Karl pointed out other landmarks while Willy and Nick went back to tying flies. As they wound hackle and occasionally glanced out the window, the conversation came around to the toughest part of their work: dealing with death. It came down to the same thing, though one man dealt with it from a medical point of view, the other from a spiritual perspective.

"When it happens, I just have to think I did everything for that child that could be done," Nick said. "But that doesn't really make it easier."

"You're right, Nick," Willy agreed. "It surely never gets any easier."

By the time we got to Bad Ischl the rain had stopped. Walter greeted us again with a *"Servus"* and a grin, and he made sure we sat at the Stammtisch, the table permanently reserved for favored guests. Hanging on the wall above was the six-and-a-half pound rainbow Karl had caught four years before in the Traun.

After ten or fifteen minutes we were joined by two local fishermen, then a third. We started out with small talk, but about a beer and a half later the conversation got livelier as Walter, Karl, and the other Bad Ischlers began regaling each other with local lore and fish tales. Some of the stories were pretty good, and I translated the best ones for Willy and Nick. When our meals came, the conversation flagged momentarily but soon recovered. I was beat and headed upstairs to bed at eight-thirty, but the rest were still going strong. In the morning we would finally fish the Traun.

*   *   *

The Traun and its tributaries have been renowned in European fly-fishing circles since before the turn of the century. In the early days, the anglers wading the pools were the aristocrats and the very rich. But just as spun graphite has largely replaced split bamboo, today's Traun angler is more likely to be a yuppie or prosperous tradesman than a baron or count.

The river and its string of lakes—St. Wolfgangsee, Hallstaetter See, Grundlsee, Traunsee, Altausseer See—make up the pearl necklace adorning the throat of the Salzkammergut. Pinned over its heart and limned with a patina of imperial splendor, Bad Ischl is the region's antique brooch.

Once the sometime headquarters for an empire stretching from Lake Constance to the Carpathians, Bad Ischl was a gathering place for the powerful and the privileged. Diplomats and heads of state from across Europe walked its streets. Empresses and aristocrats took their leisure in its mineral baths.

The beginning of the end of Bad Ischl's glory days came with the gathering storm clouds of 1914. The nattily dressed and impeccably mannered men did nothing to stop Europe's headlong plunge into catastrophe. Four years and twenty million deaths later, the old order paid its price. The Treaty of Versailles dismembered the Austro–Hungarian Empire, leaving only a quaint vestige, and exiled its rulers. These days, the most visible reminder of Bad Ischl's former role on the world stage is the Kaiser Villa, summer palace of the last Hapsburg ruler, Franz Josef.

Because it is less than an hour's drive east of Salzburg, the *Sound of Music* city, Bad Ischl is—fortunately—overshadowed as a tourist destination. No tourist mobs throng the byways, no souvenir hawkers accost visitors.

It is a town that presents interesting possibilities. There are few first-rate fly-fishing destinations where you can walk back to your hotel, change out of your waders and vest, and head down the block to hear a world-class orchestra.

* * *

The last day began with blue skies marred only by a few high, thin cirrus. Driving out of town and up the valley we were in high spirits. Today would be the day, Karl repeated, when we would all land trophy trout. "Don't you guys go catching anything TOO big," Willy said. "I don't want to have to stop fishing to help you carry it back to the car."

Above Bad Ischl, the Traun is a large river: one hundred to one hundred fifty feet wide and in most places wadeable only along the edges. In the big river are big fish—many trout of five pounds or more and grayling to three and four pounds. Eighty percent of the trout are browns, and—except for a handful of brookies—the rest are rainbows. We would be fishing a four-mile stretch leased by a German businessman for the equivalent of $60,000 a year.

When we got to the place Karl wanted us to start , another angler was already casting from a mid-river gravel bar. Karl supposed it was a friend or relative of the leaseholder and seemed slightly peeved that we could not fish his choice spot. But we drove a third of a mile upriver, walked across a pasture and squeezed through a fence, and there was the river.

The Traun seemed swifter here—and much deeper; it looked dark blue and bottomless. Karl eyed the bank and seemed surprised. "That little bit (*'kleines bischen'*) of rain in the mountains last night has given us high water," he said.

We spread out and began fishing in earnest, dreaming daydreams of monster fish lurking in the depths. Two hours of hard fishing later, I'd had only one hit. Willy had caught one small brown, and Nick had nothing. Karl drove downriver to do some scouting and we kept on, though the fishing did not pick up. After lunch we moved a mile downriver to an old mill pool. At its foot was a concrete weir. Karl advised us to work the water just below the weir, and I pulled a nice fifteen-inch grayling from the mist, foam, and spume at the base of the spillway. Willy and Nick got nothing.

With the afternoon waning, Karl drove us back up to a straight, riffled stretch where the river seemed even wider. The high bank was grass and rip-rap sloping down into the water, but the other shore, we could see, was lined with willows and overhanging brush. Karl got down close to the edge to check the water level and told us we could wade it. Willy said he hoped so because he did not think he needed to be rebaptized. I translated for Karl and he laughed.

"This stretch has some big fish," he said, "but most are on the other side, up in the branches and the foliage. Just be careful in the going over."

In the powerful, inexorable current, the crossing on cobbles and gravel was a slow, tricky business. Most places the water was knee- to thigh-deep, but there was no way to avoid one waist-deep channel and we had to pick our way around a few holes that were beyond wader depth. We were relieved to reach the far shore, where the bottom was mostly firm sand sloping up to the low, brushy bank and a marshy area beyond.

We spread out and began fishing upstream and in, from the riffled water to the bushes. I caught a six-inch rainbow on a Deer-Hair Caddis, and just below me Nick took one that was a little bigger. Upriver we could see the thunderheads building over the mountains, and the first clouds began showing in the sky over-head, thick gray renegades blown down the valley on downslope winds. It was now or never for our big fish.

Nick moved twenty yards farther downriver, and a minute later he let out a whoop. When I turned to look, a huge fish came smashing and thrashing to the surface. I stopped to watch as, pipe clenched between his teeth, Nick shoved the rod butt into his stomach while the full eight feet of graphite bowed and bounced crazily.

I heard the varied scream of the reel above the noise of the river when he turned away as the fish ran toward shore, then turned back again as it headed upstream toward me. When the trout broke water again I was close enough to see that it was a brown, a trophy brown. Nick fought it back down, but suddenly his line went slack and he let out a string of curses. "Goddamn son-of-a bitching . . ."

When he stopped I shouted over. "Did he break you off?"

"No, the goddamn hook pulled loose."

"Which fly?"

"Caddis."

Up in the mountains the thunder was a steady rumble, echo-ing and re-echoing down the valley. The sunlight was gone and there were intermittent sprinkles. The river seemed to be coming up, the current growing fuller.

Nick and I both went back to fishing, and ten minutes later I caught a nice thirteen-inch brown, thick across the back and bright with color. But it was not the big fish I wanted so much that I could already see it laid out in the grass, the trout whose heft I could feel on my arm as I slipped my fingers under its gill cover and held it high.

A quarter-hour later I hooked a big grayling while floating the No. 10 Adams downstream and in tight to the brush. But five feet from the net, the hook tore free and the fish was gone. The rain was almost a drizzle, and I ducked in under a willow to get out of it. Just as on the first day, I had no rain jacket, and the temperature was getting chilly. But five minutes later the drizzle had slacked off, and I went back to fishing.

Then I hooked the big brown, taking a break after it was gone to collect my thoughts.

Nick was still fishing seventy-five yards below me, but I could not see Willy anywhere. The rising river was not a thing to be trifled with, but my big fish was still out there. I knew it. In the deepening twilight I began casting again, working the brush line methodically. Within a minute I hooked another big fish that surged out of the willow branches. But this time I had it on for only fifteen seconds. It was time to give up.

I looked to Nick, and he motioned toward the opposite bank. I waded downstream thirty yards and began crossing over. Dead tired and fighting the rising river, I struggled. A couple of times one foot slipped, giving me a momentary weightless feeling. I was sure this spot was where I had crossed before. I had marked the route by a tree on the shore. But the river was deeper now. Nick seemed to be faring little better ten yards below me.

I took another few careful steps with the water above my waist, then both feet slipped. I was lifted free, sat down, and instantly the glacial river was up around my face and seeping down into my waders as I was swept downriver.

I held the rod and scrambled with my feet to gain some kind

of foothold, but the rocks slipped away upstream. I was now almost down to Nick, but he was a few yards behind and there was no way he could reach me. Forty yards below, the Traun opened out into a deep, three-hundred-yard pool that I had no desire to swim in waders and full gear, with a surging river, on a chill, rainy mountain evening.

I scrambled some more, and this time one foot held, then the other. I regained my feet and just stood there for a minute to get my bearings and breath.

"You okay?" Nick called.

"Yeah, I'm all right."

The worst stretch was over, but we took the rest slow and steady. The adrenaline surge canceled out the fatigue, and neither of us had any trouble making the rip-rap. Then I began to feel really cold.

When we got back to the camper, Willy was standing in the door of the RV in his underwear, wringing out his socks. He had taken a dunking, too. Because it was our last day, we had foolishly fished too hard, too long, and too late in pursuit of our trophy brown. But on this day the Traun was unyielding.

"In my whole life I have never seen it this bad," Karl said. "You always see some rises. And standing on the bridge when you look down you can see some lunkers. But today was nothing. They were gone, disappeared. I am very sorry."

I pulled off my waders and emptied them, then wrung out my pants and socks while Karl poured out glasses of brandy. Soon our cold dunking was a joke and not a potential double drowning. I asked Willy how his mishap had occurred.

"I was home free but I lost my balance climbing that darned rip-rap and fell backward," he said. "Just like a back dive, only not as pretty. I lost my hat but I stabbed it with my rod before it got away out of reach. I guess the two Baptists got rebaptized together after all."

Later, back at the hotel after man-sized *Jaegerschnitzel* (pork cutlets with mushroom sauce), boiled potatoes, and white asparagus, we quaffed our draft beers and sized up the trip.

"Naturally, I would have liked everyone to get a big fish," Karl said.

But all three of us had gotten over our big-fish fever and knew it had been a wonderful four and a half days of fishing in great company and spectacular country.

"I thoroughly enjoyed every minute of it," Nick said. "It was truly wonderful."

Willy grinned. "Sometimes I felt my soul soar. Like I wanted to put on a blond wig and start singing "The Sound of Music.""

12

Castles, Caves, and Reue

Season's End on the Wiesent, September 1992

They all became part of the river. It was the goal of all of them, yearning, desiring, suffering; and the river's voice was full of longing, full of smarting woe, full of insatiable desire. The river flowed on towards its goal. . . . All the waves and water hastened, suffering, towards goals, many goals, to the waterfall, to the sea, to the current, to the ocean and all goals were reached and each one was succeeded by another.

—Hermann Hesse, *Siddhartha*

In the fading light, the river had lost its sheen, turning black and fathomless. The few caddises and mayflies that twenty minutes earlier had skittered across the water had vanished. Darkness was coming fast and with it the chill of an autumn night. Like the day, the trout season—longingly anticipated and variously savored and squandered—was slipping away downstream.

For more than a week, Germany had woken to brilliant blue skies and temperatures in the seventies and eighties. But the day before, September 29, had dawned cool and cloudy, the first hint of a sea change in the wake of a hot, dry summer and early fall. In a few weeks, fugitive winds would sweep in from Scandinavia and the North Atlantic to strip the leaves from the trees. The cold mists and rains of November, outriders of the Central European winter, would soon follow.

During the drive from Darmstadt the overcast had thickened and lowered, turning to drizzle and, finally, to a steady, dreary rain. But an hour later, just east of Wuerzburg, it began to let up. By the time Gus and I turned off the autobahn at Hoechstadt, we had driven out of the rain. As we headed up the valley of the Wiesent, sunlight beamed through ragged holes in a thin stratus layer, dappling hillsides and meadows.

As we approached the town of Streitberg and looked across the valley, we could see the ruined hulk of the fourteenth-century Neideck Fortress, onetime outpost of Teutonic knights. Its shattered tower loomed against the skyline, brilliant in the afternoon sunshine. A quarter-mile farther on, we turned left into the town and checked into Stern's Posthotel. After eating a quick lunch of soup, sauerkraut, and *Fraenkische Wuerstchen* (Franconian sausage), we headed for the river.

* * *

The Wiesent is one of the twisting, silver blue threads in the riverine lacework of the upper Main drainage. These spring-fed, limestone streams—the Wiesent, the Trubach, the Leinleiter, the Aufsess, the Puettlach and a handful of others—weave a fluid pattern through the plaited green tapestry of the Fraenkische Schweiz, one of Germany's loveliest and least-discovered regions.

The area's name, coined by Bamberg writer Joseph Heller (no, not the *Catch-22* author) in an 1829 travel book, combines the German words for Franconia—the larger region in which it lies—and Switzerland, implying that it rivals that Alpine country in natural splendor. Any good journalist has an ingrained distrust of the word "unique" but, discounting the hyperbole, this region of high, rolling hills; thick forests; and twisting, sheer-walled valleys does have a special something. Still, curiously, it is largely bypassed by the tourist masses. Most proceed on to nearby Wuerzburg and Nuernberg, or head farther south to Munich and the Alps.

The Fraenkische Schweiz lies roughly within a triangle—thirty miles on a side—with points at Bamberg, Bayreuth, and Erlangen. In addition to scenery and outdoor pursuits from kayaking to rock climbing, it is rich in history and legend.

With neither big cities nor heavy industry, the region offers the genteel tranquility of European country living. It is also distinctly Bavarian. In the villages, window boxes of geraniums adorn half-timbered houses. And the Fraenkische Schweiz boasts the world's greatest concentration of breweries, many of them tiny pub breweries where the locals drop in daily to quaff a couple of half-liters or fill plastic pails and carry the foamy liquid home.

The central geological feature of the region is the Franconian Jura, the massive limestone formation that underlies much of northern Bavaria. Formed beneath ancient seas more than one hundred fifty million years ago, it provides a soft and porous substratum for the countless springs that feed the rivers.

Over the eons, the flowing waters scoured out some twenty valleys, here and there adorning them with fantastic rockscapes of towering cliffs, stalactite caves, and giant dolomite towers that jut above the valley walls. The most dramatic landscape is the valley of the Wiesent River.

Tumbling out of the limestone hills near Steinfeld, the Wiesent snakes its way down through the middle of the Fraenkische Schweiz. For most of its forty-five-mile length, all the way to its confluence with the Regnitz at Forchheim, it is a classic chalk stream: deep and smooth-flowing, only occasionally punctuated by riffles, weirs, or boulders. Though the river is generally too deep to wade, streamside meadows on many stretches provide ideal bank fishing.

The Wiesent and its eleven major tributaries have two qualities essential to top-notch trout habitat: a consistent flow of cold, clean water—source springs average forty-six to forty-nine degrees—and an abundant, varied population of aquatic insects. These are amiable, contemplative waters, as different from the roisterous freestone streams of southern Bavaria as the Fraenkische Schweiz's wooded hills and pastoral valleys are from the craggy, snow-capped Alps.

Fly fishing has a long and storied tradition on the Wiesent. One of the earliest accounts is by author Johann Fuessel, whose 1788 diary tells of trout and grayling "caught on a hook wrapped with feathers to represent an insect." A half-century later, the river became a favorite of British anglers, a status enhanced by H. J. Whitling's 1850 book, *Pictures of Nuremberg and Rambles in the Hills and Valleys of Franconia*. In the twentieth century, the river attracted fly-fishing notables such as Charles Ritz and Frederick Duncan.

The Wiesent is most famous for its early-summer hatches of giant mayflies. During these times it fairly boils with fish. Four years before, I had fished the river in late June, and for three days the action had been furious and nonstop. Walking to the river this time, I recalled that first trip.

* * *

Gus and I had stayed a few miles upstream, in Doos. A friend in Bamberg had told me about Gasthof Heinlein, a historic hotel that held fishing rights to a 1.3-mile stretch of the river. I called and made the arrangements, excited about the prospect of exploring one of Germany's storied fly-fishing waters.

But when we arrived, I was dismayed to learn that there had

been a misunderstanding. The hotel required a minimum stay of four days to issue a fishing permit, but our schedules allowed us to be there only two.

The owner, Erich Heinlein, a man in his late sixties with an imperious mien, was at first adamant. Rules were rules, he said, and if he started making exceptions, there would be no end to it. But after a quarter-hour of careful and supplicant negotiations on our part, he finally relented, sighed, and got out his permit book.

"However, you must promise me that you will not tell anyone," he said

While I rigged up at the car, Heinlein's son-in-law, Georg Ritter, gave me a few tips—large, light-colored flies are best; be sure to fish the shady areas—and he made me a gift of several huge, cork-bodied mayflies, tied on No. 10 hooks. They were so big they resembled the balsa-wood gliders that kids fly in their backyards.

The river was just a two-minute walk away, across the road and through a damp meadow newly mown for hay. The first half of the day had been cool and cloudy, with a puffy east wind. But in the past hour it had turned partly sunny and the wind had died, bringing out swarms of mayflies. They filled the air like snowflakes, and when I arrived at the water's edge, trout were gulping, sipping, and snatching the ephemeral insects, both up- and downstream for as far as I could see. It was not necessary to cast to rises; the fish were everywhere.

It was not a scene to inspire calm. I made three or four bad casts, letting line and leader fall on the water in coils or slapping them down hard. I almost hooked myself in the ear while rushing a forward cast. Then I stopped for half a minute to take a few deep breaths. When I resumed fishing, the trout fever had subsided. I dropped one of Georg's gift mayflies just ahead of a rise ring, and half a second later it disappeared with a splash.

When I landed the fish—a brilliantly speckled, foot-long brown—I gauged the heft of it in my hand before lowering it back into the current. After it scooted for the depths, I settled into a methodical pattern. For the next couple of hours I worked my way upstream, taking pleasure in exploring the new water as well as in the fishing itself.

The hatch and rise were still in full swing when I walked back to the hotel, intending to grab a quick bite and return to the river. But my plans got waylaid by smoked filet of trout followed by venison strips in a wild-mushroom cream sauce, with cranberries on the side. The coup de grace was strawberries topped with whipped cream.

Because there were only a handful of people in the dining room, dinner felt like a private catered meal. Herr Heinlein, ever imperious, stiffly introduced us to Frau Heinlein. We briefly exchanged small talk and pleasantries before they retreated into their official duties.

When I finally got back to the river, the sun had disappeared behind the hills and the temperature had fallen six or eight degrees. A few stray mayflies fluttered here and there, but the hatch—and the feeding frenzy—were over. I fished for another hour, catching one ten-incher on a Royal Coachman, and quit with a crescent moon rising in the twilight sky.

There was a big European Cup game that night—Germany against Italy, I think. When I got back to the hotel, Gus had staked out a corner of the dining room near the TV. A foam-topped *Pils* was on the table in front of him.

"Hey Norm, pull up a chair. This should be a great game," he said.

As a young man, Gus had been a top-notch soccer player. But despite growing up in Frankfurt, his loyalties were ecumenical: Talent, effort, and demeanor mattered more than nationality.

"I don't know if I want the Germans to win," he said. "These guys think they are too good."

I sat down and ordered a beer. About halfway through the game we invited Herr Heinlein to join us. I wanted to learn more about the fishing, and I think Gus saw loosening up our host as a challenge. At first, the conversation was somewhat detached: local sights, the weather, business. Herr Heinlein was rightfully proud of the hotel, which had been in the family since 1829. He and his wife had taken over in 1952.

He became more engaged, even wistful, when talking about fishing and his *Heimatsort*, the valley of the Wiesent. Most of his sixty-six years had been spent on or near the river. As a boy growing up in the 1920s and 30s, in accordance with local custom, he was not allowed to fish. He could only accompany his father or other adults, carrying the gear and the Faesschen, the traditional small wooden barrel used to transport the fish alive.

In those years, anglers came from throughout Europe to fish the meandering chalk stream with its cliffs and castles. Heinlein got to know many of them: the Dutch, Belgians, French, Swiss, English, and others who made pilgrimages to Doos.

But as the gathering Nazi storm darkened the political skies over Europe, the hotel had fewer foreign guests. Soon they stopped coming altogether as the holocaust of World War II engulfed the Continent. The war took Heinlein away from his beloved Wiesent, and he remembered with great clarity the spring day in 1945—Whitmonday it was—that he returned to his own flowing waters.

The conversation turned to the present. One of his daughters, also an avid angler, ran a fly-fishing shop in nearby Ebermannstadt. These days the majority of fishermen were German, but once again there were also many foreigners, mainly French, English, and Dutch.

"Do you get many American anglers?" I asked.

Herr Heinlein stiffened, hesitated. Because we had been speaking German, he seemed to have forgotten our nationality, but now it came back to him.

"No, almost never (*'fast nie'*)."

As a naturalized American, Gus was especially sensitive to

certain European attitudes, especially among his former country-men. He pressed the issue.

"Did you have many American guests after the war?" he asked.

"Yes, there were many Americans," Herr Heinlein answered.

"Were they good anglers?" Gus asked, "*Waren sie gute Angler?*"

Herr Heinlein's eyes flashed for an instant, then went neutral.

"Our American *guests* after the war," he said, putting sarcastic emphasis on the German word *Gaeste,* "were an occupation force ('*eine Bezatzungsmacht*')." They hunted and fished without regard to the customs and regulations, he told us. "They did not conduct themselves in a sportsmanlike manner ('*Sie haben sich nicht waid-mannsrecht benommen*')."

Gus's naturally ruddy complexion turned bright red, and his mouth opened as if he were about to speak. But then he picked up his beer, took a big swallow, and set it back down. He turned back to the game, and I asked Herr Heinlein a few more questions about the area and the fishing. In a few minutes, our host excused himself and went back behind the bar into the kitchen.

Gus did not say much for the rest of the game. When it was over we paid our bar bill and went up to our rooms. Climbing the stairs he finally spoke up.

"Did you hear that guy? Those bastards just got through de-stroying half of Europe, killing thirty or forty million people, but the Americans were not *waidmannsrecht.* They didn't obey the game laws! They took too many fish! That's why I still don't know about these goddamn Germans. I can only take them for a little while. Maybe the younger generation is different, but the older ones . . . I just don't think they will evah change."

Getting ready for bed I thought about what Gus had said. Then I thought of Herr Heinlein, who was about my dad's age. I knew it was remotely possible that he or one of his countrymen could have killed my father, who had fought with his unit from St. Lo to Frankfurt an der Oder. Then, of course, I would not be here to hear him expound about those victorious American occupation troops being unsportsmanlike.

* * *

The next day dawned cool and gray, with a brisk east wind, so we decided to forgo fishing in the morning and explore the area. First we headed down the valley to Ebermannstadt, where I bought flies, leaders, and dry-fly dressing at Der Wiesentfischer. We introduced ourselves to the shop's owner, Maria Eckert, whose face lit up at the mention of her father.

Afterward we drove up to Tuechersfeld, nicknamed *Felsendorf* (rock village) because of its half-timbered houses, clinging to cliffs and squeezed between dolomite towers. From this quaint tourist high point, we went a half-hour west to Heiligenstadt and a landmark with a very different, darker symbolism: Greifenstein Castle.

Its walls and towers gleaming with the patina of old ivory amid the surrounding hardwood forest, this feudal relic towered above the valley of the Leinleiter, a monument to one of the few bright spots in German history during the Third Reich. For Greifenstein was the ancestral home of Count Klaus von Stauffenberg, who planted the bomb in Hitler's Wolf's Lair head-quarters on July 20, 1944.

When the assassination attempt failed, the whole von Stauffenberg family, including aunts, uncles, nephews, and nieces, were sent to prisons and concentration camps: Streihthof, Buchenwald, Dachau. And from high up in the Nazi hierarchy came the order: Blow up Greifenstein Castle, the ancient von Stauffenberg family seat and the symbol of the blue-blooded no-bility that Hitler so despised. In the end, however, it was not razed because of the intervention of an unlikely protector: the Gestapo chief of Nuernberg, Benno Martin.

This day, high-flying clouds tore across the sky above the mountaintop. Walking from the parking lot to the entrance, three-hundred-year-old lindens lined the access road through the castle gardens, creating an eerie, tunnel-like effect. In the courtyard we gazed down a three-hundred-foot-deep well—chiseled through solid rock over a period of fourteen years in the seventeenth century—a monument to indominability, or hubris.

Inside the castle we followed the tour guide past Baroque and Renaissance furnishings, weapons of war from medieval times to World War II, the family library with books dating from the 1500s, and a hall of hunting trophies reaching back across the centuries.

It was absorbing, but when the tour was over I heaved a sigh of relief. After the whiff of musty history and ancient horrors, it was good to get back out into the forest and a fresh breeze, the scent of linden blossoms and damp leaves.

We followed the twisting road back down to the valley and farther, past other castles, high green meadows, and forests. Near Rabenstein Castle we stopped to tour the *Sophienhoehle,* a quarter-mile-long cave that became an archaeological sensation upon its discovery in 1833, when more than two dozen cave-bear skeletons—some of them thirty thousand years old—were found there. Only one remains on the site, wired together in a standing position to awe visitors.

In one massive limestone chamber we viewed the region's oldest stalagmite, a seven-foot-high, snow-white mound measuring ten feet in diameter at its base. Formed drop by drop over two million years, it provided a different perspective on nearby "ancient" human constructs built over a few centuries—mere blinks of the eye in geologic time.

We like to think our lives significant. But in two million years will they truly be any more noteworthy than those of the untold trillions of diatoms that, dying a quarter-billion years ago, turned to limestone under Mesozoic seas? And when the sun begins winking out and the Earth turns cold, of what import will be our puny hopes, dreams, and fears, or our foibles, failures and heroic deeds?

"When you look at it a certain way," a Cape Cod friend once said, "none of it matters. But you have to live your life as if it did."

Over the eons came the rains, dissolving the limestone, carving out the caves and valleys, the subterranean channels and chambers that fed the springs and swelled the rivers. And sustained the trout.

We got back to Doos a little after four. I was tired of castles and caves, of pondering infinity and humanity's follies. On the river, the wind had calmed and the sun had burned through the hazy cloud cover, triggering another massive mayfly hatch. The fish were gorging themselves, and again I had the action all to myself.

The only problem, if you can call it that, was too much natural feed. I would make a cast and follow the fly carefully downcurrent, only to have it fall victim to neglect by virtue of numbers, as trout slurped down real mayflies within a few feet of their artificial counterpart.

I landed five browns from ten to fourteen inches, missed at least a dozen that struck short or spat out the fly, and lost two big fish. One broke the leader.

Walking back across the damp meadow in the gathering dusk, I heard in the last twilight songs of the birds that I would return.

*   *   *

Four years before, in the newly minted summer days of June, the action had been frantic. But in the gray days of autumn, the pace on the Wiesent becomes slower and more pensive as astronomical and biological clocks wind down toward winter. Hatches are meager and spotty. The trout, having been fished over all summer, are wise and finicky. It is a season for small, sparse-hackle flies and long, fine leaders. And patience.

A few weeks before, I had planned again to fish the upper

river. But there had been big changes in Doos. When I tried to call Gasthof Heinlein, the number had been disconnected. I called information and got Herr Heinlein's home number. When he answered, his voice sounded different. The imperiousness was gone and there was a tiredness to it, almost a sense of resignation. At first he did not know who I was, but then he remembered. "Ah yes, the American."

I asked what had happened to the hotel. He had sold it, he said. The new owners had converted it into a rest home, a newly popular and lucrative business venture since the advent of higher government subsidies for the elderly. I asked if he did not miss the hotel, after all the years it had been in the family. No, he said. A year before, his wife had died and after that his heart was not in the business anymore. I expressed my regrets and said I could not imagine how hard it must be to lose someone you had spent most of your life with.

"Yes, she was my life's companion, *meine Lebensgefaehrtin*," he said.

I asked Herr Heinlein if he still fished. Yes, he said. When he sold the hotel he had retained the fishing rights. "Those I will not give up."

"Is the fishing still good in the Wiesent?" I asked.

"I can only judge by my own water," he said. "My water has never had more fish. And not only small fish. There are trout in there that weigh seven hundred, eight hundred grams."

I asked how I could set up a fishing trip and he suggested calling Maria at her fly shop. She sold permits for the stretch near Ebermannstadt and could make a reservation for me at a hotel nearby. When I asked if he knew how booked up she was, he demurred.

"We have drifted apart ('*Wir sind etwas auseinander gegangen*'). We have not spoken for some time."

I wished Herr Heinlein the best and said I hoped that we might fish together sometime. This seemed to catch him by surprise, and he paused a moment. Then he said when I came down I should call him. He would be glad to fish with me on his water. We talked a few more minutes, then he said he had to go. A friend of his had died a few days before, and he needed to get ready for the funeral that afternoon.

"It seems that I'm always going to funerals these days," he said.

* * *

It was only a couple of hundred yards from the car to the stream, but still I had to stop and rest when I reached the river-bank. Lately I had been having a lot of headaches, getting fatigued easily, having difficulty concentrating. The week before, my neck had locked up, and the doctor had prescribed an antibiotic and given me little electroshock treatments. I was still taking the antibiotic.

Dave B. and David L., two friends who had arrived earlier in the day, were casting at opposite ends of a long pool. They said the going was slow. Dave B. had caught one seven-inch rainbow, and David L. had none. But still the conditions looked promising. A few insects were coming off the water to do their midair mating dance in the weak sunshine, and while we were talking, three small fish leapt clear of the water. Across the river, the Neideck ruin jutted above the green, wooded hills.

But within half an hour, a gray film slid across the sky, obscuring the sun and dimming the views of the cliffs and forest. An hour and a half later, that film had become a low, drizzling overcast. The insect hatches dwindled and almost stopped. I went through my fly box but found nothing that worked. When we quit because of darkness, I'd had only one hit, on a Royal Coachman. Dave and David had landed three small fish between them.

Back at the hotel, Gus and I relaxed over dinner. But after one beer, my headache came back. I excused myself and went up to the room. I got into bed but could not sleep and lay awake in the early dark, thinking.

With winter just beyond the horizon and the year winding down, autumn—more than any other season—is a time for regrets. For things not done, opportunities not seized. Things you wish could be undone. Tomorrow would be September 30, the last day of trout season. I thought of all the places I had wanted to fish this year: Ireland, Garmisch-Partenkirchen, Denmark again, France, Macedonia. (At least I had made it to Czechoslovakia.) And I thought about other plans that had not panned out: books I had not read, letters I had never written to family and friends, trips and outings with my wife and kids I had not found time for.

Reue was the German word for it: regret, or remorse. Alone now in his old age, what regrets did Herr Heinlein have while watching the Wiesent flow on? In his mind did he follow the limpid waters down to merge into the Main, on down through hills and swales, past cities, towns, and vineyards to Father Rhine, then north through the heart of his homeland to disappear in the cold, blue black waters of the North Sea?

Did he see his own past and future spilling down through the years and did he wish he could hold them back? Was he pleased with his life? What things would he change? Was he sorry he had joined fifty million fellow lemmings in following a madman into the abyss of world war and genocide? Did he wish he had spent less time working with his wife in the kitchen, dining room, and guest quarters of Gasthof Heinlein and more time holding her in the night?

Maybe a lifetime is mostly a balancing out. We all hope that, in the end, contentment outweighs regret.

We follow or lead, face the options, and make our choices—or let them be made for us by circumstances, the wishes and will of others. We hope our mistakes, foibles and failings will be few.

"All politics is local," said one of our great leaders. Likewise, all happiness is personal, not societal or geopolitical. And truly seeking it brings a risk: the possibility of loss and failure. But though rashness is nothing to aspire to, neither are timidity and complacency. For are not mistakes of commission preferable to mistakes of *o*mission? At least you took the chance, made the attempt. Otherwise you wind up like John Marcher in Henry James's story "The Beast in the Jungle": unwilling to take a risk for fear of losing and, in the end, losing all.

I thought of the three women, besides my mother, whom I had truly loved.

With the first, we were callow kids. When we finally grew up, we also—inevitably—grew apart.

The second, a wounded spirit haunted by irredeemable horrors, I thought I could save. When I failed, it tore a hole in my soul that took the better part of a decade to heal. The eschar, I knew, would mark me always.

The third—the only one with whom I truly made a life together—I found by propitious fortune. Our lives were evermore twined, and I knew that if we got the luck we deserved, we would spoil grandchildren together and walk the beach with our trousers rolled.

When I finally dozed off, I slept fitfully.

* * *

The next day dawned cool and overcast. There would be no major hatches until the temperature rose, so we had a leisurely breakfast like good Europeans and got onto the water at nine-thirty.

At streamside, the morning could have been scripted for the last day of trout season: still air and muted gray sky and the vaguely melancholy feel of early German autumn. Beeches and maples flashed their first brilliant reds and golds on the hillsides and above the cliffs. The glassy smooth, deep-flowing Wiesent mirrored the landscape and the wistful mood.

There were a few mayflies coming off the water but no fish rising. I worked hard for more than an hour, casting a variety of flies in different sizes. Now and then wild apples bobbed past, dropped from trees that overhung the river; and masses of water weeds, broken loose and swept along in the current.

Finally, a little before eleven, a scrappy brown smashed a No. 14 Deer-Hair Caddis I had flipped into a swirling backwater. It battled and tugged furiously before being netted, a brilliantly spotted, wild fish. When released, it shot down into the depths like a torpedo.

The next few hours were hard fishing. I tried a dozen or more flies with little success before finally hitting on a No. 14 orange-body, sparse-hackle Mayfly. Fortunately I had half a dozen of these tiny, elegantly tied creations from my Czech friend Milos Sr., for on this day they were the only thing the fish wanted. When we went for lunch at three P.M. I had landed six fish between eight and eleven inches, and I had missed or lost about as many more.

While eating, I remembered that I had not phoned Herr Heinlein. It was too late, now, to fish with him this trip. I felt a little bad about it. He was an old man. I did not know when I would return to the Wiesent, or if he would still be alive when I did.

When we got back on the river, a little after five, a bluish gray haze was settling over the hills and bluffs. I quickly caught a nine-inch rainbow, then a ten-inch brown, on the orange Mayfly. But then the action went slack.

As dusk came the temperature turned cold. The insects all but disappeared, and white puffs from our breath hung suspended for several seconds before dissipating in the still air. I moved upriver to a large pool and managed to raise one tiny fish by casting to a rise near the far shore. When it hit, I missed the strike. That morning I had decided that if I got a good trout I would kill it for dinner. The hotel chef was renowned for the magic he worked with guests' catches. But I had not kept a fish all day, and in less than ten minutes the season would be over.

With the light fading fast, I walked a hundred yards back downstream to the backwater pool. I cast the Mayfly up into the inflow sluice, squinting to watch it bounce down the riffle into the dark, whirling pocket. On the fourth cast, as the fly drifted into the foam of the slip current, it was slammed hard. I set the hook and the rod doubled over, bouncing and bucking as the fish dove, then rocketed into the air.

The trout battled furiously to reach midstream, then shot in toward shore, cartwheeling out of the water a foot from the bank. It tugged and thrashed, trying to get in under the rocks along the bank. But, leaning back on the rod, I was able to force it out, and it shot back toward midstream.

Tiring but still tugging and yanking stubbornly, the fish yielded line a few inches at a time. In another half-minute it was coming more easily as I retrieved line by the foot. Finally I slid it over the net, worn down and turning on its side, and lifted it free of the water. I held it up in the fading light: a beautiful, deep-bodied, fifteen-inch brown with just a hint of the hook jaw it would have if it continued to grow.

I paused to gaze at the trout for several seconds. I was picturing it on a plate, garnished with parsley. The fish worked its mouth and gills, and flipped once in the net.

With the hemostat, I quickly removed the fly from the corner of its jaw and lowered the brown back into the river. It hesitated a moment, fanning its gills and regaining its balance, then shot away in a steep dive toward the bottom of the pool.

I snipped off the fly and reeled in. Trout season was over for another year. Across the river, high atop the bluff, the castle ruin was a jagged shaft etched against the twilight sky.

13

Lost Trout of the Tatra

April 1993

We all have a demon in us.

—Zenon Neumark, resistance fighter

Leslaw Frasik unhooked the grayling, holding it up briefly before slipping it back into the water. Then he turned his back to the wind, put his rod under his right arm, and cupped his hands, bringing them up to his mouth and puffing into them.

Spring in the High Tatra is not always a gentle season. This year it was nearly a month late. Though I was fishing in the third week in April, the temperature was in the low forties and a cold mountain wind was blowing upriver, whipping pellets of snow ahead of it. Along the banks there were still patches of crusty "corn snow" littered with leaves and needles. The high meadows rolling away to the mountains were dotted with the purple and white of wild crocuses, but the grass was still brown and matted.

The Dunajec River was swollen and green with snowmelt. But despite the high water and gray, chilly weather, the fishing was good. Frasik had already landed a half-dozen trout and grayling. I had caught three trout and lost or missed a dozen more.

Now I paused to watch and reflect. My dad would have liked these high, cold mountains, I thought.

Raised barely above the high-tide mark on the elbow of Cape Cod, he had come to love mountains in midlife—Montana's Absarokas and Crazies, the Bighorns of Wyoming, and the Bigelow Range in western Maine, where he moved to escape the Cape's creeping suburbanization. Now he would remain forever in the Bigelows. This was the first trip of my first spring without a father.

Gazing on the High Tatra peaks, my mind wandered to those other mountains, five thousand miles west across an ocean, where snow lay on his grave. I missed him terribly.

Frasik hooked another fish, and I turned to watch him land it.

We had driven up from Krakow in his Lada, following the twisting, two-lane road that snaked into the Gdrsce Mountains beside the Raba River. Along the way we got acquainted, and Frasik kept up a running travelogue: "This small river we are driving on is very good streamer fishing," he said. "The Dunajec is not so good for streamer. Better nymph and dry fly."

This was my first trip to Poland, and I had looked forward to it with anticipation. Three years after the rending of the Iron Curtain, the country was on the move politically, economically, and emotionally. At the urging of President Lech Walesa and in an effort to heal half-century-old wounds, Poland was also set to welcome Holocaust survivors from around the world for the fiftieth anniversary of the Warsaw Ghetto Uprising. I was to cover the commemoration and to interview survivors.

When I began planning the trip, I had called a Dutch fly-fishing friend, Bas Verschoor, in The Hague. Over the previous five years I had waded riffles, rapids, and pools throughout the Alps and the Pyrenees, drifted a fly down a Lowlands burn, roved the peat-bank meanders of Jutland's spring creeks, and counted rise rings in the reflection of a Teutonic fortress. The Tatra would be a sparkling addition to my mindscape of European angling memories.

Fishing in the former Eastern Bloc was still largely an enigma, information being either nonexistent or impossible to obtain. The Polish tourist bureau in Cologne was no help. Nor was Orbis, the official travel agency, in Krakow and Berlin. But Bas had fly-fishing contacts all over Europe. It took him only a minute to retrieve Frasik's name and telephone number from his Rolodex. "I don't know him so well," Bas had said, "but he should be able to help you."

The phone lines to Krakow were problematic. but I finally reached Frasik's wife and we set a time when I would call him late the next evening.

It took four tries to get through—a half-hour later than planned—but Frasik answered on the first ring. His English was quite good and he assured me that there was "yes, good fly fishing" in the Tatra. He would like to show me; I should call when I got to Krakow.

The drive from Darmstadt with Ken was long and enervating—nine hours and four major *Staus* (traffic jams) to the border at Goerlitz. Like the German personality, traffic flow was either frenetic or dead-stopped. Buying *zlotys* (Polish currency) and the hurry-up-and-wait at customs killed another hour, so it was after ten-thirty when the giant Novotel at Wroclaw rolled into view.

An early start the next morning did nothing to improve the

difficult driving on the mostly two-lane roads that wound through towns and cities. There were long backups of trucks, and kamikaze drivers passed anyplace, forcing oncoming cars, fishtailing, onto the shoulder. At mid-afternoon, Krakow's modest skyline finally rose out of the spring fields.

With one of Europe's largest and most carefully preserved old towns, Krakow has been designated one of the world's great historical cities by the United Nations. The heart of the old town is the stadium-size *Rynek Glowny,* or grand square, faintly evocative of Venice's *Piazza san Marco.* On a brisk April afternoon, with a wan sun sinking behind the buildings, the babushkas peddling hand-knitted woolens huddled together against the *Sukienice,* the colonnaded medieval hall at the center of the square. Tourists, sidewalk artists, students, and old-time Krakowers mingled, posed, performed, and went about their business. Pigeons scattered underfoot, hopping ahead or rising in a rush against the sky, to wheel and swoop around the twin Gothic towers of the cathedral, *Kosciol Mariacki.*

Back at the hotel I called Frasik's home but got no answer. When I tried his work number I could not make myself understood in English or German and had to hang up. Ken and I went back out to further explore the city.

At the Orbis office I inquired about fishing and was met with raised eyebrows: no brochures, no license information, no list of guides. "I must tell you," said agent Ivana Lachman, "that this is the first case in my career that someone like to fish." I showed her Frasik's name and asked her to call him. She let it ring a long time, then hung up and dialed the other number. After a few seconds she began speaking in Polish, turned to me and nodded, then talked some more. She handed the phone to me. "He say he already make plans for you."

Frasik was excited, and his English suffered a little. He was working until six, he said, but would pick us up at the hotel later, around seven.

We met outside the lobby and shook hands. I later found out that Frasik was forty-two, but he looked older, with the gray, doughy complexion and bad teeth that mirrored the grinding drudgery, polluted air and water, and poor nutrition so common east of the Oder-Neisse line. But he had a ready smile and eyes that had not lost their spark.

Frasik led us to a waiting car, where we met his boss, Tomasz Stella-Sawicki. He owned a construction company, and Frasik was his construction engineer. They were longtime fishing buddies and were eager to show me their home waters. But first I needed a license. With the dismantling of the old communist bureaucracy, fishing and license regulations were in a state of confusion. Orbis and the hotel had been clueless. But Frasik and Stella-Sawicki were sure I could get one at their club.

First we drove across town to a fly-fishing shop, Test Fly, where I was introduced all around and bought a selection of local favorites: Woolly Buggers, Beadhead nymphs that were close to March Browns, and a few dries. Owner Krysztof Sasula and three other fishermen in the shop were surprised and pleased that an American had come to fish in Poland.

From there, it was a ten-minute drive to the club—a basement with a refrigerator, some furniture, and a file cabinet. Frasik and Stella-Sawicki explained the situation to the club secretary, a bearded guy who eyed me curiously. He asked for my passport and flipped through it, then turned back to my companions. The three of them talked for a few seconds, then Frasik asked if I had another photo of myself. I did, but it was in the hotel.

This was apparently a problem, and they conferred again for a minute or so. The secretary turned up his palms and shrugged his shoulders. Frasik came back to me. "He say you need photo now for . . ." He made a fist and hit the flat of it into his other palm.

"Stamp," I said.

"Yes. But this club close in one half-hour. We have no time."

Stella-Sawicki continued working on the secretary, then

Frasik rejoined him. The bearded guy was relenting a little under the double-barreled onslaught. He gave a quizzical look and rocked his head from side to side. They talked some more, then Frasik came back to me.

"He say okay, you buy license now and promise to put picture." I nodded my head yes and asked how much. My brain went into momentary shock at the figure—750,000 zlotys—but then I remembered just how almighty the U.S. dollar was in the East and did a quick conversion. The exchange rate was about 16,000 to 1, so I was paying forty-five dollars for a year. There were no day or week licenses.

The secretary smiled when he made out the license, stamping it below where the picture would go. He got change from a steel cash box in the file cabinet.

On the ride back across town we talked about fishing and life in Krakow. Frasik and Stella-Sawicki had spent their boyhoods on the Dunajec, and it was still their river, though not what it used to be. "Now it goes down, down," Frasik said. "More nicer is San River; that is our best."

"The main method of fly fishing here is nymph," he said. "Every place where there is grayling we are very successful." As for the trout, "We have lots of fish, but not big fish," Frasik explained. Most, he said, were thirty to thirty-five centimeters [some twelve to fourteen inches]. "The biggest I have caught is about fifty centimeters [almost twenty inches]."

How long had he been fishing? "More than thirty years," Frasik answered. "And more than twenty years only fly fishing, or nearly only fly fishing."

"World champion," Stella-Sawicki said, jerking his thumb toward his construction engineer. Frasik shyly explained: He was a longtime member of the Polish National Fly Fishing Team, which in 1985 had won the world championship on the San, about a four-hour drive east from Krakow. A couple of years later he went to the competition in New Zealand, the trip of a lifetime, paid for by the national fishing organization.

Both men loved their city—its history, its people, its architecture. But for them, like residents of tourist centers anywhere, its historical landmarks were mainly background ambience to everyday life. Frasik could not recall the last time he had visited Wawel Castle, towering above the Vistula; or strolled Planty Park, the green belt that encircles the old town where the city wall used to be. His wife and two little girls spent more time downtown than he did.

"My life is home, office," Frasik said. "And there is some dark parts of living here." One of those, he said, was the pollution from Nowa Huta, the huge blighted complex of smelters, mills, and factories grafted onto the city's eastern edge in the 1950s and '60s.

Despite their affection for the Dunajec, Frasik and Stella-Sawicki spoke of other, better rivers: the Brda, the Gwda, the Pasteka, the Reda. "We have much trout in northern Poland," Frasik said, adding that I should come back when I had more time.

On this trip, Ken and I had only tomorrow. Stella-Sawicki had family obligations, but Frasik would take us to the Dunajec. When they dropped me at the hotel, we agreed to meet at Orbis.

* * *

The next morning was cloudy and cool, with ragged gray strati scudding before an east wind out of Russia. We shook hands in the parking lot and loaded my gear into the Lada, then headed south on Highway 7. Ken followed in our Passat.

For the first several miles, apartment buildings, factories, and a few stores lined the road. Gradually the cityscape gave way to trees, fields, single-family houses. At Myslenice, the road began its tortuous route up the Raba Valley. Down in its canyon, the river was high and gray with silt.

From Rabka we followed Route 95 to Nowy Targ, a modestly

prosperous market center renowned for its handicrafts. We turned onto the local road toward Harklowa, and soon the landscape was dominated by meadows and hillsides grown thick with evergreens. In the spring-damp fields, farm couples with creased and weather-worn faces trudged behind horse-drawn plows or worked the dark brown earth with hand tools.

The narrow pavement wound through towns and villages tucked into valleys or perched on mountain plateaus. Some of these settlements were merely clusters of wood-and-stone houses bisected by a muddy main street. Dogs, goats, and fowl wandered leisurely among the houses and the few cars.

"It is a hard life here," Frasik said. He told of the grinding poverty and the waves of emigration in the late nineteenth and early twentieth centuries. "Many of Polish people living in America, they are coming from this part of Poland," he said. "In every house you can ask, they have somebody in America—cousin, brother, uncle. . . . In Chicago, for example, are many people from this area."

Our first glimpse of the Dunajec came at Waksmund. Even a first-time visitor could tell that the river was high and discolored.

At Ostrowsko we turned down a dirt road that wound between red-brick farmhouses. Once we had to stop while a boy and girl, their arms spread wide, herded four fat, snow white geese ahead of them to a barnyard. The geese moved ahead honking loudly, breasts thrust out and orange bills in the air in that arrogant way they have. In another yard, a couple of tow-headed kids carried a woolly puppy.

Frasik pulled into a cart path and followed a pasture fence to the river. Downstream, fields and pastures sloped down gently to both banks. About a hundred yards upstream on our side, a wooded copse edged close to the river, and beyond the woods were the village and a stone bridge. Ken had pulled up behind Frasik's Lada, and we all got out to survey the country.

Originating as a mountain stream near the Slovak border, the

Dunajec switchbacks northward for some two hundred miles before joining the Vistula north of Tarnow. Frasik's favorite section is the fifty-mile stretch of the river's upper reaches, between Nowy Targ and Tylmanowa. Here the river winds through forests, farms, and villages, as well as Pieninski National Park.

At Ostrowsko, the Dunajec is a big stream, not yet a full-grown river. Frasik surveyed the water and we began bundling up against the wind that was whipping across the fields. I had on long underwear, a wool shirt, a down vest, and a flannel windbreaker, but he handed me a thick wool sweater. Then he set up both rods with tandem streamer rigs: a black Woolly Bugger in front, a silver-and-black version of the same pattern on the rear. "This early spring, it's the best fishing with streamers," he said. Clouds that were beginning to spit snow reinforced the point. Even borderline dry-fly fanatics usually try to avoid exercises in existential futility.

To someone who usually fishes a single floating fly smaller than No. 14, the tandem rigs looked like grappling hooks and nightmare tangles waiting to happen. But they worked like dreams. I watched Frasik and did the same: Cast down and across, let the streamers swing down and in with the current, then slowly strip them back.

He caught the first fish, a ten-inch brown, then the second and the third. After standing thigh-deep in the current for ten minutes, I was glad for the extra sweater. Waders, wool pants, and long johns only distanced and delayed the chill. My hands were stiff and going numb from the cold. Ken had wandered back to the Passat, and I could see he had the motor running.

Because I was used to seeing fish hit a dry fly, I found it easy to mis-time the strikes. At least, that was the excuse I made to myself when I was late on the first two gentle taps. If you are inexperienced or rusty, it is like feeling your way across a dark room, not knowing when you will touch the wall. On the third tap I struck hard and was fast to my first Dunajec trout. It fought like an eight-inch trophy, and when I released it, the fish's gleaming copper underbelly and brilliant spots contrasted sharply with the muted hues of river, field, and sky.

A heavy snow squall blew up, the hard pellets stinging our faces so that we had to turn away from the wind. Frasik caught trout steadily. Not big ones but healthy, plump Tatra trout. He moved slowly downstream while I edged my way up. Near the woods a feisty twelve-incher surged from under a brushy overhang. It hit with a hard tug instead of a tap, and I thought it was a bigger fish. My fingers would not work after I landed the fish, so I used the hemostat to remove the hook.

At lunch we sat in the Lada out of the wind to eat our sandwiches, washed down with steaming coffee.

Ken was gone with the Passat, and I figured he had driven back to the village to look for photo opportunities. It took a few minutes for my hands to thaw and the chill to leave my legs. I asked about life under the Communists, and Frasik said it was not life, just existence. "We have just started the life three years before," he said. Now things were beginning to get better, and he was hopeful for his daughters.

But Frasik was concerned about his avocation. A combination of factors—pollution, clear-cutting of forests, towns drawing on the rivers for municipal water supplies—had caused the fishing to deteriorate over the last fifteen years. Most harmful had been the logging because forests help the soil retain rainwater for longer periods, providing a reliable flow for the rivers. "Now," he said, "it's going down, down very quickly."

After we finished eating, the wind was still whistling, but we had come to fish. Because the action had slowed in the last half-hour before lunch, Frasik said we should switch to weighted nymphs, fished singly. He favored Beadheads because they sank rapidly. Polish regulations allowed fishing with two flies but prohibited any additional weight on the leader—no split shot, no strike indicators. "So we learned to put much lead into the fly," he said.

We waded back out and I watched a master go to work. This was short-line fishing, with seldom more than fifteen or twenty feet of line out, including the leader. There was no real casting involved. Frasik flipped the line partway upstream, following it down with the rod. If it stopped drifting, he struck. Sometimes he snagged a rock or a weed. But often he set the hook and was fast to a fish. Now they were mostly grayling.

It took me a few minutes to get the hang of it, maybe because the take was softer than on the tandem rigs. I missed a bunch of hits, then caught another trout. I finally landed a sleek thirteen-inch grayling. Coming out of the cold water with its scent of thyme, the fish was redolent of a smorgasbord entree on ice. I examined it for a few seconds before releasing it, tipping the grayling like a hologram to watch the changes in its quicksilver-and-rainbow iridescence.

Eventually the snow squall tapered off, but the wind did not lose its bite. I had to keep stopping to blow on my hands or put them up inside my shirt. Once I paused to watch a muskrat. It swam close in along the brushy shore for twenty-five or thirty feet, then disappeared into the bank. Twenty minutes later we headed back to the car, broke down the rods, and drove back out through the village. Ken had returned and followed close behind. A quarter-mile away, cresting a low, grassy hill, a family rode a wooden wagon home from the outlying fields.

Three or four miles downstream from Ostrowsko, the Dunajec begins to live up to the promise of its watershed. The river broadens, deepens, and gathers force as it enters a wooded gorge and slips down the steepening gradient toward Tylmanova.

We parked in a roadside turnout and climbed down a steep bank. The river was now a hundred feet across, full of riffles and mini-rapids. In the swollen current, its gravel and cobble bed called for careful footwork. Frasik led the way across, picking a ford where the water shallowed out to mostly calf- or knee-deep. The struggle of crossing the river left me winded. Despite the

exercise, however, I was freezing cold and had a throbbing headache. Ken, with no boots, remained on the far bank.

Frasik and I fished together for fifteen minutes, then I headed
up to slower water. My host began working his way down toward
some wide rapids where the river made a sharp curve to the right.

As I fished my way upstream, I thought again of my dad. Of
all the time we spent together, the hours on the water were always
the best. Casting into a blaze orange autumn sunrise on Nantucket Sound while hungry stripers and blues tore into baitfish.
Watching the stars wink out in the lightening summer sky over
Chatham Harbor, the sea transformed from charcoal to ash to
silver blue as the boat glided out into Pleasant Bay. A chilly November evening, drifting on the tide in Herring River while we
filled a wicker basket with thumping flounder. The big brown he'd
had mounted for his den, a fish he caught trolling a streamer in
Cliff Pond. I thought, too of how, standing side by side, or sitting
in the same boat using the same bait, he always outfished me.

Mainly we used spinning gear, though we turned to boat rods
when we trolled for big cow stripers in Cape Cod Bay.

When I fell in love with fly fishing, in my twenties, I became
a proselytizer and wanted my dad to learn it, too. He liked the
idea, even talked about fishing out West together, but somehow
we never followed through on it. We were always working or traveling at different times. Mostly it was my fault. I had a more flex-
ible lifestyle, and I should have made room in my schedule. When
I moved to Europe, the idea got put on hold. The previous August, my dad and I had finally fly-fished together. He had retired
a few months before, and he and my stepmother had moved to his
old deer-hunting camp in Maine. I traveled from Europe with my
family to visit.

My dad's sudden move, coming on the heels of a bitter break
with my brother over the family business, had surprised me. I had
thought of my father as a dyed-in-the-wool Cape Codder, with
sand in his shoes and salt water running through his veins. De-

spite his love of the mountains, which had grown over the years on his many hunting and fishing trips, I thought Cape Cod would always be home to him. I asked him about it during our visit.

"Cape Cod's nothin' like it used to be," he said. "It's buildin' up everywhere. A lot of the places we used to hunt and fish are gone. And I just got tired of all these old fahts movin' down from the city and tryin' to tell everybody else how to live. You can't even walk your dog on the damn beach any more."

He had bought a modest 6-weight fiberglass fly rod and a boxful of local flies. He had tried it out a couple of times, caught some brook trout, and now had a spot in mind he wanted to check out.

We got up early in the morning, while everybody else was still sleeping, and left a little before sunrise. After driving about twelve miles, we turned onto a logging road that climbed up Crocker Mountain, alongside the Carrabassett River. It was an old road, with gullies and washouts, and we had to drive slowly. About six miles in, we stopped and got out of the truck.

I was glad I had put on a sweatshirt and jacket. Already the nights were cool in Maine's western mountains. The birches were beginning to turn gold on the upper slopes. On this morning, the smell of hemlock and spruce was in the air, and in the distance a red squirrel chattered shrilly. As we were rigging up, a couple of ravens flew over, squawking brazenly with the call that is as appealing as fingernails on a blackboard.

The water was down in a little ravine off to the left, and we had to fight through deadfalls and a spruce thicket to reach it. Ten miles downstream, the Carrabassett was a fair-size river, but up here it was a mountain rill, no more than six feet across. It was heavily shaded and full of tight pockets between big, smooth rocks. Many of the rocks were covered with a thick carpet of green moss.

The stream was so narrow, the ravine so tight with trees, that it was not possible to make a conventional cast. But we caught trout. Lots of little brook trout. We fished by standing back five or six feet from the edge and dapping the water with McGintys and Hornbergs, big ungainly flies that seemed about half as big as the trout. They bounced down through the pockets, and spun and swirled in the eddies like toy sailboats. And the tiny trout smashed them. Not one of the fish was over eight inches, and the smallest was four. They fought like dervishes and squirted away into the slender flow when we released them.

"They're all fulla piss and vinegar," my dad said.

I remember how happy I was that we were together on that morning in that place, with the sun slanting through the trees, the water purling down the mountain, and the air redolent of evergreens. Life is made up mostly of little moments, I thought; lovely, coruscant flashes in time, evanescent and numinous, snatched from the stream of life just as the tiny brookies we were plucking from the Carrabassett. And if, like the trout, these moments were released undamaged, we might someday return to catch them anew.

We did not say much on the way back, but it was not out of reluctance or an inability to communicate. Words just did not seem necessary. We did talk about going fishing again the next morning, but in the end it fell through because my stepmother had made other plans.

The day my family and I left, I helped my dad with some painting and yard work. The last time I saw him, he was standing among the tall firs and hemlocks, waving as we drove away. Four months later, on Christmas Eve, came the call. A bereft little boy's third-grade nightmare had finally come true, as I always knew it would.

There is no worse trip than going home to bury a loved one. It was the dead of winter in Maine. The lakes were sealed under thick sheets of ice, the woods and fields covered deep with snow. The ground was as hard as iron, and at first it was not certain there would be a burial. But the backhoe operator was able to break through the frozen crust, and the next day, standing with my wife and kids, I watched my dad lowered into the bitter, cold earth. When it was done, I stepped to the edge of the hole and dropped in the note my seven-year-old son had put in my hand. It fell atop the polished cherry casket. "Goodbye Grampa," it said, "I love you forever."

Before they walked away from the grave, my brothers and sister and stepmother tossed in handfuls of dirt, but I could not bring myself to do it.

I had a lifetime of memories of my dad. But what I saw in my mind's eye on this cold Tatra day was him lying in that box. And his hands, those rough, meaty hands that once flexed and gripped with power, hands made for hefting tools and tousling hair, now gone stiff and shrunken, skin stretched over carpals, resting on purple satin.

After an hour of nymphing the pockets and brushy edges, I had caught only one trout, a skinny six-incher that put up a sluggish fight. Three-hundred yards above where we had crossed, a garbage dump spilled down the bank on the road side of the river. Papers, cans, and trash were mixed with broken plumbing fixtures, appliances, and threadbare furniture.

I worked my way back downstream and met Frasik at the ford. When I got to midstream, my legs felt shaky and I had to stop, panting. Here the current was at its swiftest—thigh deep—and I thought I might slip and go down if I did not rest. Frasik had almost reached the bank, but he waded back and stood on my downstream side, putting one hand up under my left armpit to support me. We crossed together.

When we reached the bank, I sat down on a log to catch my breath.

"I thought you weren't gonna make it," Ken said.

"I had some doubts, myself," I said. "I can't figure out where my stamina went."

I asked Frasik about the dump. He looked embarrassed and

angry. The dumping was illegal, but it happened in many places and was a hard thing to stop. "It is a shame," he said. "I don't fish here for many years. I don't like it so much because it is not so pretty."

Ten minutes later, we loaded up the cars again and continued on. As we followed the winding road downriver, Frasik told more about the region's geography, history, and culture. As he talked, snow showed at intervals in the woods and on north-sloping hillsides.

At Deebno we passed one of the oldest wooden churches in Poland, dating to the fourteenth century. In another village—a scattering of wooden hovels—gypsy children, filthy and ill clad, huddled around a campfire in a muddy front yard. It looked even rougher than the grinding poverty we had seen elsewere, and I asked about that.

"They don't want work," Frasik said.

After about fifteen miles we began to come down out of the high country, and the valley broadened out. On the floodplain were homes and farms that looked better kept. And in the towns, stores and houses had clean paint and landscaped yards with many crocuses showing.

It was late afternoon when we stopped beside the Dunajec at Tylmanova. Frasik took a deep breath and surveyed the water, the countryside. It was a spot he loved, with great numbers of his favorite fish. "This is the main center of grayling fishing," he said. "I think every fisherman in Poland knows it."

"Looks fishy, all right," Ken said.

Here the river was broad, a hundred and fifty feet at least, and depthless with promise. But this day it was swollen to its banks and threatening to spill over. Even in summer, Frasik said, the Dunajec was a powerful, deep, difficult river to fish. Today we would only be able to skirt the edges.

For nearly an hour we worked our way along the bank, probing the pockets and pools with Beadheads. I thought I had one hit, but it may have been a snag. Frasik raised nothing. When we got into the car he was let down and apologetic. He wished I could come in summer.

But I was not disappointed. I was happy to see the country-side, catch some fish, and wade a new river. And there was more. Frasik had shared his day and what he had: knowledge and com-panionship, of course, but also his gear, his clothes, his food. The gas alone would set him back several days' pay. As we drove along the river I thanked him for his generosity, his friendship to a stranger.

We talked of our families, and his face lit up. My little boy and girl were close in age to his daughters, and we both hoped they could meet sometime. I invited him to bring them for a visit.

We came into another village, and Frasik slowed the car. He pointed to a squat house with a barn looming behind it. The win-dows on the house seemed too small and the barn's high sides were streaked dark gray where tiles had broken or fallen from the edge of the roof. Frasik told me that he had recently purchased several antique, split-cane rods there. Then he began describing the Dunajec as it used to be.

Before World War II the river was a mecca for British fly fishermen. They came in pursuit of its legendary sea trout, a dis-tinctive variety of sea-run browns. Born among the peaks along the Czech border, these fish slipped away as smolts down the roaring Dunajec to the Vistula, gliding on powerful currents across the broad expanse of Poland to spend most of their lives in the chilly, dark depths of the Baltic.

When they returned a couple of years later to spawn in the rock channels and gravel beds of their birth, they were powerful, silver-sided fish—sometimes upward of twenty pounds. Because they were spectacular fighters and migrated such great distances, the Dunajec sea trout were regarded as almost a subspecies of salmon.

Like the fish, the fishermen returned year after year, often to the same guesthouse in the same village. Instead of hauling their gear back and forth from Britain, many left rods, reels, and other equipment with guesthouse owners from one season to the next. They knew they would be back next year, just as they knew the great silvery fish would again struggle a thousand miles upstream to the place of their birth.

The beginning of the end for this angling idyll came in September 1939 with the invasion of Hitler's *Wehrmacht*. The five-year firestorm of war, followed by the descent of the Iron Curtain across Eastern Europe, doomed the Dunajec sea trout. The final blow was the Stone-Age mentality of Communist Party central planners, who dammed, poisoned, and paved the fish to extinction in the 1950s and '60s.

Decades later, finely crafted rods turned up in rural sheds and attics, dusty and long-neglected mementos of a once-great fishery.

When Frasik finished the story, his voice was low. We did not speak for a few minutes, but then I asked about Poland's future. Along the main highways and outside the cities, I had seen stirrings of change: the rafters and beams of homes going up; restaurants, shops, and businesses that looked new or refurbished; fresh pavement on roads. How fast did he think change would come, and was it progress?

Frasik did think things were getting better but said there were some problems. Not everybody was doing good things. "There is this banker," he said. "He come here and he get much money. Millions and millions." Now the banker had disappeared, and many people had lost their money. It was rumored, Frasik said, that the man was in hiding in Israel. He gave me a brief, sidelong glance.

"We have much Jewish people here now, you know? They come back for the ceremonies."

Yes, I said, there were many visitors, and hotel rooms were tight. Ken and I had been lucky to get two.

"These Jewish people, they . . . some have much money,"

Frasik went on. "They have nice clothes, many things Polish people not have. So there is some people angry."

I did not say anything. Why do people have to let you down? I thought. Why do they always have to let you down?

I have always thought of myself as a Heinz (fifty-seven varieties) American rather than a hyphenated American. My mother's family heritage was French, Native American, and English—my umpty-ump great-grandmother and grandfather Bassett arrived in 1621 on the *Fortune,* the supply ship for the *Mayflower.* But on my dad's side, the genealogy was a blank. Because he was an orphan, my father had no memory of his birth family; he knew only the orphanage and, later, the foster family he grew up with. But from the Boston neighborhood where he was born and from our last name, there was a good chance his parents were Jewish.

At Zabrzezda, we turned off the valley road and headed back into higher country, away from the river. Night was coming, and already the hills and trees were only dark outlines against the sky. Frasik turned on the headlights. When we rounded a curve, the beams swept the edges of woods and thickets. Once a roe deer bounded into the lights, captured for a split second as if by a strobe. With another bound it disappeared back into the forest. We did not say much till Lubien, where we got back on Highway 7.

North of Myslenice, two cars pulled out to pass us on a blind curve. Frasik muttered an epithet in Polish and edged over onto the shoulder, allowing the other vehicles to squeeze between us and an oncoming truck. He hated these kinds of drivers, he said, they were a danger to everyone.

"I think in Poland is the biggest number of killed people to compare to numbers of cars," he told me.

At the hotel we shook hands all around and said good-bye. In the sky to the east, the lights of Krakow reflected off low clouds and the smoke from the smelters in Nowa Huta. Thirty miles to the west, I knew, were the now-cold smokestacks of Oswiecim, better known by its German name: Auschwitz.

* * *

WARSAW, Poland—In a bone-chilling wind and under a twi-light sky mottled with black clouds, thousands of spectators heard Pol-ish President Lech Walesa, Israeli Prime Minister Yitzhak Rabin, and Vice President Al Gore pay homage to the few thousand Jewish freedom fighters who stunned the world and their Nazi oppressors by taking up arms a half-century ago.

The three spoke late Monday in front of the Monument to the He-roes of the Warsaw Ghetto, flanked by its flaming twin sculpted meno-rahs.

In his opening speech, Walesa hailed the men, women, and children who "fought heroically . . . for the right to die with dignity."

Though they had no chance for victory—only a few hundred of the estimated 40,000 to 60,000 inhabitants survived the subsequent mass executions and deportations to death camps—Walesa asserted that "your cause prevailed. That is why today we stand on this spot."

Gore, in a speech that drew on biblical quotes, hailed the "few hun-dred poorly armed freedom fighters [who] fought on against impossible odds, with their greatest weapon: the courage of a righteous cause."

He said the uprising "shines in our consciousness like a pole star of the human spirit."

After the speeches and the laying of three wreaths, a sound-and-light simulation of the uprising began with the dousing of lights and the wail of an air-raid siren. The sounds of machine-gun fire and ex-plosions, the blood red glow of spotlights on trees and the thick billows of smoke rising from the monument caused some in the gathering to break down in tears.

Among the thousands of guests and spectators at the memorial cer-emony were uprising veterans, Holocaust survivors, and their offspring from around the world.

Eva Kupfert, from Montreal, who survived the uprising as well as Nazi death camps at Maydenek, Auschwitz, and Bergen-Belsen, was so moved by the ceremony that, "I started to cry terribly. I was shaking."

Kupfert was nineteen on April 19, 1943, when the sound of gunfire and explosions signaled that "a few Jews started to fight."

She said the ceremony made her "come back completely with my memories to that day."

Zenon Neumark, a physicist and engineer from Los Angeles, survived the war by living a double life. For nearly six years he passed as an ethnic Pole while fighting with ZOB, the Jewish underground organization. Blond hair and blue eyes, combined with false papers, were his salvation.

Though he hated the terrible malignancy of the Holocaust, Neumark said he did not hate the German people or the Poles, many of whom reacted with "hostile indifference" to the Jews' plight.

"In all the tragedy I did find many kind people . . . Jews, Germans, Poles," Neumark said. "I think any nation has the ingredient for barbarism. . . . We all have a demon in us."

The uprising ended May 8, 1943, with the near-total destruction of Warsaw's Jewish quarter, at one time the largest in Europe, with some 400,000 inhabitants. At the outbreak of World War II, one out of every ten Poles—more than three million—was a Jew. The country's Jewish population today is estimated at between 20,000 and 30,000.

The memorial ceremony marked the culmination of months of effort by the Polish government and Jewish officials worldwide.

14

In the Shadows

October 1993–November 1994

But he remembered the time when he stood alone,
When to be and delight to be seemed to be one,
Before the colors deepened and grew small.

—Wallace Stevens, "Anglais Mort A Florence"

For nine months my health had been broken, and I had been barely able to function. But lately I had made a small rally, and I was determined to get back on the water. I had not fished in nearly a year, and I missed it so much that the longing was in my bones. Nearly every night I dreamed about standing in a trout stream.

283

The previous October I had ended up in a German hospital, capping an endless string of misdiagnoses, mistreatments, and relapses.

The first manifestation had been the fatigue. It began with the "weekend flu" that came after I fished the Jihlava and Svratka. The lassitude never left, and innumerable other indications ensued.

My left elbow swelled to the size of a softball, red and hot to the touch. The doctor in our German village gave me a week's worth of antibiotics, and slowly the elbow got better. Then my neck got so sore and stiff it locked up. I could not turn my head. The doctor gave me a week's worth of another antibiotic, plus electric muscle stimulus treatments, and slowly the neck got better.

I was so exhausted all the time that I could barely make it to work. At home I had no energy for household tasks or playing with my kids. Broken items went unfixed, renovations remained unfinished. My infallible memory—an asset I had counted on my whole life, both professional and private—had vanished. I could not remember where I put things, the names of old friends, plans I made. Sometimes I juxtaposed words when I spoke. I had trouble doing the simplest math. I had been a champion speller since the second grade, but I began having to look up four- and five-letter words in the dictionary.

It became harder and harder to write. News stories I should have finished in half a day took two days. Features I should have finished in two days took a week. I began to stutter when I spoke German. For no reason, my heart would sometimes start racing out of control, continue on for several minutes, then return to normal. Sometimes it skipped a couple of beats. Often I could not read for days at a time because my eyes would not focus.

In the hospital the mystery was finally solved: The tick that had hitched a ride on me from Czechoslovakia, the insignificant arachnid I had taken so lightly, had injected poisonous parasites. Slowly but insidiously over the previous year and a half, they had multiplied, settling in my joints, muscles, and central-nervous system.

The disease was rampant in Czechoslovakia, the young doctor said, and was not always curable. He prescribed four weeks of powerful intravenous antibiotics. I would be in the hospital through October and on into November. But the following week he was overruled by the pompous old head of the clinic, and the therapy was cut off after two weeks. I was told that I was cured and sent home.

By early December I was bed-bound, slipping deeper into a black hole of debilitating illness that seemed to have no bottom. I had been away from my native country almost fifteen years, but I had always planned to return. And all that time I was sure that, when I did, it would be to a new future.

When I first met my wife, she asked where I planned to go when I left Europe. "Montana," I said. It was still my dream to live in the West, in wild country with big mountains, big rivers, and big trout. Libby had thought that was a neat idea but, though I did not know it then, this plan caused some consternation for my future mother-in-law. "Montana?" she said. "Montana? He's not the man for you." After we married, Libby told me and we laughed about it.

My goal had become our goal. We would share another adventure together. Libby had always wanted a horse, and there was no better place to own one. But now our dream future in Big Sky Country seemed as improbable as a condemned man's clemency hopes. For the first time, I thought I might never return to the United States. Or that I would return in a box.

I had always known that, as much as I loved Europe, it was not and never would be my homeland. I could not, would not die in a foreign land. Libby made all the arrangements to leave, and a week later a friend drove us to the airport in Frankfurt. I was pushed onto the plane in a wheelchair, and I flew to Boston with my family.

At my in-laws' house in Connecticut I began another

treatment with massive doses of intravenous antibiotics. At the end of two weeks, I began feeling better. After a month, I could get up and go for walks. I could read again. The joint pains had largely disappeared.

The doctor prescribed follow-up therapy with oral antibiotics for at least six months. But after several weeks I got a bad stomach bug and, blaming it on the pills, stopped taking them.

After nearly three months, we returned to Europe, and I went back to work part-time. I was not my old self but was better than I had been, and, sick of needles and pills, I again put off the follow-up therapy. Everybody gets sick, I thought, but eventually everybody gets better. Slowly I got worse until I had to stop working again.

Then another doctor gave me another antibiotic, again for a couple of weeks. I began to feel better and made plans with my buddy Vic to travel to the Black Forest. I had to get back into a stream, had to catch a trout. But when the antibiotic ran out, again I slid back. I had to cancel out on the trip.

A couple of days later Vic called. He knew I could not make it to the Black Forest, but he had gotten a line on a stream just fifteen miles away, the Gersprenz, in the village of Babenhausen. A buddy of his had caught a trout there the week before and had given Vic the name of the fishing club where we could buy day permits. It was not a big or spectacular river, he said, but it did have stocked trout. And other fish that would take a fly. Maybe we could try it together on the weekend.

I begged off but Vic was insistent. "Aw come on. I'll drive and I'll get you right up to the bank. All you'll have to do is stand there and catch the fish. We can be there inside a half-hour, and I'd really like to try it."

I had driven through Babenhausen many times, and I could not imagine that Vic had a burning urge to fish there. It was a farming village of drab, nondescript buildings and run-of-the-mill farms. I could not recall seeing a river, but the town was on the edge of the Odenwald (literally, Odin's Forest), a thickly forested region that had several trout streams.

Throughout the whole health ordeal Vic had been one of the kindest and most thoughtful of my friends, and I knew he was feigning enthusiasm for my sake. He understood how much I ached to cast a fly again, to watch a fish rise to it, and to feel the throb in the rod when it took. Missing the Black Forest trip had put me in a black mood.

"Okay Vic," I said, "you're on."

Sunday I almost called him to beg off again. But I did not. When he arrived a little after eleven A.M. he carried my gear to the car. On the way to the river I wasn't sure I could do it. We stopped in the village, and Vic bought our permits. Then we turned down a side road and finally onto a rutted mud-and-clay cart path that skirted the edge of a bright yellow rape field. In a few hundred yards, the dirt way edged up close to a low levee. Vic pulled over, and we got out and walked to the dike.

I looked at my friend, and he looked at me. This was not what we had expected. The water was flowing all right, but this was not a scene that would come to mind at the words "trout stream." The bed was channelized, the banks muddy and worn. At the edges, the flow was brown and viscid. In mid-channel it was diluted to the color of watered-down cola. What it was, was a drainage ditch.

"He said he got his fish right about here," Vic piped up. "Said it was fourteen inches."

We both knew this was no trout stream. It was a put-and-take holding water for the local club, a place that was stocked and fished out every few weeks. Trout could not survive long in such conditions and would certainly never reproduce. But neither of us said anything. We geared up.

Vic helped me down the bank, and I stood in the shallows. I expected to sink into mud, but luckily the bottom was gravel and stones. The act of casting quickly winded me, and I had to stop. I began to sweat, my head throbbed, and I felt nauseated. My joints ached. I sat down on the bank and watched Vic gamely trying to make a fishing day out of it.

"You let me know when you're tired," he said. "We can ride around and look for a better spot. Or we can go home."

"No, just resting," I said. After five minutes I got up to cast some more.

Ten more minutes and we gave up on the spot. I dragged myself to the car and flopped onto the seat. Vic backtracked to the paved road, then turned down another cart path that followed the waterway downstream. After a quarter-mile we came to a narrow bridge that crossed to the other side. Vic drove over it and parked.

"This looks like a better spot to me. What do you think?"

"Yeah, let's try it."

Here the creek edged up to a hardwood forest along the right bank. Some of the trees were forty or fifty feet tall, with expansive canopies that shaded the water. On the left bank, fields of head-high fodder corn grew right up to the levee. The water had slowed and cleared up as it broadened out in a series of pools.

I was still sick to my stomach and my head throbbed. My neck and hips ached, my shoulder hurt when I cast, and I felt dizzy. But I stood in the shade of a linden and flipped out the line, waiting for a trout that I knew, like Godot, would never come. Still, irrationally, hope surged anew when I got a hit. But when I brought in the fish, it was a listless five-inch *Doebel*, a chub. Momentarily I trudged back to the car to sit down. Vic arrived a few minutes later.

"Sorry, I just can't cut it," I said. "You go ahead and fish."

"Hey, no way, bud. How about if we just ride a little more and look for another spot. See if you feel any better."

I did not, and shortly we headed for home. On the ride back I dozed off and on. And I came to a realization. Finally, despite months and months of fierce resistance to the obvious, I had to admit it to myself: My life as I had lived it was more than changed; it was gone. Most days I was in bed or on the couch. On good days I could barely walk out of the house to the mailbox.

A few weeks before, another German doctor, a youngish woman with a compassionate mien, had spelled it out for me: "This disease has compromised your immune system. If you want to get well, you must move somewhere where there is no winter and the air is clean." After fifteen years in Europe, it was finally time to go.

This was not the way it was supposed to be. Libby and I had talked about it many times. When we made the decision, we would take a couple of months in the summer and travel as a family. I would show her and the kids some of the places I had been, and we could say a proper good-bye to our life overseas. That would make it easier to move on.

The situation was filled with absurd irony. I had contracted a life-changing disease doing some of the things I most loved: exploring a new land, camping, writing, and questing for trout.

Travel, my lifelong avocation and then my cherished profession, was now part of my past. No more, I knew, would I ski the glacier at Zermatt under the heartbreak-blue summer sky. No more would I tramp the streets of Copenhagen, Moscow, Barcelona, Athens. No more would I watch the greylag geese coming out of the dawn over Ruegen. And no more would I wade Europe's storied streams, the rivers of shadow and sun.

Libby began making arrangements to sell our house and ship our possessions to the United States. But over the next weeks my health deteriorated, and once more I found myself lying in a hospital bed, staring up at the white ceiling.

I could see that my kids were scared when they came to visit. It was getting hard for them to remember when I had been healthy. My little girl, Katrina, who was six, made a mini-get-well card. On the front was a picture of both of us, drawn in red felt-tip pen. She was waiting with open arms as I walked toward her carrying my hospital suitcase. In the balloon coming out of her mouth was the word "Daddy!" Inside, the card read, "Dear Daddy, I want you to come home. I love you."

This time I could not stand the hospital for long. Against the doctors' advice, I signed myself out and went home to my own bed.

While Libby did all the hard work, I vegetated.

Finally the house was sold. Most of the furniture was gone, and we were living with a few borrowed chairs, mattresses, and cooking utensils. It was a cold German autumn, dreary with ice fog and rain. So this was how it would end. Not with a bang of jolly parties and farewell jaunts to Paris, Venice, Warsaw, and Prague, but with a whimper of illness and invalidism.

I spent the last few days sleeping or lying on the couch in our house—the house where Libby and I had started our life together and brought our babies home to, where we had become a family, the only house we had ever shared. I could only stare out the window at the dismal sky.

Two days before we were to leave, it was clear that I would not be able to get on the plane. The people who had bought our house drove me back to the hospital. While I was being examined, probed, poked, and scanned, my family had to move into a hotel.

Two weeks later, I had regained enough strength to make it to Frankfurt and board the flight to Florida. Looking out the window as the plane took off, I watched the countryside—forests, fields, rivers, and towns—grow smaller, then disappear as the jet climbed into the clouds.

In my mind, I said good-bye. Good-bye to the splendid cities and mundane burgs, to the mountains, hills, and plains. Good-bye to the lovely Irati, to the storied Traun. Good-bye to the frigid Dunajec and the bonnie Clyde. Goodbye to the Wiesent, with its castles and caves. Good-bye to the Skjern and its windblown moors. Good-bye to the waters that flowed through a third of my life.

Epilogue

It is good to recognize certain facts that simply will not change, without regretting that they are as they are and without judging them.

—Rainer Maria Rilke, *The Notebooks of Malte Laurids Brigge*

The clichés are limitless: Every cloud has a silver lining. Good things often come out of bad. The end of something is always the beginning of something else.

In the worst times, such sayings seem irrelevant, even fatuous.

Now, sitting here on Sanibel Island, a three-minute walk from white-sand beaches and ocean swells, I can look back dispassionately at the wrenching dislocation that brought me and my family to the shores of the Gulf of Mexico.

There have been hard times. Years, even. And I still have limits, but so does everyone. We learn to live with them.

I have not returned to the streams of the Alps, the Pyrenees, or the High Tatra. But I have learned a thing or two about saltwater fly rods and about streamers that fool snook along the Gulf shoreline, sea trout over the turtlegrass flats, and redfish in the mangroves.

I never gave up on my Big Sky dreams. Last summer I waded the Beaverhead, the Big Hole, the Jefferson, the Yaak, the Ruby. And others. After all, I was born to fish. But those are stories for another book.

Glossary

Advent (G)—The pre-Christmas season. Starts four Sundays before Christmas.

Aerschle (G)—A small, sparse-hackle dry fly with a blaze orange spot on the tail.

Altweibersommer (G)—Old wives' summer, roughly analogous to our Indian summer.

Augenweide (G)—A treat for the eyes. Literally, a meadow for the eyes.

Autobahn (G)—The German superhighway system, on most sections of which there are no speed limits.

Autoroute (F)—A French superhighway where tolls are charged.

Backforelle (G)—Brown trout.

Backsaibling (G)—Brook trout (literally, brook char).

Bauernbrot (G)—A type of hearty, dark rye bread.

Bauern und Arbeiter Staat (G)—Farmers and Workers State, term used by the former East Germany to describe itself.

Beinhaus (G) Charnel house, literally bone house.

Beleidigung (G)—A social offense, a faux pas.

Berghuette (G)—Mountain hut. Often with the facilities of a mini-lodge.

Berglandschaft (G)—Mountain landscape or region.

Bildungsreise (G)—Journey of education or self-discovery.

Blauer Burgunder (G)—A German red wine, similar to Burgundy.

Broetchen (G)—A type of breakfast roll, hard on the outside, with a chewy, soft inside.

Completo (S)—Full, or no vacancy.

Demiblonde (F)—A light, golden French beer.

Donde (S)—Where.

Deutsche Alpenstrasse (G)—The German Alpine Road, which winds through the southern Bavarian Alps.

Enzian (G)—Mountain gentian.

Export (G)—A full-bodied German beer, brewed with more malt than *Pils*. Served in a mug.

Extranjero (S)—Foreigner.

Faesschen (G)—The diminutive form of Fass, or wooden barrel.

Feinbrand (G)—The finished product in the distillation process for alcoholic spirits.

Fernweh (G)—The longing for faraway places.

Flan (S)—The rich, creamy custard popular in Spain.

Fleischwurst (G)—A pork sausage, usually served cold as sandwich meat, similar to bologna.

Gemuetlichkeit (G)—A relaxed, friendly, and inviting atmosphere.

Gewitter (G)—Thunderstorm.

Glassklar (G)—Crystal clear.

Gluehwein (G)—Hot, mulled wine.

Goetterddaemmerung (G)—Twilight of the Gods.

Gutbuergerliche Kueche (G)—Home-style cooking.

Heimatsort (G)—Home region.

Hola (S)– Hello.

Helles (G)—The light, golden lager beer popular in southern Bavaria.

Irgendwo (G)—Somewhere.

Jaegerschnitzel (G)—Pork tenderloin with mushroom sauce. Literally, hunter's cutlet

Kaffeepause (G)—Coffee break.

Keiner weiss bescheid (G)—Nobody knows anything.

Krone (C)—The Czech monetary unit.

Kuhdorf (G)—Literally, cow village, a derogatory term for a small farming town.

Kurzentrum (G)—Spa.

Lebensgefaehrtin (G)—Life's companion.

Licencias de pesca (S)—Fishing license.

Luftkurort (G)—Fresh-air spa.

Mark (G)—The German monetary unit.

Muy grande (S)—Very big.

Muy bueno (S)—Very good.

Monte Perdido (S)—A high peak in the central Spanish Pyrenees. Literally, Lost Mountain.

Ossi (G)—Eastie, a resident of the former East Germany.

Peces (S)—Fish.

Peseta (S)—The Spanish monetary unit.

Petri-Heil! Petri-Dank! (G)—Traditional angler's greeting in German-speaking countries. Rough translation: hail the angler, angler's thanks.

Pils (G)—Pilsner, a foamy, slightly bitter beer made with extra hops. Served in a goblet, not a mug.

Prost (G)—A drinker's toast, cheers.

Pyrenees Orientales (S)—The eastern Pyrenees.

Raadhus (D)—City Hall.

Regenbogenforelle (G)—Rainbow trout.

Renovierungsbeduerftig (G)—In need of renovation.

Reue (G)—Regret, remorse.

Rohbrand (G)—The first product in the distillation process for alcoholic spirits.

Servus (G)—A salutary greeting used mainly in Austria and Bavaria. Can be either hello or good-bye.

Slivovitz (SC)—Plum brandy popular in Eastern Europe, especially the Balkan countries.

Sociedades Populares O Gastronomicas (S)—Gastronomic societies, private social clubs in San Sebastian.

Solamente tres (S)—Only three.

Spaetzle (G)—Egg noodles, a popular Bavarian and Austrian side dish.

Staatssicherheitsdienst (G)—The State Security Apparatus, or secret police, of the former East Germany. Also, *Stasi.*

Stammtisch (G)—A table reserved for regular, favored guests in a guest house restaurant.

Stau (G)—Traffic jam.

Tannenbaum (G)—Fir tree.

Tatra (P)—A sub-range of the Carpathian Mountains on the Polish–Czech border.

Todo Rio (S)—The whole river.

Tortilla (S)—Omelette.

Totes Gebirge (G) Literally, the Dead Mountains, a mountain range in Austria along the border between the provinces of Steiermark and Oberoesterreich.

Trabi (G)—Nickname for Trabant, the subcompact fiberglass cars with two-cycle engines produced in the former East Germany.

Trucha (S)—Trout.

Uisge beatha (Gae)—Reverential term for Scotch whisky. Literally, water of life.

Vascongadas (S)—The Basque provinces, in northwestern Spain.

Waidmannsrecht (G)—Sportsmanlike.

Weltanschauung (G)—Outlook, or world view.

Weisswurst (G)—A thick, white pork sausage, served grilled with a crispy, brown skin.

Wessi (G)—Westie, a resident of the former West Germany.

Wir sind ein Volk! (G)—We are one people! Rallying cry during massive public demonstrations in East Germany in the autumn of 1989. These led to the fall of the Berlin Wall and the eventual reunification of Germany.

Zauberwald (G)—Enchanted forest.

Zloty (P)—The Polish monetary unit.

(C)—Czech
(D)—Danish
(F)—French
(Gae)—Gaelic
(G)—German
(P)—Polish
(SC)—Serbo-Croatian
(S)—Spanish